AF528504

Social Work and Poverty Reduction Strategies

Social Work and Poverty Reduction Strategies

Pradeep Kotwal

AKHAND

AKHAND PUBLISHING HOUSE

NEW DELHI (INDIA)

Published by

AKHAND PUBLISHING HOUSE
L-9 A. IST FLOOR, STREET NO. 42
SADATPUR EXTENSION
DELHI-110094 (INDIA)
CELL- 0-9013387535, 0-9968628081

Social Work and Poverty Reduction Strategies

© Publishers
Edition 2011
ISBN 978-81-910525-9-6

The responsibility for facts stated, opinion expressed or conclusions reached and plagiarism, if any, in this book is entirely that of the author/editor. The publisher bears no responsibility for them whatsoever.

Printed in India
at Asian Offset Printers, Delhi

Preface

Poverty is an issue of grave importance to social workers, as there is ample evidence that living in poverty places individuals and families at greater risk for a host of factors that can impede prosperous functioning. For instance, poor adults have higher morbidity and mortality rates than non-poor adults, and also have lower life expectancies and a greater likelihood to work in dangerous occupations. Moreover, they are more likely to reside in high-crime neighbourhoods and in close proximity to toxic waste sites.

Poverty is also associated with a plethora of detrimental effects on infants and children, as it increases the rate of low birth-weight babies and malnutrition, which heightens the likelihood of their later developing serious and chronic illnesses. Poor children also have a greater likelihood than non-poor children of being depressed, experiencing difficulties in peer relations, having low self-esteem, and being diagnosed with behavioural and conduct disorders.

Given the deleterious effects of poverty and how the social, political and economic conditions indicative of the new economy contribute to the extent to which this social ill pervades throughout society, it is incumbent upon present-day for social work educators to seriously consider how poverty-related information can be included within the social work curriculum. Evidence suggests that social workers' attitudes and beliefs about poverty influence how they frame clients' problems and the interventions they employ to address these problems.

The present book comprehensively narrates the strategies and practices used by social workers for poverty reduction. Focusing on social work values, it offers an overview both of the practicalities of social work and the principles underpinning practice.

Pradeep Kotwal

Contents

1

Social Work for Social Development

The social work profession promotes social change, problem solving in human relationships and the empowerment and liberation of people to enhance well-being. Utilising theories of human behaviour and social systems, social work intervenes at the points where people interact with their environments. Principles of human rights and social justice are fundamental to social work.

Social work in its various forms addresses the multiple, complex transactions between people and their environments. Its mission is to enable all people to develop their full potential, enrich their lives, and prevent dysfunction. Professional social work is focused on problem solving and change. As such, social workers are change agents in society and in the lives of the individuals, families and communities they serve. Social work is an interrelated system of values, theory and practice.

Social work grew out of humanitarian and democratic ideals, and its values are based on respect for the equality, worth, and dignity of all people. Since its beginnings over a century ago, social work practice has focused on meeting human needs and developing human potential. Human rights and social justice serve as the motivation and justification for social work action. In solidarity with those who are dis-advantaged, the profession strives to alleviate poverty and to liberate vulnerable and oppressed people in order to promote social inclusion. Social work values are embodied in the profession's national and international codes of ethics.

Social work bases its methodology on a systematic body of evidence-based knowledge derived from research and practice evaluation, including local and indigenous knowledge specific to its context. It recognises the complexity of interactions between human beings and their environment, and the capacity of people both to be affected by and to alter the multiple influences upon them including bio-psychosocial factors. The social work profession draws on theories of human development and behaviour and social systems to analyse complex situations and to facilitate individual, organisational, social and cultural changes.

Social work addresses the barriers, inequities and injustices that exist in society. It responds to crises and emergencies as well as to everyday personal and social problems. Social work utilises a variety of skills, techniques, and activities consistent with its holistic focus on persons and their environments.

Social work interventions range from primarily person-focused psychosocial processes to involvement in social policy, planning and development. These include counselling, clinical social work, group work, social pedagogical work, and family treatment and therapy as well as efforts to help people obtain services and resources in the community. Interventions also include agency administration, community organisation and engaging in social and political action to impact social policy and economic development. The holistic focus of social work is universal, but the priorities of social work practice will vary from country to country and from time to time depending on cultural, historical, and socio-economic conditions.

1.1. Principles and Standards of Social Work

Ethical awareness is a necessary part of the professional practice of any social worker. His or her ability to act ethically is an essential aspect of the quality of the service offered to clients. The purpose of International Federation of Social Workers (IFSW's) work on ethics is to promote ethical debate and reflection in the member associations and among the providers of social work in member countries. The basis for the further development of IFSW's work on ethics is to be found in "Ethics of Social Work - Principles and Standards" which consists of two documents, International Declaration of Ethical Principles of

Social Work, and International Ethical Standards for Social Workers. These documents present the basic ethical principles of the social work profession, recommend procedure when the work presents ethical dilemmas, and deal with the profession's and the individual social worker's relation to clients, colleagues, and others in the field. The documents are components in a continuing process of use, review and revision.

1.1.1. Declaration of Ethical Principles of Social Work

The IFSW recognises the need for a declaration of ethical principles for guidance in dealing with ethical problems in social work. The purposes of the International Declaration of Ethical Principles are: to formulate a set of basic principles for social work, which can be adapted to cultural and social settings.

— to identify ethical problem areas in the practice of social work (below referred to as 'problem areas'), and

— to provide guidance as to the choice of methods for dealing with ethical issues/problems (below referred to as 'methods for addressing ethical issues/problems').

1.1.1.1. Compliance

The International Declaration of Ethical Principles assumes that both member associations of the IFSW and their constituent members adhere to the principles formulated therein. The IFSW expects each member association to assist its members in identifying and dealing with ethical issues/problems in the practice of their profession. Member associations of the IFSW and individual members of these can report any member association to the Executive Committee of the IFSW should it neglect to adhere to these principles.

National Associations who experience difficulties adopting these principles should notify the Executive Committee of IFSW. The Executive Committee may impose the stipulations and intentions of the Declaration of Ethical Principles on an association which neglects to comply. Should this not be sufficient the Executive Committee can, as a following measure, suggest suspension or exclusion of the association.

The International Declaration of Ethical Principles should be made publicly known. This would enable clients, employers, professionals from other disciplines, and the general public to have expectations in accordance with the ethical foundations of social work.

1.1.1.2. The Principles

Social workers serve the development of human beings through adherence to the following basic principles:

1. Every human being has a unique value, which justifies moral consideration for that person.
2. Each individual has the right to self-fulfilment to the extent that it does not encroach upon the same right of others, and has an obligation to contribute to the well-being of society.
3. Each society, regardless of its form, should function to provide the maximum benefits for all of its members.
4. Social workers have a commitment to principles of social justice.
5. Social workers have the responsibility to devote objective and disciplined knowledge and skill to aid individuals, groups, communities, and societies in their development and resolution of personal-societal conflicts and their consequences.
6. Social workers are expected to provide the best possible assistance to anybody seeking their help and advice, without unfair discrimination on the basis of gender, age, disability, colour, social class, race, religion, language, political beliefs, or sexual orientation.
7. Social workers respect the basic human rights of individuals and groups as expressed in the United Nations Universal Declaration of Human Rights and other international conventions derived from that Declaration.
8. Social workers pay regard to the principles of privacy, confidentiality, and responsible use of information in their professional work. Social workers respect justified confidentiality even when their country's legislation is in conflict with this demand.
9. Social workers are expected to work in full collaboration with their clients, working for the best interests of the clients but

paying due regard to the interests of others involved. Clients are encouraged to participate as much as possible, and should be informed of the risks and likely benefits of proposed courses of action.

10. Social workers generally expect clients to take responsibility, in collaboration with them, for determining courses of action affecting their lives. Compulsion which might be necessary to solve one party's problems at the expense of the interests of others involved should only take place after careful explicit evaluation of the claims of the conflicting parties. Social workers should minimise the use of legal compulsion.
11. Social work is inconsistent with direct or indirect support of individuals, groups, political forces or power-structures suppressing their fellow human beings by employing terrorism, torture or similar brutal means.
12. Social workers make ethically justified decisions, and stand by them, paying due regard to the IFSW International Declaration of Ethical Principles, and to the International Ethical Standards for Social Workers adopted by their national professional association.

1.1.1.3. problem areas

1. The problem areas raising ethical issues directly are not necessarily universal due to cultural and governmental differences. Each national association is encouraged to promote discussion and clarification of important issues and problems particularly relevant to its country. The following problem areas are, however, widely recognized:
   - — when the loyalty of the social worker is in the middle of conflicting interests between those of the social workers own and the clients
   - — between conflicting interests of individual clients and other individuals
   - — between the conflicting interests of groups of clients
   - — between groups of clients and the rest of the population

— between systems/institution and groups of clients

— between system/institution/employer and social workers

— between different groups of professionals

— the fact that the social worker functions both as a helper and controller

The relation between these two opposite aspects of social work demands a clarification based on an explicit choice of values in order to avoid a mixing-up of motives or the lack of clarity in motives, actions and consequences of actions. When social workers are expected to play a role in the state control of citizens they are obliged to clarify the ethical implications of this role and to what extent this role is acceptable in relation to the basic ethical principles of social work.

The duty of the social worker to protect the interests of the client will easily come into conflict with demands for efficiency and utility. This problem is becoming important with the introduction and use of information technology within the fields of social work.

1.1.1.4. Methods For The Solution of Issues/Problems

1. The various national associations of social workers are obliged to treat matters in such a way that ethical issues/problems may be considered and tried to be solved in collective forums within the organization. Such forums should enable the individual social worker to discuss, analyse and consider ethical issues/problems in collaboration with colleagues, other expert groups and/parties affected by the matter under discussion. In addition such forums should give the social worker opportunity to receive advice from colleagues and others. Ethical analysis and discussion should always seek to create possibilities and options.
2. The member associations are required to produce and/or adapt ethical standards for the different fields of work, especially for those fields where there are complicated ethical issues/problems as well as areas where the ethical principles of social work may come into conflict with the respective country's legal system or the policy of the authorities.
3. When ethical foundations are laid down as guidelines for actions within the practice of social work, it is the duty of the associations

to aid the individual social worker in analysing and considering ethical issues/problems on the basis of:

— The ethical/moral and political context of the actions, i.e. an analysis of the values and forces constituting the framing conditions of the action.

— The motives of the action, i.e. to advocate a higher level of consciousness of the aims and intentions the individual social worker might have regarding a course of action.

— The nature of the action, i.e. help in providing an analysis of the moral content of the action, e.g. the use of compulsion as opposed to voluntary co-operation, guardianship vs participation, etc.

— The consequences the action might have for different groups, i.e. an analysis of the consequences of different ways of action for all involved parties in both the short and long term.

4. The member associations are responsible for promoting debate, education and research regarding ethical questions.

1.2. Responsibilities of Social Workers

Full-time social workers usually work a standard 40-hour week; however, some occasionally work evenings and weekends to meet with clients, attend community meetings, and handle emergencies. Some, particularly in voluntary nonprofit agencies, work part time.

Social workers usually spend most of their time in an office or residential facility, but also may travel locally to visit clients, meet with service providers, or attend meetings. Some may use one of several offices within a local area in which to meet with clients. The work, while satisfying, can be emotionally draining. Understaffing and large caseloads add to the pressure in some agencies.

Social workers held about 468,000 jobs in 2000. About 1 out of 3 jobs were in state, county, or municipal government agencies, primarily in departments of health and human services, mental health, social services, child welfare, housing, education, and corrections. Most private sector jobs were in social service agencies, hospitals, nursing homes, home health agencies, and other health centers or clinics. Although most social workers are employed in cities or suburbs, some work in rural areas. Social workers should be emotionally mature, objective, and sensitive to people and their problems. They must be able to handle responsibility, work independently, and maintain good working relationships with clients and coworkers. Volunteer or paid jobs as a social work aide offer ways of testing one's interest in this field.

Advancement to supervisor, program manager, assistant director, or executive director of a social service agency or department is possible, but usually requires an advanced degree and related work experience. Other career options for social workers include teaching, research, and consulting. Some also help formulate government policies by analyzing and advocating policy positions in government agencies, in research institutions, and on legislators' staffs.

Some social workers go into private practice. Most private practitioners are clinical social workers who provide psychotherapy, usually paid through health insurance. Private practitioners usually have at least a master's degree and a period of supervised work experience. A network of contacts for referrals also is essential.

Competition for social worker jobs is stronger in cities where demand for services often is highest, training programs for social workers are prevalent, and interest in available positions is strongest. However, opportunities should be good in rural areas, which often find it difficult to attract and retain qualified staff.

Employment of social workers is expected to increase faster than the average for all occupations through 2010. The elderly population is increasing rapidly, creating greater demand for health and social services, resulting in particularly rapid job growth among gerontology social workers.

Social workers also will be needed to help the large baby-boom generation deal with depression and mental health concerns stemming from mid-life, career, or other personal and professional difficulties. In addition, continuing concern about crime, juvenile delinquency, and services for the mentally ill, the mentally retarded, the physically disabled, AIDS patients, and individuals and families in crisis will spur demand for social workers. Many job openings also will stem from the need to replace social workers who leave the occupation.

The number of social workers in hospitals and long-term care facilities will increase in response to the need to provide medical and social services for clients who leave the facility. However, this need will be shared across several occupations. In an effort to control costs, these facilities increasingly emphasize discharging patients early, applying an interdisciplinary approach to patient care, and employing a broader mix of occupations—including clinical specialists, registered nurses, and health aides—to tend to patient care or client needs.

Social worker employment in home healthcare services is growing, in part because hospitals are releasing patients earlier than in the past. However, the expanding senior population is an even larger factor. Social workers with backgrounds in gerontology are finding work in the growing numbers of assisted-living and senior-living communities. Employment of social workers in private social service agencies also will grow. However, agencies increasingly will restructure services and hire more lower-paid social and human service assistants instead of social workers. Employment in State and local government may grow somewhat in response to increasing needs for public welfare and family services; however, many of these services will be contracted out to private agencies. Employment in child protection services will grow due to increased concern over the safety of children. Employment levels may fluctuate depending on need and government funding for various social service programs.

Employment of substance abuse social workers also will continue to grow over the projection period. Substance abusers are increasingly being placed into treatment programs instead of being sentenced to prison. As this trend grows, demand will increase for treatment programs and social workers to assist abusers on the road to recovery. Employment of school social workers is expected to grow due to expanded efforts to respond to rising student enrollments. Moreover, continued emphasis on integrating disabled children into the general school population will lead to more jobs. However, availability of State and local funding will dictate the actual job growth in schools.

Opportunities for social workers in private practice will expand, but this growth will be inhibited to a certain degree by funding cutbacks and by restrictions that managed care organizations place on services.

The growing popularity of employee assistance programs also is expected to spur some demand for private practitioners, some of whom provide social work services to corporations on a contractual basis.

Through direct counseling or referral to other services, social workers help people solve a range of personal problems. Workers in occupations with similar duties include the clergy, counselors, psychologists, and social and human service assistants.

1.3. Tasck of Social workers

Social workers have an enormously difficult task. Social services departments have now abandoned any pretence of open-door, community-based services to individuals and families. Their resources are so very tightly controlled that only those with the greatest needs receive services. Some clients are therefore reduced to outpourings of rage and anger to get heard. Dealing with the impact of poverty and structural inequality is central to the social work role. Social workers must recognise the effects of widening inequality over the past twenty years and challenge this trend. Unless social workers use their powers creatively to bring about practical improvements in the lives of their clients they cannot claim to be any more than gatekeepers of resources, or social policemen. In some deprived communities social work is already seen as a form of oppression against the poor.

Very often the fast-track route to services for children in need is through the child protection system. With a little imagination it is often possible to redefine needs so that they fit into a category for child protection registration. Families are manoeuvred into situations where they have to demonstrate that they have failed in some way or that relationships have completely broken down before resources are made available to them. Consequently, child protection social workers spend much of their time policing the parenting of extremely disadvantaged people who need services more than surveillance. Social workers are aware that the risks allegedly posed by these parents would disappear if they had the resources of a more privileged family. Social workers should not lose sight of their broader social objectives. They should resist pressures to deal with clients in a narrowly legalistic and depersonalised way. At the same time social workers, their clients and the wider community need to work together in demanding adequate resources from the state for vulnerable individuals and families. The new social work degree will make entry into the profession more difficult for working class people. This is another example of the way that class discrimination is gradually seeping into the profession.Support for the social work degree clearly comes from the middle classes. The belief that social workers need longer basic training is an implied criticism of them and affirmation of the value of training. This has come about largely through an alliance between middle class managers, academics and politicians.

A key philosophical issue in social work is the nature of the relationship between the individual and the state. Social work seeks to establish the right balance between respecting privacy and intervening to provide care and control. The working class regards social work as part of the controlling state. However, social work trainers who are predominantly middle class, stress the caring aspect of the social work role and teach anti-oppressive practice. Consequently, newly-qualified social workers are ill-prepared for the job because the values they have been taught during training do not fit with those underpinning service delivery. These problems can only be addressed if class is put at the centre of training. Class must be discussed and thought about more clearly. Anti-oppressive practice must be taught in a way that includes getting to grips with class oppression. Unless social workers have a realistic class analysis they may unwittingly succumb to pressures to behave oppressively.

1.4. Social Work and Poverty Eradication

One of the most serious problems affecting the health and well-being of many social work clients is poverty. Poverty is not just about income but also the quality of life and the home and community environment. However, social services departments construct needs in ways that ignore needs arising out of poverty. The reason must be that poverty is perceived as something about which social services can do nothing. The links between poverty and health problems are well known. Poverty and illness together make people much more vulnerable and needy at all stages of their lives, and even more so in old age. Inequalities between social classes in the incidence of chronic illness and mental illness and in life expectancy are also well documented.

Social work may endorse anti-oppressive ideas but class inequalities remain as wide as ever. Clearly, anti-oppressive practice is at its weakest when it comes to the issue of class. Moral judgements about worth and deservedness permeate social work practice and unthinking class assumptions continue to influence the provision of services. For example, social work assessments inevitably include considerations of how well poor clients are dealing with their poverty. Furthermore, when social work decisions are challenged the more powerful and articulate middle classes are more likely to be successful in getting the services they need than the less powerful working classes.

The government assumes that social workers can deal with poverty without tackling the underlying causes. It continuously repeats the mantra of education as a panacea for all poverty and inequality. In reality, social workers can do nothing about raising household incomes, improving housing or transforming the community environment. Social workers must therefore resist the notion that poverty can be tackled by apolitical social work solutions.

Social workers have a responsibility to work towards structural change to resolve the issues their clients face which are caused by inequalities of income and wealth. It is not enough to simply resolve individual issues as they arise. The social work profession promotes social change, problem solving in human relationships and the empowerment and liberation of people to enhance well-being. Utilising theories of human behaviour and social systems, social work intervenes at the points where people interact with their environments.

In recent years, the language of poverty and inequality has been replaced by that of social exclusion. This has been introduced to disguise the true extent of poverty and to create the illusion that the problem is being tackled. This process inevitably requires the poor to be blamed for their poverty. It involves the mindless repetition of words and phrases that have lost any connection with meanings - equality of opportunity, inclusiveness, stakeholder - and the avoidance of any embarrassing facts about poverty. Public perception of poverty is manipulated so that the better-off do not have to take any responsibility for the problem. Meanwhile, poverty remains as serious a problem as ever.

Even the social work profession has become involved in this false way of thinking. The 'official' language sweeps away principles of social justice and any notion that social workers should be aligned with poor, working class people. The 'correct' view is that the social worker is simply employed to mediate between the client and the state and this can be achieved without any reference to poverty, inequality and class. Academics, too, are uncritically promoting the 'official' language. They are writing more and more in an artificial language that cuts them off from the real world. Their language is becoming so dense and convoluted that it is either incomprehensible or meaningless. They appear too eager to follow the lead of politicians - who are renowned for their manipulation of language and their concern with spin.

The 'official' language plays down the significance of power and class differentials between clients and social workers. It denies the reality of statutory social work where the struggle for power and control characterises much interaction with clients. It is designed to ensure that clients are groomed and moulded into the official system and that conflict is avoided.

In both child welfare and mental health services new strategies are emerging which have as their focus the assessment and management of risk and a clearer duty to share confidential information. As social workers are seen as carrying out surveillance and monitoring activities on behalf of the state, their clients, who are predominantly poor and working class, are becoming increasingly alienated from them. In this climate it is remarkable that there are still some social workers who are concerned with tackling the effects of poverty and who succeed in finding ways to meet their clients' financial needs. These are often social workers who have been influenced by their own experiences of poverty. They tend to have a broader view of the social work task and to be committed to principles of social welfare and justice.

Clients coming into the orbit of social services are sometimes people who have been pushed into poverty by a personal crisis and unemployment and need information about their entitlement to benefits and advice about debt problems. However, providing help with financial matters is generally given low priority. It is now policy in many departments that social workers do not deal with income maintenance issues if they can refer clients to voluntary agencies which provide welfare rights advice and advocacy. Meanwhile, there is a sense of crisis in the profession. Many of the problems have been brought about by the government and its obsession with performance targets which creates the illusion that something is being done when in reality the situation is getting worse. It is nonsense to suggest that targets are achievable if management has no understanding of the complexity of the problems that social workers address and the barriers to their meeting the real needs of people they purport to help.

Any credible analysis of poverty must reflect the class divisions in society which give rise to, and perpetuate, inequalities of income and wealth. Social work cannot be expected to have an impact on the consequential problems unless the root causes of poverty are honestly acknowledged and addressed.

1.5. Challenges of Social Development

At the dawn of the millennium, communities around the world are searching for new approaches to a very wide range of questions of fundamental importance to all of us. These questions include the nature of governance and the concept of conflict resolution including respect for human rights, mechanisms for the transfer of knowledge, systems for providing assistance to war-ravaged communities, regional free trade relationships, the form of higher education, and many others, without repeating the same old mistakes from the past.

In inida, early development efforts devised endogamous national development plans, had given priority to rapid economic growth, but they were unable to prevent widespread poverty, high inflation rates, and to provide full employment. Among their consequences have been the accumulation of wealth, largely provided by foreign development sources, by a small group of people, and the marginalization and exclusion of large sections of the population, the acceleration of the rural exodus, the deterioration of the urban habitat, the ghettoization of the suburbs, the degradation of the natural environment, and, more importantly, the escalation of conflict.

Structural adjustment policies attempted during the 1980s, under the guidance of the multilateral organizations, had severely affected social sectors such as education and health and even had compromised the prospects for sustained economic recovery. In the 1990s, a mosaic and short-term measures of free trade policies at times and excessive state regulations in other, left much confusion and arrested economic smoothing efforts of the populace. An endogemous, indigenous and grass-roots driven approach that combines the aiming for both economic growth and social development should be the major goals in the next decade.

Economic growth should serve the cause of social development and respect and promote human rights, environment, and foster economic competitiveness. For healthy economic competitiveness to happen, all superstitions surrounding the lawful making and amassing of wealth, by anyone or any group, should be discraded.

State regulations should be kept at minimum and parastatal beauracracies and regulatory agencies should replace enterprising people only to do work that cannot really be done profitably and efficiently by risk-taking men and women. Otherwise, there will be a huge economic and social prices to be paid in terms of corruption, economic mismanagement, social inequality and violence. The preponderance of the social acceptance of smuggling trade, capital flight, and tax evasion are some of the other deleterous effects of excessive regulation.

1.5.1. Measures to Promote Meaningful Social Development

Action to promote meaningful social development should be taken on six major fronts:

1. *Capacity-building in each and every community.* Education and training should be given the highest priority and investment in education should be increased so that both urban residents and socially distant and geographically remote populations can have access to knowledge. Intensive and low-cost training courses should be permanently available without regard to age, gender or level of previous studies.

   Education and empowerment of girls and women are key factors in curbing population growth, promoting gender equity and in developing the full potential of women. A new role for higher education should be found and encouarged in all communities, incorporating lifelong higher-learning facilities.

Continuing efforts should be made to promote the transfer of knowledge from abroad and the sharing it amongst communities, particularly in science and technology. Distance learning, through known and basic technologies and with the help of professionals in the diaspora, should be promoted and made accessible to all communities.

Development, to be really endogemous, should be based on the will of each individual and community and should express their fundamental identities, not those of the rulers, funders and planners. Cultural factors should be throughly investigated, through cultural impact feasibility studies, and understood well and be an integral part of all strategies designed to achieve balanced and sustainable development.

2. *Promoting the development of rural areas*. The central problems of both the emigration from rural areas and repatriations inflows from the refugee camps should be tackled at their roots, particularly through education - both religious and secular in orientation - through promoting traditional studies, craftsmanship, farming skills and cultural tourism; encouraging the development of indigenous cultures and devolution of political governance; ensuring that everyone has access to shelter and other basics, and decentralizing education and social services at municipal and village levels.

3. *Combating socio-economic marginalization and exclusion and promoting full participation in community life*. This is a key indicator of sustainable social development -- respect for basic human rights and the forming of democratic attitudes and conflict resolution techniques must be promoted from early childhood. Social integration, tolerance, respect and non-violence should be encouraged by all possible means, as should intercultural dialogue and press freedom.

4. *Protecting and safeguarding the environment*. Efforts should be redoubled to promote environmental awareness. One extremely important goal is to reduce the debilitating impacts of natural hazards (especially recurrent ones, such as droughts and dust bowls).

5. *Improving communication.* To reduce isolation, to foster awareness and participation and to promote social integration, mass communication (private, community and alternative radio, and telecom) must be developed and existing systems should be completely privatized, deregulated and improved within individual community, as well as between them and disparate regions, through the use of new communication and known information technologies. Regions and districts should draw up overall information policies in these fields appropriate to their own needs and capabilities, but strictly owned by individuals and communities themselves.
6. Establishing observatories and early warning systems that will be able to detect potential social conflicts and unrest and will be of great importance for monitoring implementation of the international instruments in protecting human rights. National, regional and local communities should work closely with U.N. and USAID agencies, who have recently launched programs - called MOST (Management of Social Transformations) and FEWS (famine early warning system) - to respond to the growing demand from developing countries and societies-in-crisis for assistance in building their capacities in social sciences and in monitoring rapid social change and transition and in complying with international human rights standards.

Development must have a human face. Sustainable social development is only possible by way of tangible and steady improvements in the quality of life: better security, better education, better health, respect for human rights, empowering women, popular democracy based on public and universal education, the rational use of resources through the application of advances in science and technology, and a universal commitment in the part of everyone to the culture of peace and national and international solidarity.

1.5.2. Solidarity Grassroots Groups and the Poor

The 1997 Human Development Report of the United Nations stresses the importance of the mobilization of poor people for building communal institutions (a structural form of social capital). Having their own organizations they can improve their life opportunities. The

Report points out that the accumulation of community-based social capital has historically helped to reduce the vulnerability of the poor. Yet, these communal ties have tended to erode in many places because of wars, internal strife, and, paradoxically, as a result of modernization itself.

Maintaining and building upon such traditional forms of social capital as well as finding new organizational forms to link the poor to new constellations of state, market, and civil society actors thus become priority tasks in eradicating poverty in the 21st century. Moreover, empowering ethnic and tribal minorities, low-caste groups, or women, who are unlikely to have the collective action capacity to achieve adequate representation and power, can also combat "social exclusion".

The argument is not that all community-level networks and institutions are actually favorable for collective action by the poor, but rather that by understanding the local institutional landscape, one can strengthen and invest in those local institutions that have the best potential to help the poor. This means:

(1) targeting investments to strengthen social capital preferentially for the poor and vulnerable, such as women's groups, the same way as human capital investments are usually targeted preferentially to literacy, primary, and bilingual education of special relevance to poor households;

(2) structuring investment packages to all-inclusive organizations in such a way that poor members will obtain a share of benefits they would not otherwise get.

Since poor households have few assets and little access to services, they can gain from associating. Such gains are often analyzed, as noted above, in terms of greater efficiency of resource use (the internal dimension of social capital) and greater equity of access or voice in making claims (the external dimension). The former is often achieved by obtaining economies of scale in coordinated production.

Recently, economists have analyzed the effect of formation of productive groups on distribution of goods and services. The mechanisms of internalization and control of free riding are norms and rules. Some of these norms and rules apply across the society; for example, Putnam's choirs build trust not just among those who belong to choirs but among the whole population.

Such social capital is likely to be proportionately more beneficial to the poor since they are less able to invest in substitutes. For example, a person or organization is defended against crime both by private expenditures on security and by the norms and rules of society. However, the poor are less able to afford private security expenditures and so are more dependent upon norms and rules.

Generally, the victims of crime are disproportionately drawn from the poor, so that strengthening the norms and rules benefits the poor more than others. Other norms and rules apply only to particular groups. Thus, the rules of an association may make it an effective agency for increasing the incomes of its members. Because the poor have more to gain from strengthening norms and rules than do higher-income groups, the poor have more incentive to join groups. For example, in credit transactions, social sanction and collateral assets are alternative means of reassuring the lender.

Wealthy persons do not need social sanction, whereas the poor do. Similarly the economies of scale that collective action facilitates are more likely to be otherwise unreachable by the poor; hence, the membership of revolving savings and credit associations (ROSCAs). Bates argued that it is the wealthy who are most tempted to exit from the obligations of kin groups. Finally, if the main cost of membership is time, the poor have an advantage since they face lower costs.

In rural finance, for effective use of credit by small farmers and the landless, small joint-liability groups are able to serve as viable channels for credit delivery. In the irrigation sector, cohesive groups of water users have succeeded in reliable and equitable water delivery where large, government-managed systems have been deficient. In the case of common access property, such as upland and forest areas or coastal regions, community action for proper management and protection has been shown to be indispensable for upgrading and maintaining the resources, which are the basis of livelihood for poor and marginalized groups.

In each of these contexts and in others as well, sustainable approaches for poverty reduction and improving the welfare of the poor are likely to be those that rely primarily on the mobilization of local initiative and the development of skills, rather than on heavy infusion of public-sector assistance. The experience of ADB's Pacific Island DMCs illustrates the point that even with large infusions of external assistance, unless sustainable local capacities are developed, it is difficult to break out of the cycle of dependency and poverty.

1.5.3. Exclusive Groups and Inclusive Services

The concept of "community" is often applied very loosely with the assumption that there is a rather homogenous or at least internally consensual entity. This represents the basis of participation and cooperation. While this indeed may be the case in some situations, it is not so elsewhere, when one must look for subcommunity networks as the basis for mobilizing social capital of the poor.

The experience of MYRADA is a good illustration. The cooperative movement has enjoyed mixed success in India, enduring for nearly a century in a variety of different sectors but seldom with many lasting benefits for the very poor. Indeed, many have suggested that the cooperatives were (and remain) simply another means by which local elites solidified their power and control. It is only in the last two decades that serious efforts have been made to correct the structural flaws of the cooperatives while retaining their central ethos of mutual accountability.

Leading this effort, particularly in the realm of microfinance, has been an NGO called MYRADA, originally formed in 1968 in the southern Indian state of Karnataka by Captain William Davidson. MYRADA's early work with Tibetan refugees centered on the development of local cooperatives, which were spectacularly successful. Some 25 years later, the Tibetan community living near the village of Huthur in southern Karnataka boasts its own school, monastery, health clinic, and fleet of modern tractors, enabling its members to enjoy a standard of living far superior to that of Tibetans in their native land.

Now completely independent of MYRADA, the Tibetan settlement is a development showcase by any standard. Envious locals soon asked the obvious question: Can you help us to form and manage our own cooperatives? Under MYRADA's leadership, a range of cooperatives was duly launched. Although there were isolated short-term successes, the project as a whole was soon declared a dismal failure. An institutional design, which apparently worked wonders with one community, failed miserably when it was introduced into another only a few miles away. Why? MYRADA had to rethink its whole approach, and in the early 1980s began experimenting with village development associations (VDAs), organizations of 50 to 120 members designed to bring communities together to resolve common problems, to serve as a forum for identifying beneficiaries, channeling funds, and monitoring development programs.

Two types of VDAs emerged, one involving the whole village and the other only poor families. Like the cooperatives before them, however, both types of VDAs experienced low attendance at meetings, and soon suffered the familiar plight of falling under the influence of local elites or breaking up into irreconcilable factions. While the VDAs became part of the credit delivery system, the objectives of equity, social sustainability, and participation were not achieved.

By the mid-1980s, MYRADA staff concluded that the VDAs had failed as agents of poverty alleviation, and that new ways had to be found to address the goals and interests of the poor. When staff consulted the poor themselves for their input, the reply they received was that villagers, especially women, were eager to form groups, but only if the members were drawn from those in a similar socioeconomic situation. Upon testing the viability of this approach, it turned out that the groups of 10-25 members that began to form were drawn from social networks— or "affinity groups", as they are called— which were essentially already in place. MYRADA "institutionalized" these affinity groups to form *sanghas* (or "selfhelp" groups) among the villagers, requiring members to give their group a name and to commit themselves to weekly meetings in order to begin receiving training in basic financial management. Staff did not have to expend undue effort in establishing groups because members were composed of people drawn from similar socioeconomic standing who were engaged in similar forms of employment and subject to similar social pressures such as those of caste. These were people who "naturally" seemed to come together when projects sponsored by the government, MYRADA, or the village itself were offered.

MYRADA decided that its task was thus to build upon, refine, and formalize preexisting social relations among the poor, while simultaneously linking them with broader commercial and political constituencies. Given that the poor also reported that access to secure and equitable sources of savings and credit was their most pressing material concern, MYRADA staff used this as the foundation for their work in the development of credit management groups (CMGs).

MYRADA adopted selected aspects of the Grameen Bank model but was of the opinion that a more sustainable, broadly replicable, and long-term strategy of providing credit to the poor lay not in trying to establish new banks exclusively for the poor, but rather in trying to persuade the existing commercial banks to recognize CMGs as legitimate legal entities to whom full financial services could and should be extended. Given that the largest sources of funds lay with the commercial banks, and that there was inevitably a host of complex, costly legal issues to be addressed in setting up a new bank, a more universally applicable solution surely lay in finding innovative institutional mechanisms whereby the poor were made more "bank-friendly" and the banks more "poor-friendly."

The main lessons are that while the local groups to be promoted should build on existing networks that often do not coincide with community boundaries, support and necessary control mechanisms to make intergroup cooperation possible require higher levels of authority. Such community or village-wide institutions must have a measure of legitimacy even if they are not fully accountable.

References

Grinnell, Richard M. and Yvonne A Unrau (2008). *Social Work Research and Evaluation: Foundations of Evidence-Based Practice* (8th ed.). Oxford, UK; New York, NY: Oxford University Press.

Mizrahi, Terry and Larry E. Davis (2008). *Encyclopedia of Social Work* (20th ed.). Washington, DC; Oxford, UK; New York, NY: NASW Press and Oxford University Press.

Popple, Philip R. and Leslie Leighninger (2008). *The Policy-Based Profession: An Introduction to Social Welfare Policy Analysis for Social Workers* (4th ed.). Boston, MA: Pearson/Allyn and Bacon.

2

Social Dimensions of Poverty

The past decades saw unprecedented progress in improving the conditions of people living in poverty. Income, education, and health indicators show overall gains in the decline of poverty. Despite these improvements, poverty continues to be pervasive the world over. In many of the poorest countries in Africa, Asia, and Latin America poverty has fallen slowly or even risen. Between 1960 and 1990, the income gaps between rich and poor widened from30:1 to 60:1. Developing countries' debts have doubled formal decade ago to US $1.4 trillion. Efforts ţo address the structural causes of poverty struggle with the theoretical and practical complexities of the problems.

2.1. Evolution of the Poverty Reduction Thinking

Poverty is as complex as development itself. Equally complex are the frameworks from which poverty reduction is understood and development approaches since the 1960s reflect this complexity. Modernisation, basic human needs, structural adjustment, and sustainable development all look at the causes of poverty and identify policies and solutions to rectify the situation.

Is poverty primarily an issue of income levels and consumption? Is it about a lack of access to the means and services to meet basic needs? Is it about the capacity and ability to participate in society? What is certain is that there is not one overarching, universal definition of poverty.

Recently, new dimensions broadened the debate. The preparation of the World Development Report 2000/2001 (WDR), set in motion the project "*Voices of the Poor*" to enhance the understanding of the reality of the life of poor people. The project claimed to do this "directly, through poor people's own voices", using participatory and qualitative research. The WDR put forward a framework for action based on three ideas: expanding economic opportunities of the poor by building up their assets through market and non-market actions; empowering the poor by making state institutions pro-poor and removing social barriers to poverty reduction; and enhancing the security of the poor by helping them to manage risks.

A number of issues characterising poverty emerge from the debate:

1. *Structural.* Poverty is a phenomenon rooted in the basic relations of institutional and collective power that make-up a society at a particular point in time;
2. *Systemic.* Poverty is a process and an outcome of collective political, ethical, legal, and institutional systems set in place to reproduce a given social formation;
3. *Multidimensional.* Poverty goes beyond basic needs, income, and consumption. It encompasses the right and access to services and non-material goods, the right to dignity and to be included in society, the right to security and the opportunity to share the benefits of growth;
4. *Dynamic.* Poverty is a non-homogeneous state that changes with shifts in the social, political, natural, and economic environments, evolving differently for individuals in similar environments;
5. *Comprehensive.* Poverty is a multi-level process affecting people's lives as producers, citizens, and spiritual beings.
6. *Longer-term.* The effects of poverty reach well beyond single episodes of shock. It affects present and future states, decisions and opportunities.

One of the commitments reached at the WSSD expands the understanding of poverty. Commitment number two states that eradicating poverty requires "decisive national actions and international cooperation as an ethical, social, political and economic imperative of humankind".

Despite the convergence of goals at the international level, various issues remain points of contention:

1. *Hierarchy of Priorities*. Poverty reduction takes different degrees of importance: an overarching goal; an explicit policy; one among many objectives; a single programme or project focus;
2. *Clarity of Definition.* Most agencies are engaged in internal debates about what poverty means; who are "the poor", and what are the areas of overlap with other priorities?;
3. *Dimension of Poverty.* While most agencies recognise the complexity of poverty, there is wide diversity in the understanding of the key dimension of poverty;
4. *Causes of Poverty.* There is a range of interpretations about why poverty occurs; how to identify the structural causes of poverty, and how to distinguish between causes and symptoms;
5. *Identification of the Poor*. Agencies often include "targeting" as a feature of their strategies, but identifying who the poor are and at what level of aggregation to target them remains problematic;
6. *Gender and Poverty.* Women are frequently identified as a target. However, there are concerns that gender equality and gender analysis are narrowly subordinated to poverty reduction actions;
7. *Measuring Poverty and Progress.* A key area of debate is measurement. There is a lack of tools and indicators to objectively measure poverty (i.e. income/consumption; individual/household; snapshot/cyclical; absolute/relative). There are weak systems, mechanisms and indicators to measure progress towards poverty reduction.

2.2. Social Development and Poverty Reduction

Social development is a process of human growth. It does not depend only on getting the "fundamentals of macroeconomic policy" right. It implies creating a supportive environment of integrated social policies and better distribution of the benefits of economic growth based on social equity. Social development is a foundation upon which human development flourishes, political development provides a framework of rights, and economic development becomes sustainable. Like poverty, social development is understood from different perspectives.

For some, it is the welfare state. Social development is also the development of systems to provide effective entitlements to maintaining the quality of life. Others see it as a series of remedial policies, mechanisms, processes and programmes to protect the poor.

When "social" is added to the notion of development, it conveys a number of meanings. It may refer to specific social sectors such as education and health; to policies that benefit the welfare of the poor; to the context affecting development outcomes; or to the formal and informal institutional base in a society.

Under the latter dimension, social development has become part a broader poverty reduction agenda such as the one outlined by the WDR 2000/2001. It addresses inequalities, institutional failures, social barriers and personal vulnerabilities by tackling key social development areas and focusing on social capital formation.

However, there are risks in conceptualising social development in this way, because it:

a) Transforms the concept into a linear "cover all" notion with a meaning not substantive different from others
b) Limits the understanding to compartments actions and gains within particular policy sectors;
c) Reduces social development to a desired state particular to specific demographic groups
d) Segments social development, and separates it from economic and political development; and
e) Lessens the scope and impact of social development ;

2.3. Linking Social Development and Poverty Reduction

Linking social development and poverty reduction in a coherent framework is more easily said than done. Governments, donors and international organisations struggle to find the right combination of priorities and delivery approaches within existing financial, institutional, and political constraints.

Key to linking social development and poverty reduction is the identification of social sectors and social sector policies as a strategic avenue to tackling poverty. Assumptions are that investing in social sectors allows governments to respond to basic human needs, target vulnerable groups develop basic capacities enhance productivity and economic growth; and complement other development areas.

Investing in social sectors has an instrumental and an intrinsic value. Instrumental, social sector investments strengthen "human capital", with an effect on productivity, economic growth, and poverty reduction. Intrinsically, social sector investments are a means to secure the rights of people in the access to and use of basic social services.

Another attempt to link social development and poverty reduction by investing in social sectors is focusing on the policy level rather than on the provision of services. This leads to reforming the systems and frameworks upon which depends the provision, access, and quality of services to the poor. Social policy reforms in education, health and social security have been viewed as a means by which to address poverty.

Evaluations of the early effects of these reforms and their impact on poverty confirm some of these assumptions, particularly in the education and health sectors. These evaluations also point out, however, that focusing on social sectors as an approach to linking social development and poverty reduction is not enough.

Social sectors have characteristics which make them a difficult avenue by which to reduce poverty. Performance and progress are hard to monitor. Investment decisions are difficult to make due to the traditional focus on sectorial efficiency and accountability, and to expectations that sectorial actions will respond to broad equity imperatives. And social sectors are vast and interrelated areas requiring coordinated actions and strong management capacities to achieve measurable results. Linking social development and poverty reduction demands not only clarity and flexibility in the strategic conceptualisation of the problems, but also coherence in the way in which agency policies are designed and relate to each other, and in the programming and delivery approaches.

2.4. Role of International Financial Institutions

Until 1995 the International Monetary Fund (IMF) had denied any linkage between its activities and social development or poverty eradication. The World Bank, on the other hand, had been looking at ways to enhance its policies aimed at reducing poverty. In its 1989 annual report, the Bank stated that "The central goal of the World Bank is the reduction of poverty, and that ways to achieve this are 'at the heart of the Bank's activities'".

In its 1990 *World Development Report* and in a 1991 policy paper, *Assistance Strategies to Reduce Poverty*, the World Bank explained its mission to reduce poverty. This strategy had two main elements. The first was concerned with the nature and rate of economic growth, including the macroeconomic framework for market liberalisation for private investment and expansion of the private sector. The second was concerned with providing services to the poor, including social safety nets 'designed to protect the poorest and most vulnerable people from extremes of privatisation'. In particular, the macroeconomic policies that were designed to foster liberalisation were creating poverty, and social safety nets were by no means effective in redressing that problem.

The 1995 Social Summit recommended that the multilateral organisations needed to create an international framework that would allow national governments to run their own countries. In addition, the Summit agreed that the policies of the multilateral organisations would also need to be reviewed, in particular the World Bank and the IMF's structural adjustment policies, trade policies, including within the framework of the World Trade Organisation, and debt relief policies.

In September 1999, the World Bank and the IMF launched the new Poverty Reduction Strategy.

As part of the strategy, the IMF's Enhanced Structural Adjustment Facility (ESAF) was renamed the Poverty Reduction and Growth Facility (PRGF). Through PRSPs, a government would produce its own national policy programmes, with a renewed emphasis on poverty eradication as the focus for its economic and social policies. One of the practical implications of the PRSP was that access to the PRGF would require a PRSP which has been endorsed by the boards of both the IMF and the World Bank. The PRSP, or an InterimPRSP (I-PRSP), would also be required for candidate countries applying for access to HIPC debt relief facilities or other forms of international assistance.

The IMF and the World Bank have concentrated on the issue of how to enhance national responsibility for social development and poverty eradication. However, they have not reassessed their own policies, which are part of the 'enabling' environment, as structured by the multilateral organisations.

As a consequence, by focusing on national responsibility, they have not reviewed the constituent elements of the structural reform policies that have exacerbated poverty.

2.5. Role of ILO

As an outcome of the 1995 Social Summit, the agreed programme of action was based on the idea that strategies for poverty eradication were the responsibility of national governments. At the same time, the international community was responsible for creating an economic and political environment that would be conducive to social development.

In committing themselves to the programme of action, the heads of government acknowledged that national 'ownership' requires a transparent and accountable government that recognises the rule of law and the independence of the judiciary. Hence, the concepts of ownership, good governance and civil society are related and stem from the recognition that the national administration, led by a legitimate and representative government, should be in charge of national policies for development.

In this regard the experience of the ILO in working at the country level is of paramount importance, since the strategy and approach of the ILO has been to pour on the participatory role of the social partners and ministries dealing with employment and labour issues in the preparation and implementation of poverty reduction strategies.

2.5.1. Empowering Social Partners

In 1999, the Bretton Woods institutions agreed that nationally-owned participatory poverty reduction strategies should provide the basis for all World Bank and IMF concessional lending and for debt relief under the enhanced HIPC Initiative. This approach, which builds on the principles of the Comprehensive Development Framework, is reflected in the Poverty Reduction Strategy Paper (PRSP) which describes a country's economic, social and political policies and programmes over a three year or longer horizon. It is intended to be a comprehensive document prepared by governments, with support from Bank/Fund teams, which identifies who the poor are and develops strategies for overcoming poverty, including policy and expenditure targets. It is supposed to be locally generated and owned and developed through wide participatory dialogue.

In this context, the ILO identified five special focus countries on which to pilot its support to the PRSP process. Cambodia was identified as one of these five countries, together with Honduras, Mali Nepal and Tanzania. The exercise provides a framework in which the ILO can work together with its constituents to introduce the decent work agenda into the development and poverty reduction process, as well as contributing, through social dialogue, to broader participation and national ownership of these processes. This involves preparing, in close collaboration with the national authorities, an analysis of the role of employment and other elements comprising decent work in poverty reduction, organising tripartite meetings in the countries to influence the design and implementation of PRSPs and an ongoing process of networking, advocacy and influencing among a variety of stockholders in addition to the ILO's social partners, such as bilateral donors, Non Governmental Organisations (NGOs), the multilateral development banks, other UN organisations, think tanks etc.

The PRSP is seen as an instrument for achieving the Millennium Development Goals (MDGs), which were endorsed by nearly 150 heads of state or government and 189 member States in total at the UN Millennium Summit in New York in September 2000.

Many countries are not in a position to complete a full and comprehensive PRSP. In order to prevent delays for countries seeking debt relief under the HIPC Initiative as well as other concessional financing, an I-PRSP can be formulated. An I-PRSP is meant to provide a road map for the development of a full PRSP (a time line for poverty diagnostics, recognition of policy areas that need evaluation and reform, envisaged participatory process, etc.). With an I-PRSP in place, reports on progress need to be submitted for continued assistance and at yearly intervals once a full PRSP is in place.

Both the International Monetary Fund (IMF) and the World Bank have aligned their respective lending programmes to a country's PRSP. In the case of the IMF, the Poverty Reduction Growth Facility (PRGF) – which has superseded the old Enhanced Structural Adjustment Facility – and the Financial Programming Framework are expected to derive from the PRSP. In the case of the World Bank's activities in low-income countries, the Country Assistance Strategy and all loans – including the directly related Poverty Reduction Support Credit (PRSC) -and grants must be based on the PRSP. They have become the key policy instruments in the relations between low-income countries and the wider donor community. Most OECD members have fully endorsed the PRSP approach and have agreed to base their respective aid programmes in low-income countries on the results of the PRSP process. Many have also agreed to co-finance poverty reduction credits, grants and technical assistance in line with the PRSP.

2.5.2. ILO and Poverty Reduction

The conceptual framework for taking forward the ILO's work on poverty reduction is grounded in the twin concepts of entitlement and equity. The ILO is fundamentally concerned with social justice and fundamental principles and rights at work. A poor person, then, suffers a "deficit of entitlements and poverty reduction". Inclusion, integration and, of course, access to incomes all imply the centrality of employment creation as an economic priority for poverty reduction. More generally, the need to build social objectives into macroeconomic policy implies a stress on redistribution, equity and solidarity.

This conceptual framework underlines the point that economic growth is an essential but not sufficient condition for poverty reduction. Poverty reduction involves growth with a substantial reorientation in favour of the poor. It includes changes in institutions, laws, regulations and practices that are part of the process that creates and perpetuates poverty and detailed, targeted interventions that will enable all categories of the poor to more fully integrate into economic processes so that they can take advantage of opportunities to improve their economic and social well being.

In principle, the ILO's comparative advantage in the design and implementation of PRSPs lies in the integrated approach of decent work which embraces rights, employment, social protection and social dialogue. Although it is generally accepted that the well being of any individual does not depend only on income, it is obvious that income from work is the overwhelmingly most important means of survival for poor people. It is, therefore, rather surprising how few PRSPs make explicit reference to, and even less, include an analysis of labour markets and employment issues. This may have something to do with the perspective in some quarters that equates employment with waged employment, the latter perhaps not being so relevant for many of the world's poorest people as well as the notion that labour markets are best left to the vagaries of the market.

Furthermore, given that the PRSP process is usually driven by the World Bank and the Ministry of Finance and/or Ministry of Planning, it has not always been easy for the ILO to engage in the process, especially in those countries where the ILO does not have official representation. It is very difficult to develop a relationship with the aforementioned bodies or with other agencies and donors in a country on the basis of intermittent visits. Some stockholders appear to question the value added of the ILO in poverty dialogues, especially those who are wary of the trade union movement; those who argue that the demand for labour should be left to the market; that social protection is affordable only for the formally employed.

Nevertheless, in many countries and most particularly in the five special focus countries chosen to pilot the ILO's support to the PRSP process, attention has been drawn to active labour market policy as a tool for poverty reduction. This typically includes an attempt to identify the economy's potential leading sectors in line with dynamic comparative advantage, the fiscal strategy and range of policies on interest rates, exchange rates, customs tariffs, wage rates, etc. that would best support such sectors and labour demand in other sectors policies to improve the quality and adaptability of labour to the benefit of productivity and hence demand for labour; and the special policies and programmes needed for social protection and to integrate the poor and particularly vulnerable groups such as indigenous people in the growth process.

The ILO's social partners are fundamental stockholders in PRSPs and should play a pivotal role in their design and implementation. The actual role played by the social partners and the issues which they focus on will vary from country to country but there are some common themes, not least the idea of participation as a process towards legitimising PRSPs.

In principle, ministries of labour will benefit from ILO involvement in PRSPs mainly because it will help bring them closer to the centres of policy making. The ministry of labour in a typical low-income country has a wide range of technical powers and duties but they often do not include a role in the determination of policy on employment and rarely in the determination of policy on poverty reduction. Moreover, given that PRSP processes tend to be heavily budget orientated intra-governmental processes, it is often difficult for labour ministries to carry the same weight in PRSP discussions compared to other ministries such as health or education.

In most countries, the private sector is the principal engine of growth and this is clearly recognised in most PRSPs. Thus, the private sector is usually given a voice in PRSP dialogues and there are a number of common themes espoused by employers' groups usually centred on what can be termed the enabling environment for private enterprise, including the importance of a stable macroeconomic environment; ensuring political stability, good governance and the rule of law; policies which promote open and transparent markets, including sound property rights and transparent fiscal policy; and the development of an adequate physical and social infrastructure. The PRSP is an important vehicle for taking forward this agenda which invariably has strong support from the Bretton Woods institutions and donors.

Generally, trade unions have not been given the voice that they deserve in PRSP discussions and in several countries they have been effectively excluded from the participatory processes. Sometimes this is a reflection of "political issues" in a given country which contrive to marginalise or exclude trade unions, other times it might be based on the limited capacity of some trade unions to engage in national dialogues on poverty. On other occasions it may transpire that the principal architects or coordinators of a country's PRSP perceive that trade unions, because they primarily represent the interests of organised labour in urban settings, do not add sufficient value to poverty reduction strategies which focus on the poor in rural areas and in the informal sector. This is probably a common point of view but it is also narrow and misguided and the ILO has sought to refute this viewpoint in its engagement on PRSPs. The importance of trade unions in improving the terms and conditions for public sector workers which is likely to impact significantly on the quality of public service provision especially as it affects the poor; and of the role of trade unions as a vehicle for public education and advocacy, such as on HIV/AIDS policy. In some countries, the prevention of HIV/AIDS is essential to the achievement of the MDGs and the mobilisation of the social partners and other stockholders in the world of work forms an essential strategy for mitigating the social and economic impact of the pandemic, especially for the poor, who bear the heaviest burden. It has also been argued that trade unions have a particularly useful role to play in terms of their experience in organising and giving voice to a significant part of civil society.

It should be noted that a few workers' organisations have themselves preferred not to get involved in what some regard as a continuation under a new acronym of previous policies to which they were opposed, and some employers' and workers' organisations have decided to concentrate their limited resources on other aspects of public policy. Finally, it is important to note that in some PRSP countries considerable restrictions on the freedom of workers and employers to associate and form or join organisations of their own choosing hamper the development of social dialogue on poverty reduction. Landless rural workers, small tenant farmers, small traders and producers are frequently excluded from laws providing for the legal establishment of workers' and employers' organisations or protecting such organisations and their members from intimidation and acts of violence. Reforms in these areas are essential if the poor are to be in a position to organise themselves and articulate their interests in society and the PRSP process.

2.5.3. Social Dialogue and Poverty Reduction

Social dialogue plays a key role in achieving the ILO's objective of promoting opportunities for women and men to obtain decent and productive work in conditions of freedom, equality, security and human dignity. Social dialogue is defined by the ILO to include all types of negotiation, consultation or simply exchange of information between, or among, representatives of governments, employers and workers, on issues of common interest relating to economic and social policy. It can exist as a tripartite process, with the government as an official party to the dialogue or it may consist of bipartite relations only between labour and management with or without direct government involvement. It can take place at the national, regional or enterprise level. It can be inter-professional, sectorial or a combination of all of these.

The enabling conditions for social dialogue are as follows:

1. Strong, independent workers' and employers' organisations with the technical capacity and access to the relevant information to participate in social dialogue;
2. Political will and commitment to engage in social dialogue on the part of all the parties;
3. Respect for the fundamental rights of freedom of association and collective bargaining;
4. Appropriate institutional support.

Social dialogue institutions are often defined by their composition. They can be bipartite, tripartite or "tripartite plus". The key tripartite actors are the representatives of government, employers and workers. At times, and depending on specific national contexts, the tripartite partners may choose to open the dialogue to other relevant actors in society in an effort to gain a wider perspective, to incorporate the diverse views of other social actors and to build a wider consensus.

Social dialogue can take a variety of forms, ranging from the simple act of exchanging information to the more developed forms of consultation. The following is intended as a short list of the most usual forms of social dialogue:

1) Information sharing is one of the most basic and indispensable elements for effective social dialogue. In itself, it implies no real discussion or action on the issues but it is nevertheless an essential part of those processes by which dialogue and decisions take place;

2) Consultation goes beyond the mere sharing of information and requires an engagement by the parties through an exchange of views which in turn can lead to more in-depth dialogue;
3) Tripartite or bipartite bodies can engage in negotiations and the conclusion of agreements. While many of these institutions make use of consultation and information sharing, some are empowered to reach agreements that can be binding.
4) Collective bargaining is not only an integral form of social dialogue – it is also one of the most widespread. It can be seen as a useful indicator of the capacity within a country to engage in social dialogue. Parties can engage in collective bargaining at the enterprise, sectorial, regional, national and even multinational level.

The main goal of social dialogue itself is to promote consensus building and democratic involvement among the main stockholders in the world of work. Successful social dialogue structures and processes have the potential to resolve important economic and social issues, encourage good governance, advance social and industrial peace and stability and boost economic progress. It is an essential component of participatory processes inherent to the drafting of inclusive and meaningful PRSPs and a bedrock on which the foundations for an open, transparent and democratic society is laid.

2.6. Poverty Eradication in European Union

The European Union (EU) is the developing world's main partner, providing 55 per cent of all international official assistance, and is by far its biggest trader and foreign investor. At a bilateral level, it grants non-reciprocal trade preferences, along with more favourable arrangements for the least developed. It has concluded economic and trade cooperation agreements, which will in time lead to free trade areas, with several countries or regional groupings in the Mediterranean, Latin America, Africa, the Caribbean and the Pacific.

The EU firmly believes that it is politically and morally unacceptable that more than one billion people on the planet still have to survive on less than one euro per day. That figure may well rise as the world's population grows. As a result, the fight against poverty is the central thrust of the EU's development policy efforts as it concentrates its attention on a more limited number of policy areas.

Foreign direct investment into developing countries has soared in the past decade, rising from 29 billion euro in 1990 to 185 billion euro in 1998. But it is unevenly spread.

Responding to concerns about the effectiveness of aid programmes in general, the European Commission presented a major reorientation in the summer of 2000 of its development policy. Central to the new strategy are attempts to integrate developing countries into the international economic system, to encourage them in their efforts at regional integration, to use the EU's considerable expertise and financial means to provide a critical mass, as in the transport sector, and to relate more closely to what other donors are doing.

By concentrating on core tasks, the Commission has suggested the EU should limit its activities to those areas where it can offer comparative advantages and added value. It has selected six: trade for development, regional integration and cooperation, macroeconomic policies linked with poverty reduction strategies, reliable and sustainable transport, food security and sustainable rural development strategies, and institutional capacity building to consolidate good governance and the rule of law.The new strategy with its emphasis on empowerment, capacity-building, ownership and sustainability, is based on clear political guidelines:

1. Ownership of the process must lie with the developing countries themselves and involve maximum participation of civil society representatives;
2. The need for more coordination and a better division of labour between the EU's development programme and those of other donors, especially the union's member States;
3. Contradictions between development policy and other EU activities - trade, agriculture and fisheries - which impact on developing countries must be avoided;
4. Administrative procedures must be streamlined to increase the speed and efficiency of programme delivery.

2.6.1. ACP-EU Partnership

The Lynchpin of the EU's development policy is the Colotomy

Agreement which binds it with African, Caribbean and Pacific (ACP) countries and is the most ambitious and comprehensive agreement between developed and developing countries. Its predecessor, the Loam Convention, was first signed in 1975 in Loam, the capital of Togo, and was regularly updated.

However, the basic objective of the comprehensive aid-and-trade agreement remains constant. It is "to promote and expedite the economic, cultural and social development of the ACP States and to consolidate and diversify their relations in a spirit of solidarity and mutual interest". The wide-ranging partnership is based on equality between the signatories, respect for their sovereignty and mutual interest and interdependence.

The Cotonou Agreement was signed in June 2000 in the capital of Benin, which is the origin for the informal name of the agreement. At this occasion, the existing ACP members were joined by six new countries from the Pacific, bringing the total to 77 ACP countries. It sets out an integrated and comprehensive approach to development, poverty eradication, trade and a political dialogue that includes conflict prevention, human rights and democratisation and issues of mutual concern such as migration. The new agreement includes some notable qualitative changes from its predecessors as it moves from market-access based trade relations to a more comprehensive relationship and from government to government partnerships to a more inclusive process involving all elements of civil society. It is both comprehensive and innovative.

New procedures have been drawn up for handling any violations of human rights and where these are particularly serious and flagrant, action can be taken immediately. In what is a real innovation in international relations, the two partners have agreed new procedures to deal with serious cases of corruption.

The EU has agreed to implement an immigration and asylum policy founded on the principle of partnership with the originating countries and regions. This includes new initiatives on the rights of third courtry citizens inside the Union and arrangements for the repatriation of illegal immigrants found on the other's territory.

Regional economic partnership agreements are new arrangements within the Cotonou Agreement designed to promote trade liberalisation between the EU and ACP countries and between ACP States themselves. Negotiations on these will start no later than 2002 - allowing regional integration processes to be strengthened in the meantime - and they will come into force by 2008.

The Union is committed to helping the ACP countries become more active members in the international economic and trade system. This, it hopes, will encourage other countries and international business to establish closer relations with ACP partners, boosting investment and the transfer of technology and know-how, thus helping their overall competitiveness. This should help the ACP members as the value of the preferences they have with the Union is eroded by the general liberalisation process and reduction of tariffs taking place globally.

The Union has agreed special trade concessions for all the least developed countries, of which 39 are signatories of the Cotonou Agreement. By 2005, their exporters will have free access to the EU market for almost all their products.

On the financial front, the European Development Fund used to finance ACP programmes will have a budget of 13.5 billion euro over the next seven years. To this, will be added a further 9.5 billion euro unspent from previous funds and 1.7 billion euro in loans from the European Investment Bank.

2.6.2. Africa and the EU

Traditionally, relations between the EU and Africa have had two different focuses: the Mediterranean Basin and Loam Convention members. But, largely on Portugal's initiative, the relationship was recently placed on a wider, continental basis, when the first EU-Africa Summit was held in Cairo in April 2000.

The object of the largest ever meeting between heads of state or government from the two continents was to strengthen international awareness of Africa's important potential, encourage its integration into the world economy and construct a strategic partnership to promote peace, democracy and development. While the meeting concentrated on the interrelationship between political, economic and development issues, it also dwelt on international debt relief, around 80 per cent of whose beneficiaries are African countries.

Future cooperation will be partly determined by the action plan adopted by the summit. This will focus on greater regional integration and ways to provide a solid and corruption-free environment to attract foreign investment. It includes, via better crisis management and peacekeeping capacities, ways to end conflicts between and within countries. Attention is being paid to improving health and welfare conditions, by tackling disease and HIV/AIDS in particular, reducing unemployment and combating social exclusion. Emphasis is placed on the need for sound democratic foundations anchored in the rule of law and respect for human rights.

2.6.3. South Africa and the EU

In early 2000, a wide-ranging trade, development and cooperation agreement which had taken three and a half years to negotiate came into effect between the EU and South Africa. By the end of the ensuing 12 years, the latter will have granted duty-free status to 86 per cent of EU exports, while the Union will do the same for 95 per cent of goods travelling in the other direction. The accord is accompanied by parallel agreements on science and technology, wines and fisheries and around 125 million euro of EU financial assistance to South Africa every year. The Union also played a central role in the country's successful transition to a democratic government - one of the clearest examples of the impact of EU support for human rights and democracy in recent years.

2.6.4. Human rights and the EU

The importance which the EU attaches to respect for human rights around the world was underlined by two developments in 1999. For the first time, responsibility for this area was given to one commissioner Chris Pattern, the External Relations Commissioner. The second was the publication of the first annual report on human rights documenting the EU's policies, priorities and practices in this area.

This commitment to human rights and a legal framework are reflected in the Union's common foreign and security policy provisions and in its development cooperation programme. Every new agreement between the EU and a third country includes a human rights clause allowing for trade benefits and development cooperation to be suspended if abuses are established.

The Union can impose targeted sanctions as it has done against Serbia and Burma. These range from a refusal to give visas to senior members of the regime to freezing assets held in EU countries. But its preference is to use positive action rather than penalties.

To help achieve this, the EU has an "initiative for democracy and human rights" with a budget of some 100 million euro as well as several million euros a year for use in external assistance. More indirect ways like improving the basic infrastructure of water supplies and transport links which help reduce potential tension and threats to human rights are also supported. Sending international observers to monitor elections and the use of humanitarian aid are other tools in the EU's armoury.

This concern for the respect of human rights worldwide is matched by renewed efforts to prevent any deterioration of standards inside the EU itself. This is partly being achieved through a charter of fundamental rights to provide a comprehensive code of common values with the aim of better protecting people living inside the EU.

2.7. Mainstreaming Poverty Reduction

Multiple efforts among international agencies seek to streamline their poverty reduction work and to coordinate their actions to meet the MDG commitments. Several reports assessing achievements to date show complementarity of goals and strategies in approaching poverty as well as differences among agencies.

Poverty reduction activities and pro-poor policies figure prominently in the agenda of international agencies. Most of the understand poverty reduction as a complex process both conceptually and operationally; multidimensional, focusing on the rights of people to dignity, autonomy and social inclusion; dynamic as a process affecting people differently as a result of multiple factors; and most agencies recognise that to have a visible impact poverty reduction requires a broad range of approaches.

In fact, social development as a strategic focus does not figure explicitly in the poverty reduction approaches of many agencies.

Although most pay attention to social sectors actions often lack articulation and do not respond to a comprehensive understanding of social development per se, but to the rhetoric of broad international commitments. Actions are narrowly focused and sector specific.

Shared poverty concerns among agencies translate into a variety of strategies and delivery approaches. These reflect diverse understanding, institutional traditions, views about comparative advantage, geographical concentration, and political preferences.

An examination of agencies' policy statements allows one to identify four types of strategic directions. These represent dominant emphases as in most cases agencies use a combination of them at different levels.

1. *Growth Based Strategies.* Economic growth is central to the aid policies. It is seen as a "precondition" to poverty reduction. Growth based strategies have shifted from primarily economic to pro-poor concerns. The aims to increase the poor's share of income and create economic opportunities. Despite this shift, pro-poor growth based strategies still fall short of addressing distributional issues and the structural causes of poverty.
2. *Empowering Strategies.* Many agencies include in their poverty policies a political dimension. Few, however, explicitly acknowledge politics as a guiding consideration. Issues such as "human rights", "democracy", "good governance", "empowerment", and "participation" form a coded vocabulary to highlight political considerations in poverty reduction; these concerns have sometimes a central stage. Only in the last few years, have some agencies begun to adopt more "right-based strategies" covering the political, cultural and individual rights of the poor.
3. *Remedial Strategies.* For most donors, poverty reduction needs immediate responses to emergencies and short-term crises. A common view is that addressing poverty requires, in some form, "sheltering" the poor from deteriorating conditions. Safety nets, social security and social protection schemes, and pro-poor programmes have been some solutions.
4. *Social Sector Strategies.* During the 1990s poverty reduction strategies began to give an increasing emphasis to investing in

social sectors as a means to reach the poor. Investments in basic social services are perceived to play a critical role in enhancing the "human capital" of the poor. In most cases these efforts are narrowly defined and not well coordinated with government actions or across sectors.

Independent of the approach adopted to meet poverty reduction goals, common challenges remain such as how to mainstream poverty reduction to reflect this goal institutionally at all organisational levels and across all programmes? How to ensure that policies, procedures, programmes and the organisation culture work in a coordinated manner? How to reflect this coherence in the country in assistance strategies and programmes, and how to nurture a dialogue with country partners and other donors?

A key challenge to agencies in reaching their poverty reduction goals, is achieving policy and operational consistency with government policies, internally within an agency, and externally with its partners. Donors and governments are increasingly aware of the ineffectiveness and high costs of inconsistent and uncoordinated policies and actions in poverty reduction and in social development.

Donor countries are often criticised for duplicity of purpose between, for example, their domestic and international policies; their social, political and economic stands; and their channels and agendas for delivering aid.. Ways to promote consistency in addressing poverty include: ensuring that poverty reduction priorities cut across bilateral programmes and projects; coordinating bilateral policy dialogue with partner governments and civil society agencies; creating partnerships to influence the agendas of multilateral agencies and developing country partners; ensuring consistency across agencies operating under the MDG envelope of funds; and collaborating with civil society institutions and non-governmental organisation.

2.8. Integrative Approach to Poverty Reduction

Poverty reduction strategies and social development need on integrative approach to be affective. Although differing in terminology, integrative approaches have common characteristics. They deal with the effectiveness of MDGs by contributing to the development of a positive policy environment; increasing ownership by stockholders; ensuring government's ability to respond to cross sectorial priorities; and improving local institutional capacity. They intend to meet six criteria: sector-wide in scope, follow a coherent policy framework, involve local stockholders in decision-making, reach donors agreement, find common implementation arrangements, and limit long-term technical assistance to a minimum.

These approaches claim to operate within defined sector policies and accountable and realistic strategies. However, the literature shows discrepancies between the principles and the practice. There is a danger that the weaknesses of the "project approach" are re-invented; the opportunities for strategic review and/or negotiations are limited; and there is little incentive for regular monitoring review.

2.9. Participatory Governance

Governance can be defined as the way in which people govern or assert authority over themselves through informal traditions and formal institutions. It is a particularly important issue when people cede their power to authoritative bodies to act on their behalf. People need to be assured that these institutions act in their interest. While not a new concept, governance has emerged in the past two decades as one of the most important factors in the realisation of democracy and human rights and the promotion of sustainable development. In this way, governance is also important in the labour market. National governments, in the interests of their citizens, play a role in regulating the labour market, promoting job creation and creating an enabling environment for investment and entrepreneurship. International organisations, such as the ILO, assist national governments, on behalf of the people, in creating employment and decent work for all. Trade unions act on behalf of workers to garner better wages and working conditions, and civil society organisations advocate concerns of the people on a wide range labour market interests.

As defined by Daniel Kaufmann, Director of Global Governance at the World Bank Institute, "Governance is defined as the exercise of authority through formal and informal traditions and institutions for the common good, thus encompassing: (i) the process of selecting, monitoring, and replacing governments; (ii) the capacity to formulate and implement sound policies and deliver public services, and (iii) the respect of citizens and the state for the institutions that govern economic and social interactions among them. As defined by the OECD, "In its widest sense, governance establishes the conditions whereby individuals singly and collectively seek to meet their aspirations in society... Good, effective public governance helps to strengthen democracy and human rights, promote economic prosperity and social cohesion, reduce poverty, enhance environmental protection and the sustainable use of natural resources, and deepen confidence in government and public administration." It is the way a society organises itself to make and implement decisions – achieving mutual understanding, agreement and action. It comprises the mechanisms and processes for citizens and groups to articulate their interests, mediate their differences and exercise their legal rights and obligations. It is the rules, institutions and practices that set limits and provide incentives for individuals, organisations and firms. Governance, including its social, political and economic dimensions, operates at every level of human enterprise, be it the household, village, municipality, nation, region or globe. Essentially, governance concerns the relationship between institutions and traditions of authority and the governed. Good governance is authority acting for the good of the people in whose interests it was created.

While governance is a rather nebulous concept and defined in so many different ways, it is measured in lucid and quantifiable terms on which there is widespread agreement. The World Bank uses six components to measure and better define governance: voice and external accountability political stability and lack of violence, crime, and terrorism; government effectiveness; lack of regulatory burden; rule of law and control of corruption. The UNDP Oslo Governance Centre identifies core governance indicators as "parliamentary development; electoral systems and processes, justice and human rights; e-governance and access to information, decentralisation, local governance and urban/rural development; public administration reform and anti-corruption."

However defined or measured, the one major conclusion emerging from the development debate during the post-Washington consensus years is that good governance is essential in the development and the fight against poverty. In their cross-section study of more than 150 countries using indicators corresponding to six basic governance concepts, voice and accountability, political instability and violence, government effectiveness, regulatory burden, rule of law and graft, Kaufmann, Kraay and Zoido-Lepton demonstrated that governance matters for development outcomes. In their study, they found that a one-standard deviation increase in any one of the governance indicators caused between a two-and-a-half-fold and a fourfold increase in per capita incomes. Improved governance also leads to significant increases in adult literacy, with a one-standard deviation increase in governance leading to between a 15 and 25 percentage point improvement in literacy. As stated by the World Economic Forum, "A country that significantly improves key governance dimensions such as the rule of law, corruption, the regulatory regime, and voice and democratic accountability can expect in the long run a dramatic increase on its per capita incomes and in other social dimensions."

Because authoritative bodies intervene in creating an enabling environment for decent work, investment and entrepreneurship on behalf of people's interests, the concept of governance is also important in the labour market. Justified by the perceived or effective inability of laissez-faire conditions to deliver efficient and equitable outcomes in the labour market, people cede to national and local governments the direct power to intervene in the wage-setting process, in the regulation of working conditions and in the hiring and firing of workers. Indirectly, the government is also involved in the labour market by creating and enabling an environment for investment and entrepreneurship. Government involvement in fostering a skilled and healthy workforce, maintaining a peace that respects human rights, promoting property rights, establishing a sound macroeconomic environment, encouraging a well-functioning financial system, regulating and taxing firms in a sound way and enabling investment in basic infrastructure, are all components of an effective and sound labour market. Yet, governance of the labour market is not only the responsibility of national and local governments. As stated by the ILO in the Report, *Working Out of Poverty*, "the term governance' is used to mean the regulating influence of the set of institutions, norms and policies that determine the functioning of an economy and society.

Good governance of the labour market is essential for job creation and decent work for all, and therefore of primary importance in the fight against poverty. Decent work is the route out of poverty. In the World Bank's *Voices of the Poor* study, poor people identified getting a job – whether through self-employment or from wages – as the most promising path out of poverty. This is echoed by Juan Somavia, "We know only too well that it is precisely the world of work that holds the key for solid, progressive and long-lasting eradication of poverty. Decent work and poverty reduction hinge on good governance of the labour market. Also stated by Juan Somavia, "Efforts to fulfil our collective commitments to fight poverty will fall short unless we focus on creating job opportunities and decent work for all... Getting there requires *good governance* at every level from the national to the global."

It should be made clear that governance of the labour market affects not just those currently in the labour market, but those who would like to enter the labour market, those who have left the labour market, those who will soon enter the labour market and those who pay for labour market policies. While it is common to assume that labour market governance affects only workers and their enterprises, this approach would be highly erroneous, ignoring the broader range of interests involved. Taxpayers for public services also have a stake in the costs of providing good labour market governance. Children, or the future labour market, also have very different interests than those currently working. Authoritative bodies created in the interests of the people must represent the common interest. Governance of the labour market must take into account the broad interests of society at large.

2.9.1. Good Labour Market Governance

The overall objective of public institutions in terms of their labour market involvement is to enable job creation and the realisation of decent work for all, which in turn depends on an environment that fosters investment and entrepreneurship. As stated by the ILO, "Good governance of the labour market promotes opportunities for women and men to obtain productive work in conditions of freedom, equity, security and human dignity. The characteristics of good labour market governance include the voice of the people and participation in the formulation of labour market policies, governing bodies' accountability to the people they represent in their formulation of policies that impact the labour market, institutions' implementation and deliverance of sound public services for the effective creation of decent work, the respect of people and institutions for the rules and practices that impact job creation and a wider international community committed to using decent work as the path out of poverty.

Citizens' voice and participation in the formulation of labour market policies: Just as with governance in general, the basis for good governance of the labour market is a well-functioning and democratic political system that ensures representative and honest governments responsive to the needs of the people. In this way people are better ensured that the institutions to which they cede their power establish labour market policies in their interest. It also depends on an inclusive and vibrant civil society, empowered by freedom of association and expression and representing the full diversity of views and interests in society. Strong organisation is important so that people can the labour market policies that affect their lives and ensure that policies are democratic. The poor, especially, must be granted the right to organise and participate in government decisions. Yet, today, this is sadly not the case. As declared by Juan Somavia, "The political process, which leads to decisions about taxation and expenditure as well as the mechanisms for market regulation, is a determining influence on poverty reduction. However the voice of poor communities is often not heard in the political process. The freedom of people living in poverty to organise themselves and voice their concerns and aspirations is fundamental to a determined effort to shape a more equitable patterns of development."

Institutions' accountability to the people they represent in their formulation of policies that impact the labour market: Citizens that are able to monitor those in authority and hold them accountable for their actions are better ensured that labour market policies are fair, democratic and designed in their interest. Political competition plays an important role in holding governments responsible for their results and their actions. A free and independent media plays a critical role in monitoring governments and informing citizens, helping to ensure that labour market policies benefit the common interest. Education, also, is essential in ensuring that people have the capacity for evaluating government actions and understanding whether or not public policies will benefit their long-transpirations.

Institutions' implementation of sound policies and deliverance of public services for the effective creation of decent work: Strengthened and shaped by people's participation and institutions' accountability, good labour market governance is manifest in the implementation of policies that enable decent work creation and an enabling environment for investment and entrepreneurship, the motors of productive job formation. These universal policies, which should form the base and starting point for public institutions, should include both direct interventions that enable to people to gain decent work and indirect interventions that create an environment in which decent work thrives:

2.9.1.1. Direct Interventions

Foster a healthy and educated workforce: Enhancing human capital is essential in improving productivity, incomes and access to decent work opportunities. Government institutions have an important role in this regard by increasing access to primary education and as well as creating an enabling environment for vocational training so that adults are able to acquire competencies that the market demands. Since training is a process of lifelong learning in which skills are continually renewed and adapted, not a once-and-for-all investment before the start of working life, public institutions must work jointly with enterprises – both large and small – to ensure that learning is constant.

Support the free right of association and collective bargaining: Freedom of association and institutions for dialogue and bargaining are essential in order to protect the fundamental rights of workers, provide social protection and promote sound industrial relations. Freedom of association and collective bargaining lead to decent work and constitute important instruments for participation and accountability. An important way that government can achieve equality is to ensure that all types of workers – working in the informal or formal economies, working for large or micro enterprises, working for others or themselves, etc. – have the same rights to organise.

Move children out of work and into school: Decent work for the next generation of workers depends on their current education, and for over 200 million poor children between the ages of 5 and 14, this implies moving them out of work and into school today so that they can find better work tomorrow. Child labour, by depriving children of a quality education, leads to the perpetuation of household poverty across generations and slows economic growth and social development when widespread. Public institutions have the responsibility of making it easier for families to choose education over work. They can do this by providing access to school and improving family incomes by enabling more earning opportunities for adults.

Overcome discrimination: Overcoming discrimination is essential in ensuring decent work for all and in defeating social exclusion and poverty. Discrimination denies people jobs, confines them to certain occupations or offers them lower pay simply because of their gender, religion, race or ethnic group, regardless of their capabilities or requirements of the job. Race, religion, ethnic and caste barriers condemn many communities to the margins of society and the economy. Pervasive gender discrimination makes it even more difficult for women to escape poverty than men. Public institutions have the duty to end discrimination by equalising education opportunities and adopting legislation that ensures all persons are granted equal opportunities for decent work.

Stop forced labour: Abusive control of one human being over another is the direct opposite of decent work. Forced labour robs victims of their freedom and dignity by forcing them to endure brutal living conditions, depriving them of education, ostracising them from families and communities and inflicting on them physical and mental damage. Institutions created for the common good have the responsibility to stop forced labour by enabling the creation of economic opportunities for the world's poorest and most vulnerable – the primary targets, making communities and potential victims aware of potential traps, generating awareness and respect of people's legal and human rights and integrating past victims into their society.

Devise labour market protections to benefit all workers: Public institutions can help deliver efficient and equitable outcomes in the labour market by intervening in the wage setting process, regulating working conditions and controlling the hiring and firing of workers. Ill-conceived approaches, however, can destroy decent work and exacerbate poverty by contributing to unemployment and swelling the size of the informal and unprotected economy. Government institutions can ensure that labour market interventions benefit all workers by: 1) encouraging wage adaptability and ensuring that workers are properly compensated for their work, 2) ensuring that workplace regulations reflect a good institutional fit and 3) balancing workers' preference for employment stability with enterprises' need to adjust the workforce.

2.9.1.2. Indirect Interventions

Maintain a peace that upholds the rights and dignity of citizens: Nothing undermines decent work so much as the outbreak of armed conflict. Conflict destroys human, physical and social capital and diverts resources from growth-enhancing endeavours – all leading to losses in jobs. The typical civil war in the past 50 years cut 2.2 per cent off the projected annual growth rate. On average, at the end of hostilities, GDP was 15 per cent lower in conflict ridden countries than it would have otherwise been. In the interest of decent work and poverty alleviation, government institutions have the prerogative of establishing and maintaining peace that respects human rights and dignity.

Create a stable macroeconomic environment and a well-functioning financial system: Low inflation, sustainable budget deficits and realistic exchange rates lead to a sound investment climate and well-functioning financial markets, which are essential for the sustainable creation of decent work. Instability in the macroeconomic environment deters investment by making future rewards more uncertain and undermining the value of assets. High inflation and volatile real exchange rates have particularly negative consequences on small and micro investors. Since these small and micro-sized firms employ the greater part of people in the world, including the vast majority of the poor, substantial and equitable creation of decent work depends on a stable macroeconomic context.

Ensure secure property rights: Secure property rights, including land and other property, assure that firms and entrepreneurs are able to reap the rewards of their investments. The better property rights are protected, the greater the incentives to open new businesses and invest more in existing ones. And the more investment, the more decent work. Improving the security of property rights also gives owners more incentives to rent their land because they no longer fear that a tenant may try to assert a claim to the property. Secure property rights also involve low costs and risks of exchanging them. In this way, well-functioning courts are essential. Better courts reduce the risks firms face, and so increase the firms' willingness to invest more.

Regulate and tax enterprises soundly: The way governments regulate and tax firms and transactions plays an important role in shaping the investment climate, which in turn affects the creation of decent work. Sound regulation addresses market failures, such as negative externalities, information problems and monopolies, that inhibit productive investment and reconciles the interests of firms with those of society, and sound taxation generates the revenues to finance public services that improve the investment climate and meet other social goals. Yet regulation and taxes also inflict costs – not only on the enterprises themselves, but also on society. They can also become the means through which corruption manifests itself: firms or groups seek regulation to protect them from competition, officials use regulation to extract bribes in return for favourable decisions and tax revenues are used for unofficial purposes. When in excess or used inappropriately, the costs of regulation and taxes can exceed the social interest benefits.

Enable the building of basic infrastructure: Good infrastructure connects enterprises to their customers and suppliers and helps workers become more productive. Firms with access to modern telecommunications services, a reliable electricity supply and efficient transport links are able to invest more and their investments are more productive. This all leads to decent work creation. Government institutions have the responsibility for either creating infrastructure themselves or creating an environment in which private providers invest in projects. Yet, owing to infrastructure's tendency to constitute a "natural monopoly", governments also have the responsibility for regulating infrastructure in the interest of the common good. Government institutions have often reserved the provision of infrastructure for the public domain, yet without the resources to consistently invest and provide an adequate amount. This has all led to less than optimal investment in infrastructure projects. Governments must take care to establish rules and institutions that constrain market power without weakening property rights.

Respect of people and institutions for the rules and practices that govern and affect the labour market: Respect of people and institutions for the rules and practices that govern and affect the labour market is essential for ensuring fair and predictable labour market outcomes for all. An equitable legal framework, applied consistently and equally to everyone, defends people from abuse of power and empowers people to assert their rights – to property, education, freedom of speech and other springboards into decent work. Sadly, government institutions often become the minions of elite interest groups instead of the servants of all. In general, corruption, defined as the exploitation of public office for private gain, significantly harms job growth and the investment climate in several ways. When it infects the highest levels of government, it distorts policymaking on a grand scale and leads to a badly functioning labour market. Played out through officials at lower levels of government, corruption is a tax on entrepreneurial activity, it diverts resources from public services, creates a constituency for erecting or maintaining unnecessary red tape and thereby, destroys the creation of decent work.

Wider international community's commitment to using decent work as the path out of poverty: While so far most of the recommendations have been targeted to national governments, the international community, too, has an important role in establishing good labour market governance. Global governance also matters for good labour market outcomes. This is especially true in an interconnected world in which policies in one country affect outcomes in others. Indeed, one of the major conclusions from the report, *A Fair Globalisation: Creating Opportunities for All*, is that globalisation must be subjected to better governance at all levels if the benefits of globalisation are to be enjoyed by all. To create a better global governance in the goal of decent work for all, international institutions need to establish fair rules in global competition, investment and international migration; implement better international policies to support growth, enterprise development, poverty reduction, full employment, social protection and the creation of decent work for all; and be more accountable to the people, both in terms of setting the global agenda and assessing the results of global policies.

2.9.1.3. Perform in Terms of Labour Market Governance

If good labour market governance results in the realisation of decent work for all, the continued existence of high unemployment and working poverty on a large scale shows that institutions that govern and affect labour markets are not performing well for large numbers of people in many countries. The ILO's *World Employment Report 2004-05* states there were 185.9 million people in the world who were unemployed in 2003 and even of those who were employed, 1.39 billion were still unable to lift themselves and their families above the $2 a day poverty line. This means that 49.7 percent of the world's workers and over 58.7 percent of the developing world's workers are not earning enough to lift themselves and their families above the $2 a day poverty line, and that 19.7 percent of the employed persons in the world and therefore over 23.3 percent of the developing world's workers are currently living on less than $1 a day.

Not only evident in the numbers of unemployed and working poor, the effects of bad labour market governance are also visible in the enormous size of informal labour markets, the large numbers of child workers and the continued marginalisation and social exclusion of certain socialite groups. Informal workers represent nearly two-thirds of the total non-agricultural labour force in Africa, half in South Asia, a third in the Middle East, and a quarter in East Asia and Latin America. Large informal markets mean that public institutions have not yet found the balance between regulating enterprises to protect workers while at the same time stimulating the creation of decent work. So people, in order to earn an eager living, must work outside the formal rules. Approximately 211 million children between the ages of 5 and 14 work, meaning that public institutions have not yet discovered how to enable the creation of enough decent work for the adults in society so that their children can attend school full-time. Good governance of the labour market is far from sight.

Bad labour market outcomes are widespread because the poor are consistently denied a voice in designing labour market policies, institutions of authority are not accountable to the people, labour market policies are not implemented with the common interest in mind, authority is often corrupt and the international community has not been committed to making decent work for all a priority. Most countries, even if they recognise the free right of association and the right to collective bargaining, only grant formal employees the right to organise and form collective unions. This excludes the majority of the poor and informal workers. It is no wonder that outcomes only benefit elite or powerful groups. Governments everywhere are not accountable to the people on whose behalf they exist, designing policies in blatant disregard of the common interest. Regulations and tax systems benefit favoured groups, stifling the creation of decent work for all. Property rights are stewed against the poor. Governments often use infrastructure projects for personal gain or stifle their continued improvement by making them objects of political issue. And labour market policies benefit already powerful and protected groups. Corruption and capture of state officials is a rampant issue, inhibiting the creation of decent work. And the international community, too, is much to blame. The multilateral system responsible for designing and implementing international policies is currently not sufficiently democratic, transparent and accountable. Rules and policies are the outcome of a system of global governance largely shaped by powerful countries and powerful players. In effect, the poor have little voice and are not accounted for in this governance process.

But there are signs of progress. The first being that governance has become an issue of importance within institutions of authority worldwide and recognised as essential in the path out of poverty. This view is echoed within the multilateral institutions, national governments and leaders everywhere. As evidenced in this statement by the ILO, "The quality of the institutions that constitute the governance framework for labour markets is central to strategies to promote productivity, growth and sustainable development and ensure that poverty is reduced and eventually eradicated. It is voiced by leaders worldwide, as in this statement by Paul Kagame, President of Rwanda, "Not only must we grasp concepts such as these, we must also place them in specific historical contexts, if we are to successfully confront the challenges that lie ahead in our quest for effective governance."

References

Alice O'Connor; 2000. "Poverty Research and Policy for the Post-Welfare Era" *Annual Review of Sociology*.

Betson, David M., and Jennifer L. Warlick . (1998) "Alternative Historical Trends in Poverty." *American Economic Review* 88:348-51.

Paugam, Serge. 1998. "Poverty and Social Exclusion: A Sociological View." Pp. 41–62 in *The Future of European Welfare*, edited by Martin Rhodes and Yves Meny.

3

Poverty And Human Rights

At a very basic level, well-being can be thought of as the quality or the "well-less" of a person's being or living, and living itself can be seen as consisting of a set of interrelated "functioning" of the things that a person can do or be. The level of well-being thus depends on the level of those functioning. The concept of "capability" refers to a person's freedom or opportunities to achieve well-being in this sense.

To see the relevance of capability for understanding poverty, we may begin by noting that the defining feature of a poor person is that they have very restricted opportunities to pursue their well-being. Poverty can thus be seen as low levels of capability, or, as Sen puts it, "the failure of basic capabilities to reach certain minimally acceptable levels".

3.1. Conceptual Approaches of Poverty

First, not all kinds of capability failure would count as poverty. Since poverty denotes an extreme form of deprivation, only those capability failures would count as poverty that are deemed to be basic in some order of priority. Different communities may of course have different orders of priority and hence a different listing of what would qualify as 'basic' capabilities. But from empirical observation it is possible to identify certain basic capabilities that would be common to all.

Second, once poverty is seen to consist in the failure of a range of basic capabilities, it immediately becomes a multidimensional concept. Poverty can no longer be defined unidimensionally as lack of adequate income, as has traditionally been done. In fact, in this conception inadequate income ceases to be a dimension of poverty at all because income is not a capability and hence not an aspect of well-being in itself, although it may contribute to the achievement of capabilities.

It is nonetheless important to acknowledge that the concept of income more generally, command over economic resources – does play an important role in defining poverty. The way it does so is not by adding a dimension to poverty but by helping to distinguish the phenomenon of poverty from a low level of well-being in general. This distinction is important because while poverty implies a low level of well-being, not every case of a low level of well-being can be regarded as poverty. For example, while the absence of the capability to live a healthy life is certainly a case of a low level of well-being, the specific case of ill-health caused by a genetic disorder will not in itself be recognised as poverty; whereas ill-health caused by lack of access to basic health-care resources will be.

Several clarifications should, however, be made at this point so as to avoid misunderstanding.

First, while the concept of poverty does have an irreducible economic connotation, the relevant concept here is not low income but the broader concept of inadequate command over economic resources, of which inadequate personal income is only one possible source. Other sources include insufficient command over publicly provided goods and services, inadequate access to communally owned and managed resources, inadequate command over resources that are made available through formal and informal networks of mutual support, and so on.

Second, the recognition that poverty has an irreducible economic connotation does not necessarily imply the primacy of economic factors in the causation of poverty. For example, when discrimination based on gender, ethnicity or any other ground denies a person access to health-care resources, the resulting ill-health is clearly a case of capability failure that should count as poverty because the lack of access to resources has played a role here. However, as argued before, the existence of this mediating role is crucial in distinguishing poverty formal low level of well-being in general.

Third, it is important to emphasise that even though the link with economic resources must be maintained, this does not render the capability-based concept of poverty equivalent to a uniformly low level of command over economic resources. The two would be equivalent only if everyone had the same capacity to convert resources into capabilities, but that is not the case. Similarly, people living in different cultural environments might feel that they need different amounts of clothing in order to have the capability to be clothed at a minimally acceptable level.

3.2. Human rights for the Poor

Human rights for the poor have an important relevance and we will highlight the most significant consensuses that have been formed in recent years. Particularly, if human rights are to be enforced, more attention must be focused on the poor. Similarly, it has been widely recognised that a greater respect for poor people's human rights is essential if poverty is to be reduced. Because people are discriminated against, denied education, disempowered, etc., poverty is perpetuated. Promoting basic human rights can go a long way in alleviating poverty and reducing poverty can help in the realisation of human rights for all.

As described in the Universal Declaration of human rights refer to rights that are inherent to the person. Solely by virtue of being a person, one is entitled to such rights. Human rights share two main characteristics: indivisibility and universality. Indivisibility means that they are all equally important in ensuring that all people can live a life of freedom and dignity. In contrast to needs, which can be legitimate, but not necessarily associated with an obligation on the part of the government, rights are legally guaranteed by human rights law and entail an obligation on the part of the government to enforce them. By definition, therefore, the poor are entitled to the same human rights as everyone else and the government has an obligation in ensuring that the poor receive such rights.

Yet, it is the poor who suffer the most from human rights violations. Indeed, life in poverty can be thought of as living without basic human rights. As argued by the United Nations Economic and Social Council, "Poverty and, in particular, extreme poverty and exclusion from society constitute a violation of human dignity and a denial of human rights and fundamental freedom." As described by the poor themselves, poverty means constant food insecurity, lack of adequate and safe water and living in bad housing and shelter. It means living in ill health – both physical and mental. It means living in insecurity. It means being denied the right to own property. It means powerlessness and impotence – lack of freedom of choice and action. As expressed by Amartya Sen, poverty is "the failure of basic capabilities to reach certain minimally acceptable levels".

Also, just by virtue of living in poverty, the poor are denied basic human rights. For no other reason than being poor, people are denied the right to work, the right to education and the right to participate in a political process. Poverty in itself is a reason for discrimination. As observed by the United Nations Committee on Economic, Social and Cultural Rights, "Sometimes poverty arises when people have no access to existing resources because of who they are, what they believe or where they live. Discrimination may cause poverty, just as poverty may cause discrimination. And indirectly, by not having means or power, poor people are denied a basic education, indiscriminately persecuted, denied the right to be recognised before the law, etc. Because of their poverty and powerlessness, the poor are the most likely to fall into bonded labour arrangements and work as children. They do not have access to basic human health services and often have no official documentation of their existence.

Similarly, people are poor and poverty has been so intractable because basic human rights are consistently denied. People are denied jobs due to discrimination against their ethnic, religious and caste background. And because they are denied the ability to sustain a livelihood, they feel powerless and become materially destitute. Because people are denied the right to participate in a political process, forman association and express their opinion they have no voice with which to speak out against blatant government abuse and demand respect and dignity. A significant amount of poverty could be reduced if basic human rights were enforced.

The poor are also the most ignored by the government in terms of enforcement of their basic human rights. As expressed in the World Bank series *Voices of the Poor*, in community after community poor people report that state institutions – whether in their delivery of services, provision of police protection or justice or making political decisions – either are not accountable to anyone or accountable only to the rich and powerful. As observed in *Voices of the Poor: Crying Out for Change*, "Perhaps one of the most striking revelations of the study is the extent to which the police and official justice systems side with the rich, persecute poor people and make poor people more insecure, fearful and poorer. Yet, in the face of dependency and little recourse to justice, poor people are silent even when confronted with gross abuses of power.

Clearly there is a strong correlation between poverty and human rights violations as well as the abuse of people's basic human rights and their resulting poverty. Enforcing human rights for the poor would go a long way in alleviating poverty by attacking poverty's root causes, empowering the poor and obligating the government to be accountable to the poor.

As discussed above, poverty can be the result of discrimination, low human capital, ill-health, unjust working conditions, lack of political voice, persecution and poverty itself. In a tightly woven web, disrespect for human rights leads to and perpetuates poverty. By enforcing basic human rights, such as the right to freedom from discrimination, the right to education and the right to an adequate standard of living for the well-being of the individual and his/her family, etc. many of poverty's underlying causes would be rooted out.

3.3. Empowering the Poor

As defined by Deepa Narayan, "Empowerment is the expansion of assets and capabilities of poor people to participate in, negotiate with, influence, control, and hold accountable institutions that affect their lives. Empowerment is essential for poverty reduction because powerlessness is one of the main root causes and effects of poverty itself. As expressed in *Voices of the Poor: Crying Out for Change*, "The challenge for development professionals, and for policy and practice is to find ways to weaken the web of powerlessness and to enhance the capabilities of poor women and men so that they can take more control of their lives."

A human rights approach is important, therefore, because it empowers individuals by granting them entitlements that give rise to legal obligations on the part of the government. As stated by the

Economic and Security Council, "While the common theme underlying poor people's experiences is one of powerlessness, human rights can empower individuals and communities. The challenge is to connect the powerless with the empowering potential of human rights." In this way human rights place the poor as the principal actors and engaged subjects of development rather than its passive recipients.

In this regard, empowerment also legitimises people's right to participate and contribute to their own development. According to the UNDP, "This means that participation is not simply something desirable from the point of view of ownership and sustainability, but rather a right with profound consequences for the design and implementation of development activities." The right to participate also depends on and strengthens other essential human rights, such as the right of association, right of assembly, freedom of expression, right to information and right to a reasonable standard of living. As observed in *Voices of the Poor: Crying Out for Change*, "The poor want desperately to have their voices heard, to make decisions and not to always receive the law handed down from above."

3.3.1 Role of Government

On the other side of the coin, a human rights approach confirms that the rights of the poor are binding obligations on the part of the government, not just aspirations. And therefore, enforcement of rights that can directly lead to poverty reduction becomes more than a moral obligation, it becomes a legal obligation. This distinguishes the human rights-based approach to development from a welfare or basic needs approach by bringing in legal tools and institutions – laws and the judiciary – as a means to secure freedom and human development.

As a result, a human rights based approach urges speedier results in poverty reduction and holds policy-makers accountable for their actions. Accountability is so important since poor people in many countries voice the problems of corruption, 'connections,' and violation of basic human rights with impunity as a main constraint to development.

A human rights approach, in which the principle of universality is enshrined, also confirms that the government is accountable to the poor just as any other group. This is of utmost importance because, as voiced over and over again in the *Voices of the Poor* series, poverty is often aggravated and perpetuated by governments' deaf ears to the poor and its blatant perpetration of the poor more than any other group. Nondiscrimination and equality prohibits discrimination in law or in any practice in any field regulated and protected by public authorities, such as healthcare, education, access to services and immigration.

Lastly, obligating the government to recognise and respect poor people's rights also depends on and enforces good government. This is important because from the perspective of the poor, there is a crisis in governance: contact with state institutions is disempowering and excluding. Yet good governance plays a fundamental role in creating and maintaining a conducive environment for poverty reduction. As highlighted in the UNDP's Poverty Report 2000, *Overcoming Human Poverty*, transparent and inclusive governance is an important link between the formulation of national anti-poverty policies and actual poverty reduction. As deemed by the poor themselves, transparency and accountability are essential in bringing about institutional change to reduce poverty.

3.4. Relevance of Human Rights

Despite progressive realisation of human rights, and although human rights by definition are indivisible and interdependent, some rights are of particular importance to poverty reduction. As identified by the UNDP and the United Nations Economic Security Council, the following rights are considered most pertinent:

> Human rights and human development are closely interconnected and each depends on the other for its fulfilment. Yet the strategy for achieving human rights is inherently different than that for human development, placing the poor as the principle actors in the realisation of their rights instead of passive recipients of development programmes. This is echoed by Juan Somavia, Director-General of the ILO, "People in poverty need voice to obtain recognition of rights and demand respect. They need representation and participation. They also need good laws that are enforced and work for, not against, their interests. Without rights and empowerment, the poor will not get out of poverty."

The capability approach defines poverty as the absence or inadequate realisation of certain basic freedom, such as the freedom to avoid hunger, disease, illiteracy, and so on. Freedom here is conceived in a broad sense, to encompass both positive and negative freedom. Thus, a person's freedom to live a healthy life is contingent both on the requirement that no one obstructs their legitimate pursuit of good health – negative freedom, and also on the society's success in creating an enabling environment in which they can actually achieve good health – positive freedom.

The reason why the conception of poverty is concerned with basic freedom is that these are recognised as being fundamentally valuable for minimal human dignity. But the concern for human dignity also motivates the human rights approach, which postulates that people have inalienable rights to these freedom. If someone has failed to acquire these freedom, then obviously their rights to these freedom have not been realised.

Using this conceptual equivalence between the perspectives of capabilities and rights, we can now answer the question posed at the beginning: Which cases of non-fulfilment of human rights would count as poverty, when poverty is viewed from the perspective of human rights? Recalling the features of the capability view of poverty discussed earlier, we can now stipulate that non-fulfilment of human rights would count as poverty when it meets the following two conditions:

1. The human rights involved must be those that correspond to the capabilities that are considered basic by a given society;
2. Inadequate command over economic resources must play a role in the causal chain leading to the non-fulfilment of human rights.

The idea that non-fulfilment of only certain kinds of human rights and not others will count as poverty may seem to militate against the principle of indivisibility of rights, which states that all human rights are equally important. However, it does not.

The principle of the indivisibility of human rights does not mean that all social phenomena must be defined by reference to all rights. The principle does not mean that torture, sexual stereotyping, or unfair trials must be defined by reference to all the rights enumerated in the Universal Declaration of Human Rights. On the contrary, a human rights definition of these phenomena would certainly be confined to a limited range of international human rights. However, a *strategy* to combat torture, sexual stereotyping or unfair trials would have to address a much wider range of rights than those by which these phenomena are defined. On the other hand, an effective *strategy* for tackling the problem of unfair trials would not only include issues relating to ICCPR, article 14, such as the presumption of innocence, but also the terms and conditions of judges' employment.

The same argument applies to poverty. The principle of the indivisibility of human rights does not demand that poverty be defined by reference to all the rights set out in the International Bill of Rights, but it does demand an inclusive strategy for addressing poverty.

It is useful to distinguish three different ways in which human rights can be relevant to poverty: constitutive relevance, instrumental relevance and constraint-based relevance. If the non-fulfilment of a certain human right meets the two conditions mentioned above, it can be said to have constitutive relevance to poverty. But even when a right does not have constitutive relevance in this sense, it may still be relevant to poverty for the other two reasons. Instrumental relevance refers to the ability of certain human rights to promote the cause of poverty reduction. Two different types of instrumental relevance may be distinguished, viz. Causative and evaluative.

The *causative relevance* of some human rights is illustrated by the well-known example provided by Amartya Sen in his pioneering work on famines.

His analysis points to the empirical regularity that famines never occur in a functioning democracy with a reasonable degree of civil-political freedom, especially with a relatively free media that is allowed to openly criticise the powers of the day. The reason for this regularity lies in the fact that democratically elected politicians cannot afford to be oblivious to the hue and cry that a free media would raise in the event of a famine, with the result that the Government tends to take appropriate preventive measures before an impending famine has the chance to strike. Obviously, however, the same causative relevance can also exist even in a situation of less extreme but persistent poverty.

The idea of evaluative relevance stems from the observation that the analysis of poverty requires social evaluation of various kinds. Recall, for instance, the point made earlier that the characterisation of poverty calls for a prior judgment as to which capabilities are to count as basic. In order to be ethically defensible, this judgment must be arrived at through a process of social consultation in which people from all walks of life are able to participate fully. The fulfilment of these rights is, therefore, an essential precondition for an ethically defensible evaluation of poverty. As such, all these rights have evaluative relevance to poverty, even if they do not form part of the definition of poverty.

The final way in which human rights can be relevant to poverty, even if they are not part of the definition of poverty, is to act as a constraint on the types of action that are permissible in the quest for reducing poverty.

For instance, while it is entirely sensible that a highly populous but resource-poor country would want to adopt measures for population control as part of a strategy for poverty reduction, it would not be permissible to adopt draconian measures such as forced sterilisation that violate people's personal integrity and privacy.

To conclude, although only some human rights may form part of a human rights definition of poverty, a much wider range of rights will be vital in any discourse on poverty and indispensable in the formulation of Press.

It is on the basis of this fundamental proposition that the following section delineates the main features of a rights-based approach to poverty reduction.

Social dialogue is not only a component of the Decent Work Agenda, it is also a process for achieving decent work. The annual International Labour Conference of the ILO in June 2002 reiterated the critical role of social dialogue for promoting and reinforcing fundamental principles and rights at work, achieving employment goals and improving social protection in all communities. The relevance of social dialogue is increasingly recognised as the international community searches for an appropriate response to the challenges of globalisation. In this regard, the action pursued by the ILO was to foster the dialogue, partnerships and participatory approaches, especially in those PRSP countries. Building programmes for labour ministries and the social partners are necessary if employers and workers are to participate fully in the making of major economic and social policy decisions.

A human rights approach to poverty also requires the active and informed participation of the poor in the formulation, implementation and monitoring of Press. The right to participation is a crucial and complex human right that is inextricably linked to fundamental democratic principles.

The international human rights normative framework includes the right to take part in the conduct of public affairs. Although free and fair elections are a crucial component of the right to participate, they are not enough to ensure that those living in poverty enjoy the right to participate in key decisions affecting their lives. Specific mechanisms and detailed arrangements for the enjoyment of the right to participate will vary greatly from one context to another: one size does not fit all. The active and informed participation of the poor in the formulation of Press cannot be hurried inevitabıy, it will take time.

The ILO Report, *Working Out of Poverty*, highlights the importance to the poor of the right to participate. In this regard principles and rights at work are an essential foundation for the governance of labour market which requires rules to encourage working arrangements that are both efficient and fair. Reducing poverty in most countries requires both growth and redistribution. Getting the policy mix right to achieve and sustain equitable growth is most likely where development strategies have a high degree of support across social groups. This is necessary not only to avoid destabilisation as a result of conflicting claims but also to generate confidence that action by different groups, including governments, will be matched by others. This is particularly true for policies to increase the availability of decent work opportunities. The absence of social cohesion is a severe brake on development and in extreme circumstances can undermine the capacity of States to govern, and hence to achieve poverty reduction.

In this context the enjoyment of the right to participate is deeply dependent on the realisation of other human rights. For example, if the poor are to participate meaningfully in Press, they must be free to organise without restriction to meet without impediment and to say what they want without intimidation they must know the relevant facts and they must enjoy an elementary level of economic security and well-being. Thus, without parallel arrangements to realise these other rights, the poor cannot participate, in an active and informed manner, in the formulation, implementation and monitoring of Press.

3.5. Human Rights Approach to Poverty Reduction

In the words of the *Human Development Report 2000*, "Human rights and human development are close enough in motivation and concern to be congruous and compatible, and they are different enough in strategy and design to supplement each other fruitfully". While there is now a strong consensus on the complementarities between human rights and poverty, the consequences of such recognition are less understood.

3.5.1. Empowering the Poor

Fundamentally, a human rights approach to poverty is about the empowerment of the poor. One of the clearest and most persistent themes in the series *Voices of the Poor* is the powerlessness of the poor. For example, the second volume, *Crying Out for Change*, is organised around an examination of the "ten interlocking dimensions of powerlessness and ill-being [that] emerge from poor people's experiences". The third volume, *From Many Lands*, concludes by raising an important question: "How can societies be transformed so poor people feel empowered to create lives of dignity, security, and well-being?" A major contribution of a human rights approach to poverty reduction is the empowerment of poor people, expanding their freedom of choice and action to structure their own lives.

While the common theme underlying poor people's experiences is one of powerlessness, human rights empower individuals and communities by granting them entitlements that give rise to legal obligations on others. In short, human rights can mitigate the powerlessness of the poor. To use the language from *Crying Out for Change*, human rights provide one way of weakening "the web of powerlessness" and enhancing "the capabilities of poor women and men so that they can take more control of their lives".

3.5.2. Recognition of Human Rights Normative Framework

A human rights approach to poverty will include an explicit recognition of the national and international human rights normative framework. Special attention will be given to those treaties that a State has ratified for two reasons: treaty ratification represents "country ownership" of the relevant provisions and, second, a ratified treaty is legally binding on all branches of Government. Careful attention will also be given to the commitments entered into during the recent world conferences, so far as they bear upon international human rights, such as the Rome Declaration on World Food Security of 1996 and the Dakar Framework for Action adopted by the World Education Forum in 2000, as well as the development goals set out in the United Nations Millennium Declaration of 2000.

An explicit reference to the international human rights treaties that a State has ratified serves to remind all parties that, when dealing with any government, they are required, as a minimum, to avoid policies and practices that make it more difficult for that Government to conform to treaty obligations it owes to individuals and groups within its jurisdiction.

3.5.3. Non-Discrimination and Equality

It is well documented that the poor frequently experience social exclusion, isolation, alienation, discrimination and inequality. This feeling of being looked down upon often arises from a combination of economic deprivation and sociocultural factors, such as ethnicity, colour, religion, social hierarchy and gender. Poverty not only arises formal lack of resources it may also arise formal lack of access to resources, information, opportunities, power and mobility. As the United Nations Committee on Economic, Social and Cultural Rights observes: "Sometimes poverty arises when people have no access to existing resources because of who they are, what they believe or where they live. Discrimination may cause poverty, just as poverty may cause discrimination."

The twin principles of nondiscrimination and equality are among the most fundamental elements of international human rights law. They are enumerated and elaborated in numerous international instruments, not least the Universal Declaration of Human Rights, ICESCR, ICCPR, CRC, the International Convention on the Elimination of All Forms of Racial Discrimination (ICERD), the Convention on the Elimination of All Forms of Discrimination against

Women (CEDAW), and the International Convention on the Protection of the Rights of All Migrant Workers and Members of Their Families (MWC).

In short, the international human rights normative framework has a particular preoccupation with individuals and groups who are vulnerable, marginal, disadvantaged or socially excluded. Thus, the integration of human rights into PRSPs helps to ensure that the relevant measures give proper attention to (a) those sectors and subsectors that have particular relevance to pro-poor policies and (b) the particular situation of vulnerable, marginal, disadvantaged and socially excluded individuals and groups.

Because of the special attention it has devoted to these issues over many years, including the systematic consideration of hundreds of reports from States on their relevant law and practice, the international human rights system has considerable experience regarding policy measures that impact on discrimination and inequality.

They may arise from express legal inequalities in status and entitlements; from policies that are blind to the needs of particular people; or from social values that shape relationships within households and communities. The human rights experience also confirms the importance of looking at effects, not intentions. For example, if the effect of a policy regime is to impoverish disproportionately women, indigenous peoples or any other group that is protected by one of the internationally prohibited grounds of discrimination, it is prima facie discriminatory, even if the policy-makers had no intention of discriminating against the group in question.

In conclusion, the integration of human rights into anti-poverty strategies helps to ensure that vulnerable individuals and groups are treated on a nondiscriminatory and equal basis and are not neglected. The human rights experience also provides numerous valuable insights regarding the efficacy of anti-discrimination and equality laws, policies and practices.

3.5.4. Integration of Human Rights into Poverty Reduction

With a view to achieving a human rights approach to poverty reduction strategies the office of the United Nations High Commission for Human Rights (OHCHR) developed draft guidelines on the subject. The short-term objective is to provide governments, development agencies and other practitioners involved in the design, implementation and monitoring of poverty reduction strategies with operational guidelines. The long-term objective is to enhance the effectiveness and sustainability of poverty reduction strategies.

The first phase has been characterised by the elaboration of a conceptual framework extensive consultations have been conducted with poverty specialists from the United Nations system, the Bretton Woods institutions, development agencies governments and civil society. A draft of the guidelines was prepared. In the second phase the draft guidelines will be revised. The piloting phase will include four components:

1. Awareness-building about the existence of the draft guidelines;
2. Substantive consultations with human rights experts, including treaty bodies, special rapporteurs, field officers and development practitioners;
3. Field testing;
4. Revision of the draft guidelines.

3.6. Labour Standards And Poverty Reduction

Poverty persists in large partly because people are denied core human labour rights. Forced labour drives victims into deeper and more intractable poverty, child labour robs children of future opportunities and societies of their hope, discrimination and poverty feed on each other in a vicious cycle and obstacles to the free right of association and collective bargaining silence those who have the most to say about poverty reduction.

Forced labour drives victims into deeper and more intractable poverty – stopping forced labour lifts individuals out of poverty traps and builds socially cohesive and peaceful societies.

Of all the ILO standards, the most widely ratified is the elimination of forced labour. Yet, sadly, forced labour remains a significant and rising global problem. While traditional slavery and state-sponsored forced labour are on the decline, human trafficking has been increasing significantly in recent decades, kidnapping is widely feared and the use of extreme forms of abuse and bonded labour is a rampant practice in many countries. Some estimates put the figures at 27 million forced labourers on a global scale. And according to the US State Department's 2004 Trafficking in Persons Report, 600,000-800,000 people are trafficked across international borders annually, many of them women and children bound for work in the commercial sex Industry.

Before delving into the links between the elimination of forced labour and a resulting reduction in poverty, it is beneficial to elucidate forced labour's victims and the main areas in which the phenomenon occurs, including military activities, prostitution, begging, domestic labour, agriculture, and hazardous and harmful industry such as mining and textile production. Within each of the economic areas discussed, the main mechanisms through which labour is secured and retained will be discussed, most prominently force, kidnapping, bondage and ever-increasing phenomenon of trafficking, which entail extreme dependence, vulnerability, force, coercion, exclusion and distance from familiar and helpful social networks.

3.6.1. Forced Labour Profiles

Domestic labour: Although most domestic work does not involve the use of force, it is an area that can easily degenerate into such a situation because of the workers' extreme dependence on their employers and the fact that they work within a private setting far from the scrutiny of even neighbours. Girls, particularly, are susceptible to sexual violence formal young age.

— *Begging*: Begging is another area in which forced labour is common. Children are often kidnapped and often maimed for use as beggars, and girls, particularly, may be 'sold off' by their families to beg and sell sex.

— *Prostitution:* Prostitution is often a forced labour problem in which women and children are abducted, 'cashed in' by relatives or misled into sexual exploitation. Increasingly, the trafficking of humans is an important mechanism by which people are induced into this situation.

— *Agriculture:* Agriculture is also an area in which forced labour exists, usually through debt or social bondage. In times of scarcity, rural workers are easy prey for recruiters, who offer means of subsistence through a debt that has to be paid off by future work.

— *War:* Child soldiering is a severe form of forced labour in which children are kidnapped or coerced through threats, bribes and false promises and forced to serve government armies, militias and rebel groups.

— *Industry:* In countless other hazardous or extremely low-wage activities, such as mining, brick kilns, construction, carpet making, camel jockeying, etc., forced labour is a common practice. Many workers induced into these situations accept work for an advance payment, which is structurally impossible to pay back in full. In addition, trafficking and kidnapping have also been used to secure or retain workers in these activities.

Although transcending so many modern-day activities, and recruited or retained through various means – namely force, trafficking, kidnapping or bondage – forced labour's victims have a common face: they are the world's most vulnerable and marginalised peoples. They tend to come from the poorest segments of communities, in many cases from groups that are discriminated against and often come from rural areas. They are particularly vulnerable, because they are children, are uneducated, are hungry or perhaps because they have been moved from familiar social networks. Nearly all of them, or their families that may have sold them, are desperate for work and the opportunity to make a modest living. Forced labour preys on poverty, and once in a forced labour situation the victims' poverty increases and is perpetuated, often across generations.

Because forced labour almost always places people in a worse situation than they would find themselves in otherwise – by forcing victims to endure brutal living conditions, depriving them of education, ostracising them from families and communities, inflicting on them physical and mental damage – its elimination would most definitely result in a reduction in poverty for the individual. Society also would gain significantly. As children are educated instead of falling captive to sexual and physical exploitation or kept from school because of the fear of being kidnapped and trafficked, human capital and productive capacity would increase substantially. The ILO has estimated that tens of billions of dollars would be gained as a result. And because forced labour promotes social breakdown, fuels more organised crime, undermines public health and subverts government authority the benefits of its elimination far exceed these modest estimates.

The effective reduction of forced labour requires targeting both the victims and its perpetrators. Economic opportunities must be created for the world's poorest and most vulnerable, communities and potential victims must be made aware of the dangers of trafficking and bonded labour arrangements, people should be made aware of their legal and human rights and programmes must be implemented to reintegrate past victims into their society.

On the other side, persons who exploit victims should be identified and prosecuted. In this regard, much progress could be made by combating corruption, since perpetrators' collusion with police and government officials often propagates the practice.

Child labour robs children of future opportunities and societies of hope – A future without child labour would lead to gains in the trillions through increased human capital. Although nearly all the world's governments have ratified international human rights conventions that call for the elimination of child labour, the phenomenon continues to exist to a significant extent.

As estimated in the ILO 2002 study, *Every Child Counts*, approximately 211 million children between the ages of 5 and 14 were working in the world in 2000. With nearly one-fifth of the world's children between the ages of 5-14 economically active and two-fifths of children between the ages of 5-17 working, child labour is a significant phenomenon.

Child labour is primarily a developing country phenomenon. The Asia-Pacific region has the largest number of child workers in the 5-14 age bracket, 127.3 million in total, followed by sub-Saharan Africa and Latin America & the Caribbean with 48 million and 17.4 million respectively Accounting for population size, sub-Saharan Africa has the highest relative proportion of working children: one child in three under the age of 15 is economically active. In the Middle East and North Africa, it is 15 percent.

Table 3.1. Number and percentage of children working by region in 2000

	Number of children working (in millions)	Work ratio (% in Child Population)
5-14 Years Old	211.0	17.6
Developed economies	2.5	2.0
Transition economies	2.4	4.0
Asia & the Pacific	127.3	19.0
Latin America & Caribbean	17.4	16.0
Sub-Saharan Africa	48.0	29.0
Middle East & North Africa	13.4	15.0
15-17 Years Old	140.0	42.4
Developed economies	11.5	31.3
Transition economies	6.0	29.1
Asia & the Pacific	86.9	48.4
Latin America & Caribbean	10.3	25.0
Sub-Saharan Africa	18.1	44.8
Middle East & North Africa	7.5	31.8
Total	351.0	23.0

Approximately one half of the total number of economically active children and more than two thirds of those in child labour were working in hazardous situations in 2000.[13] In addition to the number of children in hazardous work, it is estimated that there were about 8.4 million children involved in other worst forms of child labour as defined in ILO Convention No. 182, Art. 3. This includes trafficking forced and bonded labour; armed conflict; prostitution and pornography; and illicit activities (0.6 million). While the worst forms of child labour are above the intolerable level, as no level is acceptable, it is important to note that the majority of the world's child workers are not within this category.

In general, child labourers either work unpaid, in the household or on the family farm/in the family enterprise, or do paid work in the labour market. The vast majority of child workers are involved in agricultural work, typically in family-run farms. It is also important to note that these children may also be simultaneously enrolled in school. And, as evidenced by Orazemand Gunnarsson, a significant proportion of child labour spells are short-lived, many times in response to unanticipated transitory shocks to household income.

Sector	Work only	Work and School	School, no Work	Only HH Chores	Idle
Urban	9.5	14.7	46.5	12.2	17.0
Rural	19.8	21.8	24.9	14.6	19.0
Total	16.9	20.1	30.7	14.1	18.2

It is important to note, in this regard, that working does not necessarily displace school enrolment in developing countries, as is often assumed. For example, increases in enrolment in a sample of girls in Bangladesh were not associated with appreciable decreases in child labour. Yet, while the evidence on the effect of child labour on school enrolment is not very strong there is evidence of a strong negative effect on school attendance, test scores and grade completion.

Boozer and Suri, studying children aged 7-18 in Ghana in the late 1980s, conclude that an hour of child labour reduced school attendance by approximately 0.38 hours. Orazem and Gunnarsson, using data-sets of children in Latin America and Central and Eastern Europe, find that child labour has adverse consequences for test scores and that the effects get larger as work hours increase. They also find that the damage is greater at younger ages and that even modest amounts of child labour lower cognitive achievement. Similarly, Sanchez et al., using data on 3rd and 4th graders in Latin America, found that in all ten countries tested, performance on mathematics and language tests was lower when the child worked outside the home, and the impact became greater when the child reported working many - rather than a few - hours. Heady, studying Ghana, found that child work had relatively little effect on school attendance, but had a substantial effect on learning achievement in reading and mathematics, most likely attributable to exhaustion or lack of interest in academic performance. Roseate and Rosy, studying grade retardation in Pakistan and Nicaragua, found that increasing the probability of working raises the likelihood that the child has fallen behind the correct grade for age.

In effect, therefore, child labour has significant negative effects on human capital formation. As stated by Betcherman et al., "child labour is widespread and bad for development, both that of the individual child and of the society and economy in which she or he lives". Additionally, the hazardous and worst forms of child labour have obvious harmful effects on the lives of children and their possibilities for a hopeful future.

So, if the costs child labour incurs are enormous, why do so many children in poor countries continue to work instead of focusing their efforts in school? Basically, the answer is poverty, although individual decisions are much more nuanced. Children may work when the economic benefits of working are greater than the expected benefits of schooling when families are constrained from sending their children to school because of poverty or insurmountable short-term economic concerns or when parents are unaware of the economic benefits of education or orphaned children do not have any parents to act on their behalf because of HIV/AIDS or conflict.

The elimination of child labour would have an enormous impact of poverty reduction. It is estimated by the ILO that gross economic benefits from the elimination of child labour over the period 2000 to 2020 would be over five trillion dollars or a net benefit of approximately four trillion dollars after taking into account costs associated with eliminating the practice.

The elimination of child labour in a developing country context, however, is not as simple as banning the practice. Most obviously, developing countries lack the legal and political infrastructure for enforcement of a ban. Also, taking a child out of work may immediately plunge families into an even more dire poverty situation when income from the child is necessary for the family's survival. Additionally, many children that are "rescued" from labour arrangements often, driven by poverty, shift to less visible sectors or into the informal sector where conditions are more exploitative, thereby augmenting and perpetuating poverty.

In a developing country context, therefore, eliminating child labour must be achieved by attacking the roots of its occurrence. As outlined by the ILO, governments must address the reasons that families choose work over education; reduce poverty or insurmountable short-term economic concerns that force families to send their children to work; and ensure that people are aware of the benefits of education. In terms of addressing the reasons that families choose work over education, making schools accessible, improving their quality and reducing direct schooling costs can all have a large impact in this regard.

Discrimination and poverty feed on each other in a vicious cycle – Equality at work leads to enormous gains as people's skills and capabilities are used instead of being needlessly wasted.

Discrimination in employment and occupation exacerbates poverty, while poverty furthers discrimination by limiting educational and employment opportunities for generations beyond. Tightly linked, the two feed on each other in a vicious cycle. By denying certain groups equal education opportunities as well as equivalent entitlements and rights, they and their future generations are indirectly discriminated against in the workplace as their capabilities are never fully realised.

Its victims are disproportionately women, older people, rural inhabitants, indigenous groups, ethnic and religious minorities and the historically disenfranchised. In developing countries, they include the Roma in Bulgaria, the low castes and untouchable in India, "the hated poor" in Bangladesh, indigenous and Afro-American groups in Latin America, and slum dwellers everywhere. All over the world discrimination leads to poverty and marginalisation and at the same time the poorest and most marginalised peoples are the primary victims of discrimination.

The reason why discrimination exists is not fully understood. Through the theory of "statistical discrimination" or "employers' taste," neoclassical economists explain discrimination based on the premise that firms cannot scrutinize the productivity of individuals. As a consequence, they tend to rely on easily observable characteristics, such as race or gender, as an indicator of likely productivity – often assuming members of certain groups to have lower than average productivity. It follows that discrimination at work should be short-lived because it is costly and inefficient. Employers who discriminate against certain groups should disappear because they cannot compete with employers who do not discriminate. Yet, the fact that certain groups have remained disproportionately discriminated against throughout history reflects the insufficiency of most theories proposed so far.

Regardless of why discrimination in employment and occupation exists and persists, it inflicts many costs, not only on the individual, but also on society. Most importantly, it results in an enormous waste of skills and capabilities. And because it often leads to inequality, discrimination can foment political instability and therefore reduced economic growth. Inequality in general has been also shown to be bad for growth and poverty reduction. Because discrimination can be extremely severe, accounting for up to 50 percent of wage differentials as the table below demonstrates, its costs are estimated to be substantial.

Enormous benefits would be gained by countries that are successful in eliminating discrimination. The projected gains would be generated froman increase in aggregate production and income arising from the full use of the existing education, skills and experience of Afro-descendant and indigenous individuals in the jobs that they actually hold in addition to an increase in aggregate production and income due to expanding the education and skills of Afro-descendant and indigenous individuals to levels similar to those of the white population in those countries.

The equalisation of education, not only in years of schooling, but also in terms of quality, can go a long way in reducing discrimination. Affirmative action has also been useful, particularly in Malaysia, South Africa and the United States. Legislation and its effective enforcement is also an important way to ensure that all persons, regardless of their gender, religion, race or ethnic group are granted their due opportunities.

Denial of freedom of association and right to collective bargaining silences those who have the most to say about poverty reduction – the right to organise for social justice leads to empowerment, placing the poor in the driver's seat of their own development.

Freedom of association and the right to collective bargaining is far from widespread. While most OECD countries guarantee the freedom of association, restrictions exist in much of the developing world. Even it is possible to establish workers' organisations and union confederations, governments commonly limit the right of collective bargaining to formal employees. This silences the voice of the poor majority who often operate in the informal economy or are self-employed.

Table 3.2. Freedom of association in world countries

Group	*Definition*	*Countries*
1	Freedom of association, on the whole, is guaranteed by law and practice.	All OECD countries, except the Republic of Korea, Mexico and Turkey. In addition, Bahamas, Barbados, Israel, Malta and Surname.
2	Some restrictions exist, but it is possible to establish independent workers' organisations and union confederations.	Argentina, Brazil, Chile, Ecuador, Ethiopia, Fiji, Hong Kong, India, Jamaica, Mexico, Niger, Papua New Guinea, Peru, South Africa, Republica Bolivariana de Venezuela and Zambia.
3	Restrictions on freedom of association are significant, that is, stringent registration requirements exist, and political interference or acts of antiunion discrimination make it very difficult to form indep.. dent workers' organisations or union confederations.	Algeria, Bangladesh, Bolivia, Taiwan, Colombia, Ghana, Guatemala, Honduras, Kenya, Mali, Malaysia, Morocco, Nigeria, Pakistan, Philippines, Sri Lanka, Thailand, Tunisia, Turkey and Zimbabwe.
4	Freedom of association is practically nonexistent	Cameroon, China, Egypt, Indonesia, Iran, Kuwait, Syria and Tanzania.

Much of the reason for the diversity in countries' enforcement of freedom of association and the right to collective bargaining results from the controversy in its effects on poverty. Yet, most of that controversy stems from the fact that freedom of association and the right to collective bargaining have been historically granted to or practised by an elite few. When only elite insider groups have the power to voice their concerns, leaving outsiders and the poor excluded from the process, bad socialite outcomes - far from the common interest - are the result. This can be devastating in a poor country context if, unions push more people into a large and exploitative informal sector, drive up costs of basic noncompetitive goods, such as electricity or gas lower informal sector wages and further inequalities. These bad socialite outcomes are essentially the following monopoly costs, described below:

1. *Higher prices:* Firms will try to pass on the wage demands to consumers as higher prices. This increases inflation and therefore reduces the real wage of all workers.
2. *Increase in unemployment:* The wage mark-up of unionised workers increases the relative price of labour in the union sector, inducing firms to lay-off unionised workers;
3. *Reduction in the non-union wage:* As workers are laid-off, this tends to reduce the non-union wage. Also, an output loss may result because workers are now employed where their marginal productivity is lower than before;
4. *Reduction of investment:* As unionised firms share their profits with the union, a hold up problems created that reduces investments in physical capital and R&D below the socially optimal level. Empirical evidence supports this theory: in the UK and the US, the investment rate tended to be lower in unionised than in non-unionised firms with similar characteristics.

It should be emphasised that these are potential costs. Economic theory and empirical evidence show that if collective bargaining is able to incorporate the interests of all citizens, by ensuring that the poor, the unemployed and the informally employed are also granted the right to organise and voice their concerns and participate in any collective bargaining process, workers organisation can lead to significant benefits for society as a whole. As long as unions are open and incorporate the interests of excluded parties, outcomes in the common interest will result, some of which are outlined below:

1. *Reduction in inefficient turnover:* By communicating the preferences of workers directly to management and participating in the establishment of work rulesand seniority provisions, workers can express their grievances without having to leave the firm. Also, by helping establish seniority provisions, rivalry between experienced and inexperienced workers is lessened, thereby increasing the amount of informal, on the job training that the former is willing to provide to the latter;

2. *Increase in skills:* By enforcing contracts between workers and management, workers are more willing to acquire firm-specific skills because of greater uncertainty about future employment;
3. *Increase in productivity:* By providing a channel through which labour can draw management's attention to changes in working methods or production techniques that may be beneficial to both parties. Empirical evidence, however, is indeterminate in terms of productivity gains.

Apart from higher wages, longer job tenure, increased productivity and lower discrimination, the most important contribution of collective bargaining and freedom of association is empowerment. Empowerment refers broadly to the expansion of freedom of choice and action and was highlighted as one of the three important tools for promoting economic growth and reducing poverty by the 2000/2001 World Development Report. As defined by Deepa Narayan, "Empowerment is the expansion of assets and capabilities of poor people to participate in, negotiate with, influence, control, and hold accountable institutions that affect their lives." The right to collective bargaining and freedom of association enhance all four key elements of empowerment, namely access to information, the inclusion/participation in decision making, the accountability of public and private officials, and the ability of people to organise locally to solve problems of common interest, make their voices heard and ensure their demands are met. "

The challenge for governments, therefore, is to ensure that freedom of association and the right to collective bargaining is granted to all – including the poor, the informally employed and the self-employed. Additionally, outsider interests should be voiced in any collective bargaining process. Important strides have been made in recent years. In South Africa, for example, the provisions of the basic Conditions of Employment Act and the Unemployment Insurance Fund were extended to domestic workers. Taxi workers have been organised through the South African Transport and Allied Workers' Union (SATAWU) and have gained a powerful voice in recapitulation the industry and formalising employment. Also in South Africa, the Southern African Clothing and Textile Workers' Union (SACTWU) has played a key role in high-level negotiations that recently culminated in the adoption of legal and institutional reforms which allow for organising and bargaining around informal work. In India, after the Self-Employed Women's Association (SEWA) fought for and won the rights of groups of self-employed workers to be registered as trade unions, numerous efforts successfully mobilised and organised informal and poor workers across the country. As a result, enormous benefits were granted to the once, voiceless poor.

The focus, therefore, for an effective reduction in poverty through the free right of association and collective bargaining should be on how to remove the potential costs of unions and organisations while at the same time retaining their benefits. In a developing country context, the greatest potential benefit of a "voice at work" – whether the voice is that of a domestic worker or a taxi driver – is derived from greater empowerment. This is so because empowerment places the poor as the principle actors and engaged subjects of development rather than its passive recipients. And empowerment most definitely is good for poverty reduction.

Effective implementation of core labour standards leads to important reductions in poverty. Stopping forced labour lifts individuals out of poverty traps and builds socially cohesive societies, placing children in school instead of at work leads to increased human capital, equality at work results in enormous gains as people's skills and capabilities are used instead of needlessly wasted and the right to organise for social justice endows the poor with the power to drive their own development outcomes. If rescued from forced labour arrangements, victims must be ensured opportunities on their reintegration into normal society so that they will not become perpetrators themselves. Efforts to reduce child labour must not drive children into deeper and more exploitative activities. Good judgment needs to be used so that unions don't work against the poor, pushing more people into large and exploitative informal sector or furthering inequalities. While these challenges are significant, the enormous poverty reduction benefits are too large to ignore. The world's poor are counting on institutions to realise this.

3.7. Role of Labour Standards

Concepts of poverty have broadened in recent years beyond concerns about income and living standards to reflect a concern with vulnerability and risk, and with powerlessness and lack of voice. Increasingly, major institutions of global governance are moving toward comprehensive, broad-based and inclusive approaches to poverty alleviation that assert that workers have a right to labour standards. A focus on workers' rights to labour standards at work reflects this shift in ideas about poverty and vulnerability to a broader understanding of poverty as a lack of access to services, lack of personal security, low social status, and lack of control over labour and working conditions.

The World Bank's Comprehensive Development Framework, for example, builds on discussion in the OECD in 1995 on partnership, and aims to bring together current trends in development thinking that balance good macroeconomic and financial management with sound social, structural and human policies. And the *World Development Report 2000/2001* contrasts the World Bank's 1990 two-part strategy for poverty reduction – labour-intensive growth and broad provision of social services – with the Bank's current three-pronged approach – promoting opportunity facilitating empowerment and enhancing security.

A concern about the quality of the working environment, and the relationship between working conditions and the broader social environment has, traditionally, been a key concern of the trade union movement. Unions have always held that a consistent defence of their members' interests over the long termrequires them to work for people's overall well-being. Their vision of society includes elements such as political, social and industrial democracy, civil and democratic rights for all, the elimination of poverty, equality and the rule of law. Respect for freedom of association and effective recognition of the right to collective bargaining are thus intrinsic parts of a broad based conception of development as a process through which individuals and communities enlarge and realise their capabilities.

The relationship between the realisation of the principles of freedom of association and the effective recognition of the right to collective bargaining and development in a globalising world is complex.

In the United Nations Development Programme's Human Development Report 2000, Novel laureate Amartya Sen discusses a key underlying question: how to define "development". He advances the concept of freedom as development. This view includes as goals both civil and political freedom, of which freedom of association and the right to organise collectively are part.

The increasing discussion on core labour standards (CLS) takes place in the broader context of a globalising economy and society, and discussions on reform of financial architecture and global trade regimes. While much rhetoric is spilled recognising the urgency of integrating social and economic considerations in the new structures of global governance, the voices of those advocating for social objectives are sometimes less audible than those of finance and trade officials.

The international development community is increasingly accepting that while growth is important, sustainable development encompasses many other factors. There is growing recognition of the need to consider institutional factors in order to ensure that growth translates into poverty reduction. Among the institutions that matters are the "institutions of voice": trade unions and other effective social groups. As the ILO explains, principles of freedom of association and effective recognition of the right to collective bargaining are necessary conditions for the development of institutions of voice in the labour market – in both the formal and informal economy.

3.7.1. Labour Standards and Economic Growth

A recent literature review by the OECD concludes that there is growing consensus on the relationship between CLS, economic efficiency and growth. The 2000 study, argues that the resulting increased buy-in by workers to the goals of the immediate work group can lead to higher productivity.

The ILO presents the economic efficiency case for core labour standards as follows:

1. Child labour is detrimental to development, since it means that the next generation of workers will be unskilled and less well-educated;
2. Collective bargaining and tripartite dialogue are necessary elements for creating an environment that encourages innovation and higher productivity, attracts foreign direct investment and enables the society and economy to adjust to external shocks;

3. Discrimination faced by women and minority groups are important obstacles to economic efficiency and social development.

3.7.2. ILO's Development Agenda

The ILO is widely acknowledged as the global reference point on employment and labour issues and a centre for normative action in the world of work. It provides a platform for international debate and negotiation on social policy, and offers services for advocacy, information and policy formulation. The ILO is the only international institution that monitors labour rights.

Under its Director-General, Juan Somavia, the ILO has launched a development agenda. The *Decent Work* initiative is the expression of the organisation's shift in focus.

A cornerstone of this agenda is the *ILO Declaration on Fundamental Principles and Rights at Work* and its follow-up, which aims to enable all working women and men to have a say in defining what decent work means for them and how to achieve it. The decent work agenda addresses jobs, enterprise creation and human resource enhancement, and elimination of the worst forms of child labour. Gender is a crosscutting theme.

There are four key elements in the decent work agenda:

1. Promotion of the Declaration on Fundamental Principles and Rights at Work, and their follow-up;
2. Creation of more and better jobs and income
3. Social protection for all;
4. Increasing social dialogue, networking and organisation (the ILO recognises that it needs to work with many people in civil society; the organisation's strength is its tripartite structure, which is presently extending to include NGOs and people's organisations (POs) within the informal sector).

3.7.2.1. Experience on PRSPs

There have been a large number of studies and reviews of the PRSP process and it is impossible to summarise them in this book. However, it is important to highlight that the PRSP process is still in its early stages, that all stockholders are learning by doing and that the biggest challenge will be in implementation. It is widely accepted that the PRSP approach is extremely challenging for countries and their development partners alike due to the difficulties of its objectives as well as the tensions between them. Among the issues most frequently raised include the following: improving the participatory process; achieving an appropriate balance between speed and quality in the drafting process; improving poverty diagnostics, targets and indicators and monitoring and evaluation; clarifying the priority public actions in PRSPs; improving public expenditure systems; improving the integration of PRSPs with other government decision making processes; In a statement to the IMF, the Director-General of the ILO broadly agreed with these findings but reiterated that, "pro-poor growth has, by implication, to be about promoting employment and livelihood opportunities and this needs to be more explicitly addressed in a number of PRSPs".

There is also little evidence yet available on what impact PRSPs are having on poverty outcomes. It is important to be realistic about what progress can be reasonably expected as it is obviously necessary to strike the right balance between pushing for more rapid achievement of PRSP objectives and ensuring that the approach is realistic in light of country constraints and the need for the process to be participatory and country driven. In some cases the PRSP process seems to be overlay driven by the World Bank to the extent that some critics argue that the process has as much to do with developing a new instrument for poverty reducing strategies, as it has to do with achieving the political and institutional objectives of the World Bank.

From the perspective of the ILO, experience of PRSP processes has varied significantly from country to country depending on a number of factors both internal and external to the organisation but overall, there are three major overarching concerns which have arisen on a recurrent basis, all of which have been alluded to above. Firstly, insufficient attention has been placed on equity in contrast to growth in PRSPs. Secondly, too often trade unions, employers' organise actions and ministries of labour have had difficulty in participating in the PRSP. Thirdly, few PRSPs contain much analysis of the labour market, of employment issues, the core labour standards (CLS) and other aspects of decent work, so that the latter is too often absent from poverty reduction policy.

The ILO continues to engage with the Bretton Woods institutions and other development organisations on PRSP policy. For example, review meetings were held in Geneva with the World Bank's Director responsible for the PRSP programme in July 2001 and again in July 2002 and a paper was drafted on decent work and poverty reduction as the ILO's contribution to the IMF/World Bank Comprehensive Review of PRSPs and presented to a review meeting in Washington in January, 200. Regular contact between the field and headquarters has been maintained and ILO country staff involved in PRSP work met in Geneva to take stock of progress and to exchange information and experience in July 2001 and again in June 2002.

In taking forward the ILO's contribution to national PRSPs, the focus has been on an integrated approach to support national initiatives aimed at reducing decent work deficits. This draws on the numerous ILO initiatives already under way in most countries and seeks to demonstrate how an integrated package of policy measures around the theme of decent work is likely to have a more significant and sustainable impact on poverty than would a series of independent initiatives. However, it is evident that many of the factors which need to be tackled lie in the global economy and are to do with trade and capital flows so it is important to make these links. Thus, promoting decent work also means changing the way the global economy works so that its benefits reach more people. However, this section now focuses on the five special focus countries, to illustrate the type of practical steps taken by the ILO to integrate decent work into poverty reduction strategies and to empower the social partners to influence the design and drafting of PRSPs.

The 1998 ILO Declaration *on Fundamental Principles and Rights at Work* emerged in the context of adjustment to an emerging global economy, and represents a major thrust by the ILO to secure wide ratification of core labour Conventions by member States.

Adjustment to forces of globalisation has been marked by a series of crises, from the oil crisis of the 1970s and the debt crises in Africa and Latin America in the 1970s and 1980s, to the transitional crisis in Europe in the 1990s and, more recently, the Asian financial crisis. The Declaration urges all ILO member States "to respect, to promote and to realise in good faith" the rights of workers and employers. These core labour *rights* are not under debate; what is under discussion is support for core labour *standards*; that is, the mechanisms that implement those rights.

The follow-up to the ILO Declaration provides for the ILO to assist member States, upon request, in achieving the Declaration's objectives. This could be in the form of technical assistance, or realised through activities of multilateral organisations or projects implemented by other parties such as trade unions and NGOs.

The four "fundamental principles and rights at work" provide a framework for the meaningful application of eight labour standards and promote the expression of free choice as a key element in the healthy functioning of market economies. The high degree of international political consensus with respect to these standards, and the primacy of the ILO among international organisations with respect to key aspects of labour standards, is reflected in documents such as the declaration issued by the WTO Singapore Ministerial Conference in December 1996. The fundamental principles and rights in the *ILO Declaration* draw from the conclusions of the 1995 World Summit on Social Development. The *Programme of Action* from that Summit commits participants to safeguard and promote "basic workers' rights" based on the eight ILO Conventions listed below:

Freedom of association and the effective recognition of the right to collective bargaining:

1. Freedom of Association and Protection of the Right to Organise Convention, 1948
2. Right to Organise and Collective Bargaining Convention, 1949 Elimination of all forms of forced or compulsory labour:
3. Forced or Compulsory Labour Convention, 1930
4. Abolition of Forced Labour Convention, 1957 Effective abolition of child labour:
5. Minimum Age Convention, 1973
6. Worst Forms of Child Labour Convention, 1999 - this Convention is now designated as the eighth fundamental Convention, effective upon its entry into force on 19/11/00.

Elimination of discrimination in respect of employment and occupation:

a) Equal Remuneration for Men and Women Workers for Work of Equal Value Convention, 1951

b) Discrimination Convention, 1958

Of these, the ILO and most trade unions emphasise that freedom of association and the right to collective bargaining constitute the foundation on which all other rights are built and respected.

3.7.3. Gender Equality Issues

Labour standards are important tools to promote equality concerns. Increasingly, trade unions have become strong advocates on gender equality issues, a response to the rapid rise in female labour force participation rates, growing visibility of gender issues in the workplace, and trade union efforts to organise and support women workers in the informal sector. Labour legislation on minimum wages is particularly important to women because women predominate in lower-paid work where minimum wages are most relevant. Labour standards empower women by outlining women's rights, and even for those outside the formal sector, the standards provide a declaration of the rights of women workers.

There are, however, labour rights issues of particular concern to women workers that are not explicitly addressed in the core labour standards encompassed in the "fundamental principles and rights at work". These include issues relating to occupational health and safety, maternity leave, sexual harassment and physical abuse, reproductive rights, minimum wages and maximum hours of work. Workers in the informal sector are often in desperate need of the social protection that standards are designed to offer: the 1996 Convention on Homework, recognises that home workers are entitled to minimum standards laid down by international law, including rights to accessible training to improve skills. These are labour rights issues on which trade unions have often supported women workers.

There is also an urgent need for protection for migrant workers, who, whether legally or illegally employed, frequently are denied basic rights of citizenship in the country where they work.

3.7.4. Role of Government Institutions

National political commitment is the key to the effective abolition of child labour. In the absence of a firm policy commitment by the government, backed up by resources and translated into effective action, the best efforts of other partners in the fight against child labour are likely to result in making little more than a small dent in the problem.

International cooperation helps to build an environment in which child labour can be abolished in the national context. International organisations raise awareness of the problem worldwide, engage national governments and other social actors in a dialogue, and facilitate the availability of resources from wealthier countries to tackle child labour in poor countries.

We will present some of the ways in which national governments and international organisations can contribute to the effective elimination of child labour.

Governments, parliamentarians, ministries and other public agencies are critical actors in the fight against child labour. Cooperation of national governments and their institutions is essential to ensure that the conventions and recommendations passed by international organisations will be effective instruments at the national level.

Firstly, the participation of governments and agencies is necessary to paint a complete picture of the status and extent of child labour in a country. Cooperation from regional and local governments facilitates the necessary research and reporting components of successful policy changes and implementation.

For example, some governments, including those of Colombia, Kenya, Thailand and Turkey, have set up permanent child labour committees, specialised bodies headed by the government whose task it is to oversee all activities and policies regarding child labour in the country and to work together with international organisations. But it also includes representatives of employers' and workers' organisations, as well as informed individuals from various NGOs and other knowledgeable agencies, universities, research institutes, etc. to coordinate joint actions.

Secondly, government action is important to conduct internal reviews and initiate legislation, policies, and programmes. If national legislation is adequate, the government or one of its agencies should monitor and examine its enforcement.

Thirdly, government participation is crucial for providing adequate enforcement of all laws and international standards that protect children from child labour. Enforcement of legislation is necessary for combating child labour but not always easy to carry out. Government and public bodies can also examine means of prevention.

Finally, governments can explore the children's needs in order to identify priority target groups and formulate projects; and they can allocate the necessary resources if they are available and set up ways to utilise them. The input for formulating new programmes and for introducing projects can come from various sources. In general, it has been found that a multi-pronged attack on child labour, one that involves different approaches or actors, is likely to be the most effective.

In order to formulate successful programmes, governments can seek technical advice and expertise from international organisations, academics, and various other experts. Once a programme has been designed and implemented, a nationally appointed commission or public agency can be established to oversee its functioning and funding.

Governments also have the responsibility of evaluating the educational system in those areas where child labour is found, of exploring ways to improve children's access to education and of making it more appropriate. They must also concern themselves with the quality of schools. They might decide to introduce other kinds of educational experience, including non-formal or vocational education. This might involve determining the best ways to introduce social protection and other measures to sustain family incomes so that children are not sent out to work.

The scale of the child labour problem and nature of the underlying causes require that child labour concerns are "mainstream". Many developing countries are formulating national Poverty Reduction Strategy Plans (PRSPs) and other "multi-sectorial" programmes. PRSPs, which are formulated within the framework of

World Bank and IMF assistance to low-income countries, are, in effect, comprehensive development plans covering many economic and social sectors, including education, health, employment and agriculture. They are mostly the result of intensive consultations at national and sub-national levels with the aim of ensuring broad-based participation, national ownership and political commitment to implementation. In many countries, the PRSPs also serve as a basis for the mobilisation of development resources, especially from bilateral donors and international financial institutions.

3.7.5. Role of International Organisations

There are a number of ways in which international organisations dialogue and work with national governments to take action against child labour. These include:

1. Raising the awareness of government officials and persuading national authorities of the urgent need to act;
2. Marshalling the financial support of the governments of wealthier countries for projects and programmes and a host of other child-labour-related activities;
3. Sensitising international public opinion about child labour, including its most reprehensible forms;
4. Elaborating research methodologies to help countries examine child labour;
5. Promulgating international legal standards which countries can promote and ratify, and encouraging countries to implement and conform to them by offering technical cooperation and assistance;
6. Encouraging governments to enter into a broad range of constructive relations and programmes with other countries of the region, with international organisations and with donors and others who share a common interest in improving children's living and work situations.

3.7.6. International Labour Standards

International labour standards are elaborated in the ILO's annual

International Labour Conference by delegates representing governments, employers and workers from the ILO member States. As such, they are agreed upon by virtually the entire international community, and are a powerful tool for setting the parameters for action within countries concerning child labour and other labour issues. International standards can also serve to raise awareness within countries about the importance of the objectives they promote.

Individual countries are encouraged to ratify them and, afterwards, to conform to them in their legislation and action even though there is no international "police force" that can force them to do so.

The most important international labour standards adopted concerning child labour are the Minimum Age Convention, 1973 and the Worst Forms of Child Labour Convention, 1999. States that ratify these Conventions have the obligation to define a range of minimum ages for certain types of employment, ages below which no child should be required to work.

Convention No. 138 is the main international framework for action against child labour, and has received wide ratification. The Convention establishes that the general minimum age for admission to employment should not be less than the age of completing compulsory schooling and in no event less than 15 years of age. Countries that ratify it must "pursue a national policy designed to ensure the effective abolition of child labour and to raise progressively the minimum age… to a level consistent with the fullest physical and mental development of young persons".

Convention No. 182 concerns the wo forms of child labour, and its aim is to ensure that children in all countries, irrespective of their level of development, are protected from extreme forms of work. Ratifying countries are expected to take immediate and effective measures to prohibit them and work toward the elimination of these forms of child labour.

The ILO's *Declaration on Fundamental Principles and Rights at Work*, which was adopted a year earlier than Convention No. 182, highlights the importance of respecting the most fundamental labour rights in the context of globalisation. These include the right to freedom of association and to collective bargaining, the abolition of forced labour, nondiscrimination in employment and occupation, and the effective abolition of child labour. The Convention on the Rights of the Child (CRC), adopted by the UN in 1989, defines a child as every person under the age of 18. Several key provisions of this Convention are closely related to those of the ILO child labour standards.

Spearheading assistance programmes in combating child labour is the International Programme on the Elimination of Child Labour (IPEC), a technical cooperation programme of the ILO that was set up in 1992 (the ILO itself dates from 1919 and is the oldest agency within the United Nations family). IPEC's main goal is the progressive elimination of child labour by strengthening national capacities to address the problem and by promoting a worldwide movement to combat it. It helps its partners to develop and implement measures aimed at preventing child labour, withdrawing children from hazardous work, providing alternatives and improving working conditions in nonhazardous kinds of work for older children.

IPEC's experience has shown that because child labour is a complex problem stemming from multiple causes, action to combat it must be holistic and multifaceted so as to result in a positive and sustained impact. These children must be provided with viable developmental opportunities, including education and training, so that they do not return to the same kind of work or enter other, perhaps worse, forms of child labour. Measures against child labour should be linked to combating poverty, unemployment and low wages overall.

Credible and cost-effective systems must also be put in place to ensure that other children do not replace those withdrawn from the workplace. Solutions to these tasks need to come from many groups and share many perspectives, and IPEC-associated programmes need to be set up wherever possible in a comprehensive and integrated approach at the level of the children, their families and communities, the employers and adult workers, the government and society in general.

IPEC has also developed a systematic approach to mainstreaming child labour in the Poverty Reduction Strategy Plans and other national development programmes by supporting the networking of policy research institutions, government agencies and other IPEC partners. Highlights of the approach include the following:

1. Promotion of the elimination of child labour as an explicit development objective, particularly within poverty reduction strategies.
2. Analytical work on child labour. This includes the development of child labour impact assessments and appropriate indicators to facilitate the integration of child labour concerns into development programmes.
3. The integration of child labour into the monitoring and evaluation systems used in national development programmes, particularly those set up within the PRSP framework. This work includes the selection of core child labour indicators as indicators of poverty and social development, the incorporation of child labour modules in data collection operations and the widespread dissemination of the data collected.
4. Capacity building for government and non-government agencies concerned with child labour. This work entails the promotion of child labour research at universities and research institutes, networking of IPEC's partners and research institutions for knowledge-sharing and support, and the adoption of strategies for enhancing national ownership and sustainability of child labour programmes, including the mobilisation of local resources.
5. The pursuit of dialogue with international financial institutions and other major development agencies to promote collaboration and advocate greater attention to child labour in their operations. Similar strategies are being used in the efforts aimed at mobilising institutions working on health issues to act on hazardous child labour.

3.7.6.1. Labour Standards for Informal Sector Workers

A challenge for the ILO and national governments is in extending the rights and principles contained in the ILO Declaration beyond workers engaged in a traditional employer-employee relationship to include those in the informal sector, where a majority of the world's workers, and the poorest workers, are to be found. Decentralisation and the increasing use of subcontractors have contributed to the expansion of the informal sector globally. In high-income countries, about 15 percent of the population is engaged in work outside the formal sector;

the figure is 40 percent for middle-income countries and 80 percent for low-income countries.

The majority of these workers are women, and many have been displaced from jobs in the formal sector. In response to the recent financial crisis in Asia, many companies moved production outside the factory, offering piecework to women workers to perform in the home. Piece-rate wages are generally considerably lower than daily minimum wages. In addition, home-based workers lose all the social benefits they had as factory workers, and they must take on costs of electricity, water and sometimes tools of the trade. The putting-out system is also an effective way of discouraging worker solidarity and collective bargaining. Occupational health and safety issues and their downstream implications are enormous: former factory workers in the Thai shoe-making industry, for example, have moved dangerous equipment and toxic chemicals into their homes.

Another study on factory unemployment in Indonesia found that many companies took advantage of flexibility in new labour regulations after the crisis to retrench undesirable workers and replace them with younger, single women workers.

Discussions on labour standards globalisation and informalisation, address concerns about "throwing the baby out with the bath water". How can core labour standards be applied down the supply chain in such a way that the livelihoods of home workers are not jeopardised? How can social protection coverage be made universal, at a cost reasonable to workers, employers and the State, without lowering standards? Home workers usually talk of the need to link standards to institutional change, and the need to involve home workers in identifying appropriate, intermediate standards.

Others emphasise that voluntary grassroots schemes should not be viewed by employers as a cheap substitute for social security and thus an encouragement to informalise more of their activities. Instead, State systems already in place should be extended to all workers.

The ILO's response is that it takes a "comprehensive" approach to labour standards, recognising, as Amartya Sen elaborates, that in furthering the interests and demands of one group, it is easy to neglect the interests and demands of others. The ILO also recognises that it must broaden its partnerships to include non-governmental organisations and networks of workers, such as Home Net and WIEGO which work with women in the informal sector. An example is the collaboration between the ILO, the World Bank and WIEGO on a study and workshop on social protection for workers in the informal economy carried out in connection with the ILO STEP programme.

A key consideration is placing the diverse concerns of different groups of workers within a comprehensive assessment, so that, as Sen explains, "the curing of unemployment is not treated as a reason for doing away with reasonable conditions of work for those already employed, nor is the protection of workers already employed used as an excuse to keep the jobless in a state of social exclusion from the labour market". These considerations are critical to implementing core labour standards in such a way that the livelihoods of the poorest and most vulnerable are not jeopardised.

The major thrusts of ILO initiatives aimed at the informal sector are:

1. Revision of the statistical definition of the sector, and measurement in the urban and rural sector;
2. Promotion of rights at work
3. Access to economic services and business opportunities, vocational and technical training and enterprise development training;
4. Extension of social protection.

The trade union movement and the ILO are finding new ways to form alliances with informal workers to support social dialogue, organisation and representation. In some cases, a traditional trade union may extend its field of activity to include informal workers. The Textile, Clothing and Footwear Union of Australia, for example, organises home workers in its sector, and UNITE in Canada organises home workers in the garment industry. TESTU, the Transport and Export Service Trade Union in Bangkok, has extended its support to home-based shoe-sewers by setting up a credit union, helping them lobby for welfare, and raising their concerns with suppliers.

The Self-Employed Women's Association in Ahmadabad, India, is an example of a new trade union created specifically to organise informal sector workers. Formed 25 years ago, SEWA organises home workers, street vendors, paper pickers and refuse collectors. SEWA played a central role in instigating the ILO Home workers Convention. SEWA is also active at the international level in two networks of informal sector workers: Street Net, the International Alliance of Street Vendors, and Home Net.

3.7.7. Labour Standards and Socio-economic Development

The ILO has been urging the Bretton Woods institutions and the United Nations system as a whole to speak "with a single voice" on global minimum labour standards. While not insisting that these institutions make their programmes and funding conditional on the recipient enforcing core labour standards, the ILO is urging them to integrate standards into their policies and programmes.

In 1999, the ILO was admitted as an observer to the Development and Interim Committees of the World Bank and IMF, providing a means for high-level engagement between them, and an institutional framework within which management and staff-level cooperation could take place.

Meetings of senior members of the ILO, World Bank and IMF take place annually. At a recent meeting with World Bank staff, for example, ILO Director-General Juan Somavia highlighted the points of asynergy between the WEB's comprehensive development framework and the ILO's concept of Decent Work, in particular the Comprehensive Development Framework (CDF)'s emphasis on fostering partnerships within countries among the "social partners" with whom the ILO has been engaged since 1919.

The multilateral financial agencies are adopting, to various degrees, similar steps, including:

1. Linking up with international efforts to promote and implement CLS;
2. Sensitising staff and management on issues involving CLS, including studies into how they could address labour standards in their activities and support the efforts of other organisations such as the ILO;
3. Increasing dialogue and consultation with trade unions and non-governmental organisations engaged in workers' rights issues;

4. Taking CLS into consideration when revising relevant sectorial and non-sectorial policy guidelines.

3.7.7.1. World Bank (WB)

The World Bank took its first look at the relationship between core labour standards and macroeconomic stability with the 1995 World Development Report, in which Bank President James Wolfensohn emphasised that "work – safe, productive and environmentally sound – is the key to economic and social progress everywhere". More recently, the Comprehensive Development Framework and the Bank's work on social principles represent important responses to the Bank's recognition of the social dimensions of globalisation. The WB is increasingly taking on a promotional role with respect to labour standards, despite continuing reservations on links between freedom of association and economic growth.

The Bank has established a Labour Markets Group within its Social Protection Team, which functions as resource to the Bank by informing Bank staff on labour issues, conducting staff training, and coordinating cooperative initiatives with unions and the ILO. It acts as a resource for country directors, who may include labour standards in the Country Assistance Strategies (Cases) of borrowing countries. It identifies key issues for client countries and provides Bank staff with information on labour market interventions. Priority areas for the Labour Markets Group include active labour market programmes, vocational education and training, income support for the unemployed, industrial relations, informal labour markets, labour standards and child labour.The WB is particularly interested in working with unions in poverty reduction initiatives. In October 2000, sixty trade unionists formulation trade union centres, the International Trade Secretariats (ITSs), the Trade Union Advisory Committee (TUAC) and the International Confederation of Free Trade Unions (ICFTU), as well as ILO representatives, took part in meetings with the IMF and the Bank. Many subject areas discussed led to new commitments towards trade unions' positions by WB and IMF officials. Two important developments were the following:

1. Both institutions announced that trade unions would be invited to participate in the poverty reduction process introduced by the IMF/WB one year ago;

2. A WB official stated that the Bank is currently reviewing its procurement documents and is considering upgrading labour clauses contained in the Standard Bidding Documents for the Procurement of Works from "recommended" to "mandatory".

3.7.7.2. International Finance Corporation (IFC)

The IFC is the lending and underwriting affiliate of the World Bank, whose clients are in the private sector, not government. Following broad international consultations, the IFC developed policy on harmful child labour and forced labour; it has also developed occupational health and safety guidelines. Project proposals to the IFC undergo environmental and social assessment, and projects must include mitigation measures where necessary. The IFC is beginning to study how to apply nondiscrimination and freedom of association and collective bargaining standards.

3.7.7.3. International Monetary Fund (IMF)

The IMF has indicated that it will encourage the observation of core labour standards in member countries, but does not want core labour standards to become an object of IMF conditionally. In 1998-99, labour issues were included in the development of new programmes with Brazil and Mexico, and were raised in the context of monitoring existing programmes, including those in Indonesia, Korea and Thailand. The Fund has recognised the need to consolidate an integrated approach to economic and social policy, including stronger collaboration with other international organisations like the ILO. The ILO is an observer on the International Monetary and Financial Committee.

3.7.7.4. Asian Development Bank (ADB)

The Asian Development Bank undertook a preliminary study of how it could address labour standards in its activities in 1998. In the wake of the Asian financial crisis, the Bank moved to design a framework for operations on social protection and social safety nets. A 1999 ADB study on the social consequences of the financial crisis, however, contains no discussion of labour standards, and only briefly refers to the role trade unions played in Korea and the Philippines in reaching agreements with employers to avoid layoffs and strikes. The Bank, with the ILO as Executing Agency, is funding a regional technical assistance programme to strengthen the role of labour standards in sustainable economic and social development within the ADB and member countries

ADB supported projects that promote good labour practices which stipulated protection for worker welfare, including construction safety and health, in covenants in the loan documents. These projects also included China, among other countries.

3.7.7.5. Inter-American Development Bank (IDB)

Following the WG model, the IDB has established a working group involving equal representation from the Inter-American Regional Workers Organisation (ORIT, the regional organisation for the Americas of the ICFTU) and the Bank. At its first meeting in August 2000, the working group discussed what kinds of initiatives the Bank could undertake to strengthen unions in the region, and identify potential areas for joint activity, including a study of the impact of WB programmes on core labour standards.

The Inter-American Investment Corporation (IIC), the private-sector lending affiliate of the Inter-American Development Bank Group, has adopted a policy that prohibits the use of harmful child labour and/or forced labour in projects it supports. The policy further stipulates that projects should comply with national labour laws of host countries.

3.7.7.6. African Development Bank

A 1998 Bank position paper found a "direct link between the principles underlying the standards, and the Bank's fundamental development objectives", noting that standards are "intertwined with the crosscutting programmes on poverty alleviation, gender, governance and democracy". The Bank has identified the following strategies and arrangements to implement core labour standards:

a) Country Strategy Papers (CSPs) are to include discussion on labour standards with the social partners (government, labour and employers' associations, NGOs) and a section of the CSPs is to be devoted to a review of institutions, policies and programmes, legal framework, implementation progress, problems and future prospects on the theme;

b) Industry Sector Policy is to pay close attention to issues contained in labour standards, including mechanisms for implementation;

c) Education sector policy is to take into consideration issues relating to education and training in all aspects of core labour standards, since they are relatively new issues in regional member countries, and many stockholders may have little or no formal education.

d) The crosscutting themes of gender, environment and poverty alleviation are to incorporate relevant aspects of labour standards in their policies and guidelines.

The Bank works with the ILO, particularly in connection with the International Programme for the Elimination of Child Labour (IPEC), the Interdependent Action Programme on Privatisation, Restructuring and Economic Democracy, and the Jobs for Africa Initiative.

In a September 2000 progress report, the Bank noted that new Country Strategy Papers contain a section, as a standard component, that focuses on ratification and implementation of international labour conventions, collective bargaining rights, gender and discrimination issues in work, and child labour.

3.7. 8. Role of Social Partners

3.7.8.1. Trade Unions

Trade unions in industrialised countries engage in development activities at national and international levels. Some programmes are conducted through international sectorial trade union organisations (such as ITSs) and may be supported by public funds when national trade union federations or centres have access to such funds. In addition, there are some large national unions that conduct bilateral cooperation programmes, for example, UNISON in the UK.

The ways of working vary, with some engaged in bilateral approaches and others preferring to emphasise multilateral partnerships; some emphasise humanitarian aid and employment creation projects, and others concentrate on institution-building aimed at changing power relationships in societies.

With a few exceptions, the trade union movement as a whole is the most democratic institution in society, and the only democratic international movement worldwide. A healthy trade union movement is both an indicator and supporter of broader democratic structures:

1. All trade unions have a clearly defined constituency – the membership, to whom the leadership is accountable;
2. All trade unions have a leadership elected at regular intervals by representative governing bodies. This leadership may lose the next election, and is sometimes subject to recall;
3. Union accounts are usually public, audited, and available to the scrutiny of the membership and the general public;
4. The consequences of union policy are immediately felt by the membership; monitoring and evaluation takes place constantly, at the workplace to start with and more formally in frequent meetings of elected governing bodies.

The following are some of the major international union organisations, together with some and examples of their activities.

3.7.8.1.1. International Confederation of Free Trade Unions (ICFTU)

Founded in 1949, the ICFTU represents the collective interests of some 124 million members in 213 trade unions from 143 countries and territories around the world. There are three regional organisations that are part of the ICFTU: the African Regional Organisation (AFRO), the Asia and Pacific Regional Organisation (APRO), and ORIT, which draws in the Americas, Canada, the United States and the Caribbean region. The Canadian Labour Congress is presently president of ORIT.Based in Brussels, the ICFTU has offices or representatives in Boznia, Geneva, Hong Kong, New York, Moscow and Washington D.C.. The ICFTU has consultative status with the ILO, and is recognised as a representative body within the United Nations, its regional bodies and specialised agencies. Its aims are to:

1) Defend and promote universally recognised trade union, labour, and human rights;
2) Campaign for the eradication of child labour;
3) Assist trade union development and maintenance, particularly in developing nations;

4) Improve living and working conditions;
5) Advance democracy, full employment, and social security;
6) Combat all forms of worker discrimination and exploitation; and
7) Advance social and economic development and justice.

The ICFTU holds consultative status with the United Nations, its Economic and Social Committee (ECOSOC) and its specialised agencies.

In recent meetings with the WB and IMF, the ICFTU raised issues relating to poverty reduction, core labour standards and international financial reforms, and pressed the Bank and IMF to meet regularly with employers' organisations and unions, both nationally and internationally. In the Spring 2000 meetings of the IMF and World Bank, the ICFTU, the International Trade Secretariats and the Paris-based Trade Union Advisory Committee to the OECD called on the Bank to include the following social components in their dialogue with governments:

1. Social protection, and social safety nets including retirement pensions, unemployment benefits, child support, sickness and injury benefits;
2. Programmes aimed at maintaining and enhancing school participation, especially for girls, spreading the availability of health care, and eliminating the worst forms of child labour;
3. Ensuring that labour market reforms are based on respect for core labour standards and draw on the ILO's competence in the development of institutional frameworks for collective bargaining and labour law.

More recently, in October, the ICFTU called on the WB and IMF to extend the programmes for the Highly Indebted Poor Countries (HIPCs) to a greater number of countries, while including fundamental workers' rights as a requirement to qualify for the HIPC initiative. The ICFTU also issued a strong call for cooperation to combat HIV/AIDS, urging the Bank to include trade unions in Bank activities regarding HIV/AIDS. The ICFTU also called on both the IMF and WB to establish better participation of all sectors of civil society, including trade unions, in consultation procedures.

3.7.8.1.2. The Trade Union Advisory Committee (TUAC)

The TUAC acts as an interface between 55 trade unions from developed nations and the OECD the CLC is a member of the committee. The TUAC has consultative status with the OECD and various specialised agencies within the OECD structure. TUAC's primary goals are to effectively represent the interests and views of its affiliates in intergovernmental discussions, such as the G7 Economic Summits and Employment Conferences, and to advance the social agenda in economic policy debates.

3.7.8.1.2. International Trade Secretariats (ITS)

International Trade Secretariats are among the oldest international trade union organisations, and are industry or sector based. All the LIDC members, as well as many non-LIDC unions, are affiliated to the ITSs.There were 33 international organisations at the end of World War I, but, through a process of mergers, which reflect both changes in multilateral ownership, changes in the organisation of work, national union mergers and the need to rationalise scarce resources, the number now stands at around ten.

3.7.8.1.3. International Employers' Organisations (IOE)

Employers' organisations represent a key asset in any society: its enterprises. Successful enterprises are at the heart of any strategy to create employment and improve living standards. As one of the three constituents of the ILO, employers' organisations have a special relationship with the Organisation. The ILO's Bureau for Employers' Organisations is responsible for the nurturing and development of that relationship.

The Bureau is available, through national employers' organisations, as a gateway through which employers can gain access to some of the best information available on human resources development, industrial relations and a host of other employment and labour market-related subjects.

The Bureau also runs a programme of technical cooperation which provides development assistance to employers' organisations in developing countries and countries in transiti2on to a market economy.

This work is mostly done through projects financed by the overseas development assistance funds of donor countries.

3.7.8.1.4. Employers and the ILO

As one of the three constituents of the ILO, employers have a special relationship with the Organisation. Employers are represented on the ILO Governing Body, form part of the tripartite delegations at the International Labour Conference and participate on equal basis with governments and workers in the numerous technical and sectorial meetings organised by the ILO.

The IOE, which provides the Secretariat to the Employers' Group in all its various activities, pursues a number of policy priorities within the ILO. In essence its role is to ensure that ILO activities contribute to the growth of successful enterprises which in turn can provide employment and improve living standards. At present it focuses on a number of key areas:

1. The development and strengthening of employers' organisations. This activity is carried out in close cooperation with the ILO's Bureau for Employers' Activities;
2. The strengthening of the ILO's activities on employment enterprise creation as well as the development of Seems;
3. Reform of the ILO's standard setting activities.

3.7.9. Globalisation and Labour Standards

The economy is becoming more and more globalised, and this is mainly due to increased economic integration and the emergence of a knowledge society characterised by the information and communication technology revolution. According to the report of the World Commission on the Social Dimension of Globalisation, there are winners and losers, yet the latter are the majority. In a Global Economy rules should relate to the global trends, but this is not forthcoming. In this context, the major stockholders and players in the global arena are looking for appropriate and integrated legally binding reply to transnational (global) economic decision-making. The local (national) decision makers are peddling in empty air and look forward to countervail the international economic decision-making.

On the one hand, there already exists a global answer to the above-mentioned economic pressures. This is given by the existence of labour standards.

All major stockholders, both national and international, seem to agree that (core) labour standards have to be respected both at international and national levels. The full implementation of labour standards constitutes a sine quinine for economic globalisation to be really successful.

3.7.9.1. Conventions of the ILO

The Conventions of the ILO are agreed by the International Labour Conference, and are binding on all member States which ratify them. Since member States are represented by the three sectors theoretically, the sectors should be capable of implementing them. The four "core labour standards" in the ILO Declaration are binding on all ILO members, regardless of whether they have ratified the Conventions to which the Declaration refers. There are no formal sanctions on countries that fail to implement ILO Conventions, and, since adoption of Conventions is usually voluntary, different governments have committed to different Conventions.

There is, indeed, no doubt that economic globalisation can only reap its total rewards and prosper if there are strong social systems, which provide, among others, excellent education, healthy collaboration and social peace.

The ILO rightly observes the negative effects of globalisation on certain groups of workers can arise from the absence or inadequate application of labour standards. When standards are not applied, workers do not have the basic tools they need to defend themselves, and States do not have adequate tools to ensure the balanced distribution of the benefits of development.

This is often the case for temporary workers, migrant workers and workers in some export processing zones, as well as in the informal economy. Women are particularly affected, as well as they comprise the majority of workers in these categories. An increasing amount of research shows that the failure to apply labour standards is damaging to national development. Child labour transmits and perpetuates inter-generation poverty; releasing children from work and providing them with adequate educational opportunities goes hand in hand with providing decent work for adults.No doubt, there is a crucial role for all actors to promote and ensure that basic rights at work are effectively respected all over the world, without exception.

Over the least decade, important areas of consensus have emerged concerning the social dimension of globalisation in the context of the ILO. Since the World Summit for Social Development in Copenhagen international consensus has been achieved on following categories of core labour standards:

1. Freedom of association and the right to collective bargaining;
2. The elimination of child labour;
3. The abolition of forced or compulsory labour;
4. The elimination of discrimination in occupation and employment.

This led to the adoption by the International Labour Conference in 1998 of the ILO *Declaration on Fundamental Principles and Rights at Work* and its follow-up. Labour standards are not only at the forefront of the ILO's objectives and activities. They are also prominent on the agenda of other international bodies like the UN and the OECD. Some multinational corporation have, on their own or together with other organisations, elaborated corporate codes of conduct in which they express their willingness to implement core labour standards have also become globalised as they are standards to be implemented worldwide and constitute a framework for the social policies of the national as well as the international economic actors, especially the Mines. They are, as employers, the actors in labour and employment par excellence. Indeed, they have to apply the labour standards on a daily basis.

Enterprises have consequently been addressed, on an ongoing basis, by international organisations, governments and NGO's, employers' associations and trade unions included, urging them to follow, wherever they operate, not only national rules but also internationally agreed upon labour standards.

Governments united in international bodies like the UN, the ILO, the OECD have developed codes of conduct for multinational enterprises.Consequently, legally binding international agreements addressed to multinational enterprises, also regarding labour issues, were not realistic, since the political will to do so was lacking.

These voluntary instruments carry great weight. They are not only formulated by democratically-elected governments, but also endorsed by the representatives of business themselves and thus guidelines which enterprises believe in. In particular, as these guidelines are endorsed by public opinion at large and by consumers, who pay more and more attention to the way companies behave. When enterprises do not respect fundamental social principles they are often severely sanctioned where it hurts by consumers not buying their goods or services.

In this sense guidelines may even be more important than so-called legally-binding instruments, which are unilaterally imposed and whose effective implementation can often not be guaranteed anyway.

These guidelines are also helping companies doing their business in a positive way. They do indeed provide a passport of good conduct to enterprises, which often are confronted with difficult choices and do find in the guidelines a way of conduct, which if followed, lifts them above criticism, as the enterprises rightly can point out that they behaved in a way society at large expects from them.

Guidelines, which translate fundamental social rights, do also constitute good human resources policies, which are self-evidently endorsed by the employees and their representatives in the companies involved.

These voluntary guidelines have a strong appeal. They are a call from society, respond to the need of enterprises and serve the interests of the employees and communities as well.

Along with the above-mentioned voluntary guidelines, many enterprises have initiated codes of conduct on their own initiative, which also contain labour standards, therewith laying down the rules which will inspire their business and contain guidelines for management, employees and eventually for their subcontracts. In doing so, companies want to project a positive image to the public at large and especially to the consumer.

3.7.9.2. National legislation

National labour legislation, usually in the form of a labour code, is the mechanism that translates core labour standards into reality on a day-to-day basis. A major gap in coverage provided by much national labour legislation is the lack of protection for informal sector and some other categories of workers, such as migrant workers.Effective implementation of labour legislation depends on the existence of a work environment in which the three partners – government, workers and employers – have the obligation and capacity to understand, implement and enforce that legislation. Trade unions and workers need to understand both their rights and obligations under the terms of collective agreements. Employers need to understand and respect their rights and obligations to workers and government.

3.7.9.3. Voluntary Regulation in the Private Sector

In addition to national labour laws, many enterprises have introduced voluntary workplace codes of conduct which are a form of self-regulation for multinational corporations.They contain written statements of principles specifying the labour standards that must be complied with either by suppliers or other components of the company. The most common areas that codes of conduct address are labour standards, environmental protection and human rights. Other mechanisms include social labelling programmes, involving the use of a label or logo to indicate the product has been produced on the basis of certain standards.

Codes of conduct for international business activity are not new. In the 1970s, concern led two international organisations to adopt such codes: the ILO Tripartite Declaration of Principles Concerning Multinational Enterprises and Social Policy, and the OECD Guidelines for Multinational Enterprises. These were aimed at protecting the sovereignty of countries by defining the responsibilities, including social responsibilities, of international business.

Codes of conduct may be differentiated by their content, how they are applied, who administers them, and their industrial coverage.

A recent ILO study identified more than 200 such codes, of which 80 percent were developed by multinationals. "Model codes" are those issued by enterprise associations, trade unions, NGOs or governments for others to use as a basis for developing their own codes. Examples include the Business Charter for Sustainable Development, of the International Chamber of Commerce.

Codes of conduct can be distinguished on the basis on which party initiates, administers and monitors the code: private enterprises or enterprise organisations; workers' organisations; NGOs; professional consultants, auditors or educational enterprises. Public sector involvement in the development and implementation of codes of conduct can provide a stimulus and broader range of support to the initiative. It receives financial support from the UK aid agency, DFID.

Codes can also be categorised according to the production chain of goods and services. "Vertical" codes apply to an entire production chain, for example, in the clothing, footwear and toy industries, which are usually head quartered in developed countries and outsource production to subcontractors in developing countries. If consumers are included in the chain consumer-driven initiatives such as social labelling, and investor-driven initiatives such as socially responsible investing, could be considered in this context. Horizontal codes, on the other hand, apply to a specific industrial sector, where leading companies initiate policies in their operations and apply them across the industry.

The effectiveness of a corporate code of conduct as a mechanism to improve conditions for workers is controversial: How should a code be developed, and by whom? How should codes be implemented, monitored, and by whom? What is the impact of one company's "good practice" in the broader economy? Are there some sectors, such as high-quality sports shoes, where a code of conduct might have more impact than at facilities producing low-cost, low-skill merchandise?

How can codes be used to empower workers, particularly in countries where trade unions are banned? Trade unions often stress that codes of conduct cannot substitute union organisation, and that monitoring is done most effectively by union organisations in the workplace. How can codes of conduct be implemented in a way that does not jeopardise the situation of workers further down in the supply chain? The informal, home-based workers, who are usually women? In an effort to conform with terms of a code, suppliers may eliminate outsourcing to home-based workers, thereby depriving them of work. Some of the better new codes contain clauses requiring companies to take a "continuous improvement" approach and terminate business only where serious breaches of the code persist. They also require transitional economic assistance for children found working. Labour organisations and many activists also advocate that the workers themselves must be involved in developing a code of conduct, to ensure that the code actually addresses workers' priority concerns.

Codes of conduct can play a role in capacity building for workers to develop and strengthen associations. In countries where trade unions are not permitted, voluntary participation on health and safety committees established in connection with developing a code can be a forerunner to freely established worker associations.

3.7.9.4. Framework Agreements

Some of the obstacles to negotiated codes can be overcome and some advantages gained by distinguishing between framework agreements and unilaterally-adopted company codes of labour practice. A framework agreement is an agreement negotiated between a multinational company and an international trade union organisation such as an International Trade Secretariat (ITS) concerning the international activities of that company.

The International Federation of Building and Wood Workers (IFBWW) has signed framework agreements on workers' rights with transnational companies such as IKEA, FABER-CASTELL and HOCHTIEF. Under the terms of the agreement with IKEA, all suppliers and manufacturing companies owned by IKEA are asked to ensure that their working conditions at least comply with national legislation or national agreements. Suppliers must also respect all ILO Conventions and Recommendations relevant to their operations. This means that child labour is prohibited and that workers have unrestricted rights to join trade unions and to free collective bargaining.

References

Statham, Daphne (2004). *Managing Front Line Practice in Social Work.* New York, NY: Jessica Kingsley Publishers.

Thyer, Bruce A. and John S. Wodarski (2007). *Social Work in Mental Health: An Evidence-Based Approach.* Hoboken, NJ: John Wiley.

Turner, Francis J. (2005). *Canadian Encyclopedia of Social Work.* Waterloo, ON: Wilfrid Laurier University Press.

Wittenberg, Renee (2003). *Opportunities in Social Work Careers* (Revised ed.). Chicago, IL: VGM Career Books.

4

Social Work Policies and Practices

Local authority social work generally accepted the new roles required of it by government in its anxiety to maintain control of social care. Crucially these new social work roles and tasks followed from the 'purchaser/provider' split which not only meant that the state would be the purchaser of services but increasingly these services would be provided by the private sector. It also meant that budget holders rather than those close to service users and their needs would determine the extent and allocation of support.

Statutory social work – that is social work in state organisations – with its powers to restrict people's rights has been the focus of most social work discussion. The voluntary sector has continued to be dominated by large charitable providers whose values and philosophies have frequently shared state services emphasis on institutionalisation, paternalistic relationships, enforced dependence and segregation. Smaller innovative voluntary social work organisations have emerged and existed alongside, for example, Family Service Units, as have black and minority ethnic voluntary organisations, but these have tended to be insecure, underfunded and having to compete with big conventional service providers.

There is little evidence to suggest that social work's own discussions about its theory, philosophy and value have impacted upon service users or significantly affected the routine experience of many service users. While such theories and philosophies have changed over time, what service users say about social work practice and the problems they identify with it, have continued to be remarkably consistent and based on their actual experience. The problems they highlight include its:

1. Unreliability
2. Inconsistent quality
3. Failure to provide good quality information
4. Association with control, paternalism and dependence
5. Tendency to reinforce segregation and institutionalisation
6. Common problems of abuse, neglect, disrespect and bullying

4.1. Recent Developments

Key developments in recent times which have affected the understandings and experience of social work of service users and particular groups of service users include:

1. The emergence of the philosophy of 'anti-oppressive practice' in social work. The aim here has been to challenge discrimination along all lines of difference, including race/ethnicity, culture, sexuality, gender, disability and age. However, it was not a development in which service users were generally centrally involved and less attention over the years was paid to some areas of discrimination, for example, disables, mentalism and egoism
2. The development of 'normalisation' or 'social role valorisation, particularly in relation to people with learning difficulties and its emphasis on non-service based approaches to support, citizen advocacy, participation and people being able to live 'ordinary' lives alongside 'valued' people and take part in mainstream life and activities
3. Emerging interest among some social work practitioners in philosophies of involvement, empowerment and partnership. This resulted in some practitioners seeking to develop more group and community based approaches to social work linked with the emergence of service user organisations and movements. Important examples of this developing in the 1980s was support for the individual and collective involvement of people living with HIV/AIDS and of young people living in state care

All of these issues and developments have in related ways impacted both upon practitioners' understandings of the roles and tasks of social work and service users' experience on the receiving end.

4.2. Adult Service Users and Social Work

There is another key point to make about social work roles and tasks historically in relation to adult service users. Most adult social care service users have limited access to and contact with professional social workers. This has long been the situation. Research in the 1970s indicated that social workers preferred work with children, young people and families to work with adult service user groups. They spent less time with and seemed to attach less priority to the latter service user groups. Adult service users were much more likely to have contact with residential, domiciliary and day care social care workers than qualified social workers.

This situation is still significantly the same despite pressures and schemes to extend training and qualification. There has long been a distinction drawn between professional social workers and the much larger body of social care workers. Before these amalgamated they belonged to different trade unions. As yet only social workers have a 'protected' identity through the General Social Care Council and other social care workers have not yet been registered with it. Yet it is this largely unqualified workforce that adult social care users have most if not all their contact with.

Four stages or aspects of social work practice tend to be identified. These are:

1. Assessment
2. Planning
3. Intervention
4. Review

For most adult service users, the process does not get beyond the first stage. The continual narrowing of eligibility criteria means that they are not seen to qualify for further action. Furthermore the process of assessment is increasingly one undertaken by non-professionally qualified workers, increasingly based in call centres and operating according to a preset script. What this means in practice is that a large and costly social work/social care system is actually operating to access a strictly limited number of service users to a very limited pot of resources. Furthermore, a strong case can be made that just 'a bit of help' can play a key and much valued role in maintaining the independence of service users, notably, older people.

4.3. Contexts of Social Work

4.3.1. Structural Factors

Service users point to two key sets of structural issues affecting social work. These are first the broader barriers and restrictions which operate on them as individuals and second, the nature of the organisations in which social work is provided and the ideologies, values and beliefs operating in them. Clearly these two sets of issues operate in relation to each other.

4.3.2. Barriers Facing Service Users

Crucial in the discussions of service users, originating with those of disabled people and the disabled people's movement has been their emphasis on the *barriers* which they face and which play no less a part in shaping their lives, experience, opportunities and choices than any personal characteristics, problems or impairments that they may have. From the 1970s, the disabled people's movement developed a social model or social model for understanding disability which established this approach.

This model drew a distinction between the impairment, or perceived impairment, that any individual might experience and the negative reactions that people in this situation might experience in society. The first was described as *impairment;* the second as *disability*. Such disability or disabling effects of society were seen to include physical or environmental barriers, discrimination, stigma and oppression, resulting in the narrowing of opportunities, restricting people's quality of life, encouraging segregation, poverty and material disadvantage. Over the 30 or so years that the social model has developed, increasing attention has been paid to both disability and impairment and to the complex interrelation of the two.

While there is no consensus about the social model of disability, it is constantly being debated and developed and it has played a crucial role in directing the thinking, campaigning, strategies and self-organisation of disabled people. While the social model of disability was initially developed by disabled people, over the years such barriers based approaches to understanding people's situation as service users, have gained increasing support from other groups of service users, including mental health service users, older people, living with HIV/AIDS, people with palliative care needs, people with learning difficulties, people with alcohol and drug problems and so on. Service users' organisations like Shaping Our Lives see this model as having relevance and being applicable to all groups of social work/care service users, including families and children and young people in state care.

This barriers-based approach to understanding their circumstances and the support that they need is increasingly influencing service users' expectations of the role of social work and social care.

This is because social or barriers based approaches highlight the denial of people's rights and the importance of a rights based approach in public policy and provision, including social work. This originated with the disabled people's movement and has developed across service user groups.

Poverty, created and perpetuated by inadequate levels of benefits, inferior access to employment and education and the costs of disability and charging for community care services, have all been highlighted by service users as a key barrier they face. Critical social work commentators have also argued that social work practice and policy has often not sufficiently addressed issues of poverty and material disadvantage

4.4. Ethnicity and Difference Issues

There is no doubt that some progress has been made over addressing issues of race equality and other forms of difference over the recent history of social work and social work practice. Admittedly, the starting point was not an encouraging one. It was only in 1970 that the key text, The Client Speaks justified *not* including in its sample service users not born in the UK 'since the reaction of "non-natives" to social work are likely to be complicated by cultural differences, language problems and so forth'! Social work's commitment to policies and practices of anti-discrimination and anti-oppression, have undoubtedly been of some benefit. However, equal access to services and support, the receipt of cultural appropriate services and support have continued to be qualified.

Black and minority ethnic service users' have repeatedly reported and been shown to have inferior access to valued social work and social care services and to be over-represented in involuntary and less valued areas of intervention. Inappropriate assumptions about BME service users, for example, the levels of informal support available to them, continue to be reported. Nasa Begum also argues that the participation of BME service users in social work and social care is declining rather than being supported. Worrying issues are also raised in relation to refugees and asylum seekers, where social work may be expected to be part of the policing and control processes introduced where citizen rights have not been granted or have been refused. Where groups cross over social work and social care's administrative categories, they can also expect to face additional problems. Service users have also highlighted other issues of difference and the problems such service users still experience in relation to actual social work practice, on the basis of gender, sexuality, disability and age.

4.5. Organisation of Social Work

While professional social work is now available in many different settings, the social work that has most relevance to and most impact on service users is statutory social work located primarily in local authorities. Budgetary cuts and from the 1980s, attacks on local state bureaucracy and increasing centralisation from the New Political Right, have resulted in constant problems of underfunding and ironically a preoccupation with reorganisation as a means of problem solving in local government.

Thus service users' experience and perceptions of statutory social work has been influenced by the effect of their local government bureaucratic culture, increasingly overlaid with an emphasis on managerialist approaches to change and policy provision. This has had a damaging effect on their experience of social work services. It has undermined continuity, demotivated staff, resulted in constant changes in personnel and organisational arrangements, requiring frequent relearning and the remaking of relationships.

Similar, if not even greater problems are reported by service users in relation to social work and social care in the NHS, particularly in relation to the approved social worker role in mental health services. Constant major restructuring and the failure to ring fence mental health services, have also been experienced overall as resulting in reduced support from specialist social work. The same problem is identified with community psychiatric nurses.

Service users, in consultations, frequently draw a distinction between individual practitioners working with them, for whom they often have praise and the statutory organisations in which they work, about which they are frequently highly critical. Such statutory organisations have generally over the years adopted and internalised the ideology and values handed down by central government.

4.5.1. Globalisation

Changes in political ideology have also coincided with major changes in economics and economic policy. These have had profound implications for public services. During the 1970s there was a strong pressure to reduce public expenditure because of economic recession. Subsequently a new emphasis was placed on the 'globalisation' of the economy. It was increasingly argued that public expenditure had to be controlled if states were to be competitive. This was accompanied in the UK by a rising emphasis on the market playing a much greater role in the provision of public services, including social work and social care. This has been a key determinant of the policies and services that service users have received.

4.6. Policy Context for Social Work

Before we look at roles and tasks in social work first with adults and then with children and families, it will be helpful to look at the implications such distinctions between groups may have from service users' perspectives. For service users the distinction is often associated with a continuing sense that services for children and families that are given greater priority than those with adults because there are particular political and public concerns over child care tragedies and abuse.

4.6.1. Categorising Service Users

The recent history of statutory social work is one which has reinforced the division of service users into separate 'user groups'. This has followed both from a strengthening shift to specialisation in social work over the last 25 years and also the increasing organisation of social work through separate structures for different groups of service users. This has been most evident in relation to developing divisions between work with adults and with children and families, culminating after the government White Paper 'Every Child Matters' in the separation of the two in two different government departments: the Department of Health (DH) and the Department for Education and Skills (DfES) and the creation of 'children's trusts'. Service users have highlighted that such divisions have created significant problems for them, for example:

1. Where the identity of service users crosses over administrative boundaries, for example, that of disabled children;
2. Where people have multiple identities as service users, for example, as parents and people with learning difficulties
3. At times of transition, for example, when disabled children are growing into young adulthood

There are similar problems with adult services where these are divided administratively, for example, into older people with physical and sensory impairments, both when people move from one category to another and when they fill more than one category. The overall effect for service users is that they feel they are not treated as whole people, but divided into service led administrative categories. This results in fragmentation of the services and support available to them.

People with long term experience of using social care services have been on the receiving end of massive changes in policy, provision and ideology over the last 25 years. In terms of access to social work services, however, the message that frequently comes across from service users is how *little* in some senses their experience of social work and social care has actually changed fundamentally. The continuing trend that service users report is of reduced access to social work and social care support, with eligibility criteria that continue to narrow and focus on people seen as having the greatest need, rather than on preventing problems getting worse.

4.7. Emerging Developments

Having said that the policy context for social work with adults has changed significantly in recent years. Key expressions of this are:

1. The shift to a market based model of service provision, where the commercial sector has come to play the predominant role in the provision of social care services and where services are means tested and service users are expected to pay for support, unless they cannot afford to and are included as eligible.
2. The shift to the market has placed an increasing importance on arrangements for allocating and rationing support. The 'care manager' approach was adopted to do this. This has fundamentally altered and limited the role of professional statutory social worker in the context of adult service users.
3. The emergence from the 1980s of new organisations of service users as well as of new service user movements. This was a development beyond policy, but it was supported by parallel policy developments and spread to a growing range of service user groups, starting with the disabled people's movement. Service users and their organisations have been committed to having a greater say in social work and social care services and have argued and worked for their democratisation.
4. The emergence of a new rhetoric of participation, partnership and empowerment, linked with the shift to consumerist market welfare approaches from the 1980s. Provisions for such participation were built into legislation and guidance of the community care reforms, for example. Service users and their organisations remain uncertain what this new consumerist rhetoric means and achieves in practice and frequently express concerns about 'consultation overload', 'tick box exercises' and 'tokenism' - in participation particularly.

Concepts of participation and empowerment have been particularly central among service users, their organisations and movements. Empowerment for them includes both personal and political empowerment and takes account of the complex relations between the two. As people become more personally empowered they are able to make a more effective political impact. Similarly through collective action, people can become more empowered personally Participation or user involvement, is concerned with increasing the say and control that service users can have over their lives and services they use or which impact upon them.

5. The Valuing People initiative represents a break with traditional approaches to policy and practice with people with learning difficulties. Significantly based on principles of normalisation, the aim was to raise standards of support for people with learning difficulties and enable them to participate more actively in mainstream society. Large numbers of people with learning difficulties are still living in NHS institutional services, although the aim was for these to be closed. The recent Cornwall and Orchard House abuse scandals highlight that the accountability and quality of such provision is still suspect.
6. While one of the concerns that government sought to address in undertaking community care reforms in the 1990s was to end 'perverse incentives' for people to be placed in residential care, disproportionately high referral of adult service users to residential services continues. Service users and their organisations argue that many of these people could be supported to live in their own homes consistent with the original goals of the community care reforms.
7. At the same time service users have been able to impact on policy. A key expression of this is the introduction of direct payments schemes with new legislation in 1997. The number of people receiving direct payments has gradually increased. The range of people has also been expanded to include a wider range of service users and children and young people. But the overall numbers in receipt of direct payments is still small in relation to numbers of social care service users overall.

8. Direct payments were pioneered by the disabled people's movement. They represented a radical change in values and philosophy to underpin people's support. The aim was to put individuals in charge of the support they received by giving them control over the cash it cost; for them to decide on what support they wanted; for them to have support to initiate and run such schemes and for the support to be sufficient to make it possible for them to have 'independent living'; that is to say for people to live their lives on as equal terms as possible to non-disabled people/ non-service users.
9. While this has been the policy framework for direct payments, there have been major problems and barriers undermining it. There has been strong resistance from some local authorities, who have wanted to continue to control their own services; budgetary limits have meant that often direct payments have not been sufficient to ensure independent living and there has frequently not been equity between service users; the process of assessment has continued to be dominated by traditional professional values, direct payments appear often to have been understood officially in consumerist terms rather than as a means of empowerment, requiring infrastructure support; and contracts have increasingly been placed away from valued disabled people's organisations to commercial organisations which have undercut them and offered an inferior service. Problems have also been experienced by service users where local authorities themselves seek to be the service provider 'in house' for direct payments. The cumulative effect has been to subvert direct payments as a truly different approach to personal and social support.
10. Recently the government has made clear its commitment to individualised approaches to support more generally as a central plank in social care policy. Such 'individualised support schemes' or 'personalised budgets' are based on bringing together different funding streams to provide support for service users. These schemes have not originated with service users. While the aim is to mainstream such schemes, so far their development has been based on a relatively few pilot projects with a limited evidence base for their effectiveness.

11. Service users and their organisations have also developed their own thinking about issues affecting them, for example, their identity and how they are perceived, new ways of understanding their situation and new. User-led approaches to support and assistance.

Service users have in addition sought to gain greater involvement in four key areas, all of which have significant implications for social work roles and tasks and which in some cases have already begun to influence them. These are in:

a. Developing their own accounts and histories – offering their versions of their experience and views
b. Education and training – developing user involvement in social work education and training, user trainers, training for user trainers and user led training
c. Research and evaluation – getting involved in research, developing a more inclusive knowledge base for social care, developing their own new research approaches and becoming researchers
d. Quality definition and measurement – developing user involvement in quality standards and user-defined outcome measures.

4.7.1. Broader Developments

Broader developments have also had a major influence on the policy context of social care and social work. Key to this is the introduction of rights based legislation. This includes the introduction of the Disability Discrimination Act, the subsequent extension of its provisions to include a wider range of service users and situations; the passing of the Human Rights Act and in 2006 the establishment of the Disability Equality Duty, requiring public agencies and services not only to counter discrimination, but also to strive towards and promote, equality for disabled people

4.7.2. Mental Health Legislation

While disability legislation and proposals for change have focused on rights and entitlements, the policy context for mental health has been significantly different. Since the community care reforms, there has been a growing media and political preoccupation with the perceived 'dangerousness' of mental health service users and the 'threat' they pose to 'public safety'.

Most significantly over the last nine years it has resulted in ongoing government attempts to introduce new mental health legislation increasing restrictions to be placed on mental health service users' rights, including the extension of compulsory treatment beyond hospitals and the detention of people labelled as having 'dangerous personality disorder', prior to conviction for any crime and fears that attention has been diverted from continuing core problems and deficiencies of mental health services and policy.

There has been continuing questioning in policy of the specific contribution that social work and a social work background has to offer in health and social care. The first expression of this was embodied in the Community Care reforms, when the official assumption was that other professionals would be just as well qualified to act as care managers as social workers. More recently the intention has been to end the approved social worker role and put a mental health social worker role in its place which might be undertaken by other health and social care professionals.

4.8. Children and Family Social Work

Service users and indeed members of the public more generally, seem to understand social work with families and children as ultimately being concerned with keeping children with or removing them from their families. Whatever, the origins of this perception, whatever the part played by the mass media in perpetuating it, this does seem to be a view which is much more broadly internalised. In a study of another area of social work, this negative stereotype of social work as child remover seems to be a deeply held concern and fear about social work held by many people, worrying them about accessing other forms of social work support.

A process of child care and child protection policy and practice development in children and family social work based on a cycle of tragedies and follow-up enquiries has been widely recognised.

Service users highlight what they see as the arbitrary use of social work's controlling powers to remove children from parents with mental health problems and with learning difficulties, rather than ensuring the provision of appropriate ongoing support – especially at times of particular difficulty. Inadequate funding, problems in recruiting and retaining good quality staff, insufficient management resources, over-bureaucratisation and overloaded agencies are all seen to contribute to the inability of such social work to ensure adequate and reliable support for families and children to prevent problems worsening, to identify difficulties early and to ensure effective decision-making. Problems of communication and coordination with other agencies in work with children and families, as well as with adults is also recognised as a problem, which service users are aware of because of the difficulties they experience in securing suitable and integrated support where their needs cross over different agencies and policy sectors.

Over the last 25-30 years there have been radical shifts in child care and child protection policy and practice. Many of these have become high profile issues which have become part of broader, political, media and public debates. They include:

1. A shift from residential provision to foster care and adoption;
2. Shifts towards and away from 'same race' fostering and adoption;
3. Shifts in understanding from 'relativism' in relation to culture and ethnicity, to the need to adopt effective anti-discriminatory, anti-racist policy and practice;
4. Shifts in philosophy relating to removing children from families of origin and seeking to keep them with their families;
5. A shift from long term retention of cases to fear of 'drift' in care;
6. Shifts in approaches to fostering and adoption relating to the sexuality of potential parents and the nature of their households;
7. Shifts in approaches to adoption in relation to the age of potential adapters.

Such policies and practices have changed over the years, in some cases due to shifts in social work thinking and because of child protection tragedies, rather than as a result of strongly knowledge based policy development. One thing which has remained a constant in stated policy and practice over recent years, however, has been a view of the primacy of the child in considerations and decisions relating to child care and child protection. Both the Victoria Climbie tragedy and the more recent Child B case in Westminster, were defining cases where this did not happen, although it is argued that this is for different reasons.

The 1989 Children Act, which provided the original underpinning for current social work with families and children, like the community care reforms introduced at the same time, placed an emphasis on the participation of children. It also placed more emphasis, than the reforms relating to adult service users on rights and entitlements as well as needs.

However, participation in relation to children and young people raises additional issues to those raised with adult involvement. Service users argue that these do not particularly follow from the ability or otherwise of children to come to realistic and sensible decisions; to make choices and to contribute their views about themselves, their circumstances and services relating to them.

Children do not have the rights of full citizenship in societies like England and the UK. In some cases they may lack the capacity to pursue their own interests independently. There is a strong tradition of adults speaking on behalf of children and interpreting what they say.

Children and young people are also being involved in research and supported to undertake their own research (Ward, 1997; West, 1997; Kirby, 1999). Yet there is still a strong sense at the level of policy, provision and general-decision making that children have very little influence over social work and social care. At an individual level, both the Victoria Climbie and Child B cases highlighted basic problems of the voice of the child not being given central consideration and the child not necessarily being spoken with or listened to.

Social work with children and families includes at least five groups of children and young people. These are:

a) Disabled children and young people and their parents;
b) Disabled parents and their children;
c) Looked after children and their families
d) Children in the family where child care/support or child protection needs have been identified;

e) Children and young people within or at risk of coming within the juvenile justice and related social control/penal systems.

The wide range of issues and circumstances included under these five headings reflect the diversity and complexity of social work with children and families.

In recent years social work and social services have identified another group which they see as coming within their orbit, relating to the second group identified above, who have been categorised as 'young careers'. A new area of policy, practice and discussion has developed in relation to this externally constructed identity. Many disabled people and disabled people's organisations challenge the thinking underpinning this concept and policy approach, arguing that while it often serves to blame and stigmatise disabled parents, the actual issue is the lack of adequate and appropriate support they are able to access as disabled people and parents.

4.9. Social Work Roles and Tasks

There are some general points that need to be made before looking separately at social work roles and tasks with adults and with families and children.

4.9.1. Lacking Public Understanding

All the signs are that the roles and tasks of social work have not been and are still not well known to the public or to service users. Studies of public and service user understandings from the 1980s and 2000s both provide evidence to this effect. Thus social work may be something that 'the public' has strong often negative attitudes about, but equally it doesn't have a clear understanding of what social work actually is and what it does. The fact that service users may not know what the nature and scope of social work practice resulted in one current text recommending that social workers needed to be much clearer to service users about what they do.

Lack of public familiarity with and understanding of social work seems most likely to relate to the fact that it is generally not a universality service. Its association with deprivation, disadvantage and people who are often devalued in society mean that people are more likely to see it as for others rather than themselves. Social work is also essentially a human rather than technological service. It isn't linked with high technology, complex equipment and 'scientific discovery'. The truth is that much of it is about people talking to or communicating with each other. This is perhaps what can make it seem so unremarkable and mundane, but which is actually what makes it so complex and difficult to tie down and comprehend.

From what service users say it seems that social work is an easy job to do badly, but a very difficult one to do well. In discussions, they highlight the benefits they have got from good social workers as well as the problems when social work supports is not good. It will be helpful to look more carefully at the roles and tasks of social work and how they are defined in turn.

4.9.2. Social Work Roles

Two main roles for social work tend to be identified most often and service users certainly talk in these terms too. These are social work's

1. Support role
2. Control role

The first of these roles is largely uncontentious and relates to the goals and values that social work most often associates itself with, including advancing self-determination, autonomy and social justice.

The control role has always been part of social work. It is not only traditionally associated with social work playing a part in ensuring that people conform to prevailing values and behaviours. It also extends to social work having powers to restrict people's rights and freedom of action. This is most associated with the child protection and mental health aspects of social work practice. Social workers can also intervene where they judge people incapable of managing their own affairs and in the institutionalisation of people seen as no longer able to manage in their own homes. The control role of social work is particularly linked with interventions to restrict the rights of some people, in order to safeguard the rights of others

A third role however is also associated with social work; this is a role to bring about change in the individual. Thus the International Federation of Social Workers' (IFSW) definition of social work includes:

Professional social work is focused on problem solving and change. As such, social workers are change agents in society and in the lives of the individuals, families and communities they serve.

While social work may see this role and goal as unproblematic, for many service users the intervention of state social work to change them can seem very much the opposite. Bearing in mind that such intervention for change is significantly based on psychiatrically based interpretations of behaviour and emotions, its appropriateness as well as its effectiveness are concerns for service users.

Service users draw a distinction between social work and social workers. At least two of the core roles discussed above are cause for concern for many service users. What makes social work more acceptable to them is the extent to which good practitioners mediate underlying problems in its ideology and organisation. This places a big responsibility and creates large challenges for such practitioners.

Social work has long been associated with poverty and working with a clientele with particular problems of deprivation, although as has been said, some commentators have felt that social work has not always paid enough attention to this. New Labour governments from 1997 highlighted the related concepts of social exclusion and social inclusion and made them central in UK social policy, setting up a Social Exclusion Unit, initially chaired by the Prime Minister. Over this period, increasingly, government has seen a primary task of social work and a measure of its success the degree to which it reduces social exclusion.

Government definitions of social inclusion have emphasised the importance of people being in paid employment as a key criterion. This has also been reflected in the significance attached by government in its overall social policy, benefits and fiscal policies, to people being in paid work rather than relying on benefits. Thus a key implicit role for social work is to support such an interpretation of social inclusion by encouraging the integration of social care service users into employment Certainly key groups of social care services users, particularly disabled people and mental health service users, have been officially identified as having low employment rates and government policies have sought to integrate them into employment. There has also been a growing interest on the part of government on getting single parents back into paid employment. Service users frequently experience these pressures to take paid employment as a problematic, crudely conceived and implemented policy, which takes little account of:

1. The lack of flexibility of the labour market and its insensitivity to their needs;
2. Broader discrimination in employment;
3. The poverty traps that reintegration into employment may still face them with;
4. Their continuing needs for support when in employment;
5. The limited capacity of some service users to be in (full-time) employment, even if they are capable of making a contribution to their communities;
6. Alternative ways in which service users can contribute and develop their skills, for example, through education and training, getting involved in their communities and services and as full-time parents;
7. High costs and shortcomings of child care provision.
8. Continuing problems with benefits policy and practice in the way of people undertaking unpaid activities which can develop their sense of self-worth and self-esteem, confidence and occupational skills, which may later help them to join the labour market.

4.9.3. Social Work Tasks

If we take social work tasks to mean what social workers do and with what practice is concerned, then the range of work approaches and activities is truly enormous. Social work approaches include:

a) Individual direct work with service users
b) Indirect work with family and friends
c) Work with loved ones and others identified in roles as 'informal careers'
d) Group work
e) Community-based and community development work

Actual tasks are wide ranging including:

1. Offering information, advice and advocacy;
2. Helping people negotiate with other state agencies, particularly over benefits/financial support, housing and other services;
3. Providing counselling and other psychotherapeutic support
4. Providing practical guidance and help
5. Referring service users to other relevant agencies and service providers
6. Accessing financial support to service users

4.9.4. Social Work Practices

Strong consistent messages emerge both from formal research and what service users say about what they find helpful and value in social work practice. Issues they highlight include social work and the social worker's:

1. Social approach
2. Relationship
3. Personal qualities

Social approach: While some service users make clear that social work is not always strongly consistent with the social approach that defines it as *social* work, nonetheless the recognise it as having an underpinning philosophy which aims to see the person in their broader context and respond accordingly. This distinguishes it from other health related professions which tend to be based more on medicates individual models which focus narrowly on the individual, rather than their circumstances and the issues and barriers they face.

Relationship: Service users highlight the relationship with the social worker as key to the positives they associate with social work practice. It is this relationship which is the starting point for building trust and supporting people's self-empowerment.

Personal qualities: When asked what they want from social workers, service users consistently refer to a range of valued personal qualities. How much these qualities are inherent in practitioners and how much they are learned remains unclear. They include, warmth, respect, being non-judgemental, listening, treating people with equality, being trust worthy, openness and honesty, reliability and communicating well.

Service users also value the shared understanding that they believe comes from direct experience of using social work and social care services. They argue for this to be seen as a positive in the recruitment and training of new social workers. They also highlight continuing barriers standing in the way of service users becoming social workers on equal terms with non-service users and call for these to be removed

A picture emerges of the kind of social work practice service users want and what they want from it. This includes practice which:

1. Is participatory in process and purpose
2. Focused on supporting independent living and participation rather than dependence
3. Offers continuity
4. Is flexible and person-centred
5. Is holistic and social model based
6. Connects the personal with the social and political, offering personal/emotional and practical support
7. Addresses rights, risks and their complex interrelations
8. Is based on inclusive understanding of knowledge which includes the experiential knowledge of service users and the practice knowledge of face to face workers.

Service users value social workers who:

1. Enable them to work out their own agendas with them
2. Give them time to sort things out
3. Who are available and accessible
4. Provide continuity of support
5. Are reliable and deliver
6. Are responsive
7. Have a good level of knowledge and expertise
8. Value the expertise of the service user

This picture emerges from a wide range of service users and the whole spectrum of social work interventions, including work with adults, mental health service users, young people, families and children, in criminal justice, residential, day services and field work. There is remarkable consistency in data

4.10. New Approaches in Social Work

Approaches to social work roles and tasks with adults and with children and families, have if anything become increasingly differentiated over recent years.

There has been little detailed discussion of social work roles and tasks in recent government discussions of adult social care. Significantly, the green paper on social care: and the subsequent joint health and social care White Paper, Our Health, Our Care, Our Say, made little reference to social work. What they do suggest is that they see the future roles and tasks of social work in terms of the social worker as 'navigator'.

While it does not spell out clearly or fully the kind of social work it envisages for the future, what this suggests is some version of care management set out in different terms. It points to a model of social worker as organiser, manager and referral point. However, these are not the aspects of social work practice which service users have highlighted that they value. They place an emphasis on the benefits of the relationship and the range of support activities offered by good practitioners. The role of the social worker as assessor and referrer are in fact the aspects of social work practice which adult service users seem to find most problematic.

This is of particular significance currently when the government has made it clear that it sees individualised budgets and individualised approaches to support as central to the future of social care support and service provision. Direct payments, developed by disabled people and the disabled people's movement, pioneered such individualised approaches to support, putting the individual service user in control of the money for their support and those providing such support, for example, through employing personal assistants. In this arrangement, the service user defines the support they want and decides who provides it. This has led to service users identifying a wide range of imaginative forms of support that they want, outside the box of traditional social care provision. Research has repeatedly highlighted that service users prefer direct payments; that they make it more possible for them to live independently and improve their health and general wellbeing, enabling them to be more active citizens and to contribute in various ways, including through being in employment

However, service users have identified a wide range of problems in the way in which such direct payments have in practice been implemented. These include:

1. Lack of parity, according to when people access them and where they live;
2. The exclusion as yet of health services and funding from such arrangements;
3. The longstanding lack of enthusiasm of some local authorities for such arrangements;
4. The increasing use of private and other non-disabled people contractors providing such support, leading to a lowering of its quality;
5. The setting of rates for direct payments being determined by comparisons below the cost of residential care, rather than enabling independent living;
6. The failure to ensure infrastructure support for direct payments to make possible their uptake by the widest range of service users;
7. The failure to offer or fund legal advice should things go wrong between a personal assistant (Pas) and their employer;
8. The undermining and closure of local user controlled organisations because of inadequate and insecure funding.
9. The shortcomings of traditional professional social work based assessment processes in relation to such schemes

We will return to this last concern shortly. While disabled people and other service users have increasingly been highlighting the problems with existing direct payments schemes, other approaches to individualised support have also recently been developing. These are most associated with the In Control project and the Department of Health Care Services Improvement Partnership. Neither of them have been rooted with service users or grown from their experience. Both have sought to extend the range of income streams included to pay for support and involve the service user knowing what their budget is in advance through the resource allocation system. They have so far placed a significant reliance on the unpaid involvement of family and loved ones, rather than infrastructure support.

As has been said, the government has responded enthusiastically to these schemes, seeing them as the major plank in future arrangements for adult social care, although the research evidence for them is so far limited and the scale of pilot projects is still small. Some disabled people are concerned these schemes will be used to replace direct payments, rather than sort out the shortcomings now associated with them; that they do not have the ownership of service users and are being advocated as being capable of offering improved support for less money. This has created considerable concern, given that service users are currently reporting cuts in services, as well as in their own user controlled organisations.

This brings us back to the issue of professional assessment. In December 2006, a two day 'Self-Directed Support Academy for people who use services and family careers, organised by CSIP, brought together service users with experience of using direct payments and other self-directed support schemes. The latter tend to be seen as different from direct payments by their advocates and were also compared adversely with direct payments by service users at this event, although direct payments can be used as part of an individual budget. They compared positive experiences of SIDS, with what they called 'bureaucratic' and 'over-policed' arrangements for direct payments. It is the specific issue of assessment that we will be focusing on here. But it is also possible to see how problems and confusions over different approaches to individualised support are being created by comparisons being made between small scale specially funded pilot projects and mainstream local authority policy.

4.10.1. Professional Assessment

The problems that service users highlight with existing systems of professional social work referral can be summed up as relating to:

1. It being based on 'professional' rather than service user definitions of issues and problems;
2. That these are still not necessarily informed by 'social' or 'barriers' based models;
3. Instead they continue to be based on deficit models of service users, only offering support where 'inability' is identified, rather than seeing support as a means of enabling ability and supporting preventative approaches;
4. While they are meant to be 'professionally-led', they are still significantly budget-driven;
5. Limited effective involvement of many service users in their assessment
6. Time taken to respond to assessment and requests for information from social workers thus undermining the opportunity for service users to be in control of how their personal assistance needs are met, particularly in relation to direct payments.

Given the future role seen for social work as navigator, professional assessment can be expected to become an even more central part of the role with adult service users. Yet many service users see it currently being interpreted and operated in regressive and disempowering ways.

The policy response of government to the tragic death of Victoria Climbie was the White Paper, *Every Child Matters*, which was framed in broad terms of the rights and needs of all children and made the case for a national data system for children. Yet statutory social work has never provided a universalist service for children and families. The Victoria Climbie tragedy was related to specific failings in social work and other services and the recent history of child care practice has increasingly been dominated by a 'very narrow model of child protection work' This has not been valued by service users or indeed other stockholders.

This shift away from community-based to child protection work which emphasises the controlling powers of social work has not been the only development narrowing the roles and tasks of social workers with families and children. As with adult work, they have been under increasing pressure to manage and commission work rather than undertake ongoing direct work with families and children. Thus the very strengths that service users value from good practitioners, to capacity to be non-judgemental, to listen, to be honest and reliable and crucially to offer a key supportive relationship are weakened rather than maximised. This has been compounded as problems of recruitment and retention have increased.

While child protection work is associated with the use of social work's powers to restrict people's rights, it is the arbitrary and inappropriate use of such powers, without adequate information or warning which service users have long expressed most concern about. The existence of such powers does not in itself inherently exclude the possibility of service users being involved and having a say in what happens to them. But they do report concerns that this does not always happen and that safeguards are inadequate. Some service users who have developed relationships of trust with social workers even feel able to confide problems to them. They also talk of the problem of social workers failing to keep them informed, perhaps because of the challenge such openness poses for some practitioners. High levels of staff turnover, promotion out of practice and constant reorganisation, also create problems in the way of maintaining ongoing relationships with service users, which in turn inhibits the development of trust in sensitive situations where it is especially important.

Two groups of parents have particular concerns. These are parents with learning difficulties and those who use mental health services. Both groups may need ongoing support as parents, or support at particular times of difficulty, or over particularly difficult issues. Their concern is that rather than receive such support, they are required to change or their particular difficulties are seen as reason for removal of children.

It is not only the shortcomings of social work practice that service users refer to. They also highlight the inadequacies of placements and other follow-up action initiated by practitioners. Here they refer to poor outcomes in terms of the inferior quality of residential placements the frequent breakdown of fostering placements in some cases; the continuing stigma associated with being in state care and the poor personal performance still repeatedly ascribed to young people with experience of being looked after by the state.

As service users say, while many policies have changed over recent years, often through 360 degrees, the problems experienced by service users continue. Policy proposals continue to be imposed from the top down and opportunities for choice are restricted as standardised prescriptions continue to be adopted – even if change significantly over time. The limited say that social work practitioners have in shaping the broader landscape of social care in the context of work with children and families needs perhaps to be seen as having a key part to play in perpetuating this problem.

While social work roles and tasks with both adults and children and families can be seen to be arbitrarily constrained by managerial structures, increasing bureacratisation and funding priorities, resulting in the standardising of social work responses and referral to a limited range of support services, there is one area of social work, where a different picture seems to emerge.

This is the field of specialist palliative care social work, an area of social work that seems to have been neglected in both public and professional discussions of social work. Not only do service users report it providing a wide range of supportive roles and tasks, combining practical and psychological forms of help and support and addressing personal and social issues,, but they also indicate that the response of practitioners is very much geared to the individual service user, offering whatever combination and form of help that the particular person may value and find most helpful.

There seems to be some irony in the fact that a branch of social work which has remained so true to social work values and principles, where there is much desired continuity of practice and practitioners, has been significantly marginalised by social work and in social work discussions.

Service users have much to say about both the strengths and weaknesses of existing social work practice. They show a sensitivity to the rights and needs of practitioners as well as of service users. Taken together their accounts and the material they have produced offers a distinct set of discourses to set next to conventional professional and academic social work discussions. They have also developed their own theories and philosophies for social work to be based upon.

Thus their critiques of existing practice and services and government proposals offer a basis for how things could be different and better. But they also point directly to the kind of social work that they want to see. Key components of such social work practice are that it is:

1. Social model based
2. Inclusive
3. Participative
4. Rights based

Here we set out some of the key elements making up service users' vision for an inclusive, participatory, inclusive and rights based approach to social work. While it is not a complete list, it does include the main ones that service users, their organisations and discussions have highlighted and returned to frequently over recent years.

1. Service users want social work which is based on a barriers model/social model approach, committed to working with service users, addressing their personal and social circumstances and challenging the barriers which they face in society and supporting them to deal with these barriers and their effects as well as finding ways of minimising them.
2. A touchstone for social work practice for service users is the degree to which it safeguards and secures their human and civil rights. This needs to be recognised in both the process and aims of social work.
3. Theorising about social 'care' and support for adults has been strongly influenced by the discussions and developments of service users and their movements, beginning with the disabled people's movement and its development of the social model approach to disability and the idea of 'independent living'. These have impacted upon policy, practice, research and theory. Social work theory about child care and child protection similarly needs to be more strongly influenced by the input and perspectives of service users
4. The production of formal 'social work discourse' has generally been dominated by policymakers, managers and academics. Service users highlight the benefits of a more inclusive discourse which enables the fuller and more equal involvement of both service user and current face to face practitioner perspectives

5. Service users generally find technicians managerialist based models of social work unhelpful. They want a 'hands-on' approach from social workers rather than one where the social worker is essentially a referrer to other agencies, professionals and services.
6. They see a distinct value and contribution in social work practice which addresses both their personal, psychological needs and the broader issues and problems that face them. They see these two aspects of their lives as closely bound and inseparable.
7. Service users value the wide range of social work approaches, including individual, family, group and community work approaches. They also want to see social work which will intervene on their behalf, offer reliable information, support and advocacy and is familiar with their rights and needs.
8. Service users highlight the central importance of the relationship they have with social workers as a key value of social work. The organisation of social work is undermining and curtailing such relationships. Service users argue for promotion in social work to place much greater weight on enabling people to remain in practice, rather than moving out of it.
9. Service users want the social work role of assessment to be seen in terms of supporting self-assessment. They want assessment to be based on social and barriers based models, rather than deficit models of social care support as they frequently are now. This would support preventive approaches to social care which can make independent living possible. New related roles need to be explored and developed, for example, to support service users to have an effective say in assessment.
10. Service users highlight the importance of 'person centred support' as the starting point for social work and social care. By this they mean support that is geared to meet the rights and needs of service users rather than service or budget driven support which fits service users into traditional services.
11. Social work and the structures associated with it have developed a negative approach to risk taking. This restricts the life chances of service users unhelpfully and prevents them gaining the opportunities that are part of making the journey to independent

living. Social work needs to be supportive of positive risk taking for service users. It also needs to be more effective in safeguarding service users from the risks that they currently encounter in the social care system, including serious risks of neglect, abuse, denial of rights, bullying, racism, etc.

12. Service users want to see social workers, as a routine part of their professional and post-qualification education and training, to be offered an effective grounding to understand access issues broadly defined, for example, in relation to the physical, communication and cultural access requirements of service users.
13. The government is placing an increasing emphasis on 'individual budgets' and 'self-directed support schemes'. Building on direct payments developed by disabled people, these are intended to bring together different funding streams to support service users' independent living.
14. Much more work also needs to be done to ensure that direct payments schemes are more widely available and are less constrained by traditional assessment approaches, inadequate funding and the lack of infrastructure support as envisaged by disabled people's organisations to enable the widest range of service users access and retain them.
15. Service users emphasise that they have a particular contribution to make to each other in offering the positive support and advocacy roles associated with social work through the direct experience that they share. This raises at least three key issues, that:
    a) professional social work practitioners are encouraged and supported to be based in service user controlled organisations, as well as in other settings.
    b) service users are supported and encouraged to develop their own support, advocacy and advice giving roles alongside those of professional social work, rather than these being displaced by it, or it necessarily being offered instead.
    c) social work education and training fully involves service users and their organisations. To achieve this means ensuring:

i) strategic support and capacity building for service users and their organisations to be involved;

ii) some funding resources for such involvement are provided directly to service user controlled organisations;

iii) that the current patchiness of implementation of user involvement in social work education is addressed and raised standards are achieved generally;

iv)diverse involvement of service users, including the wide range of social work service users (including those where social work's control as well as support roles are applied) and addressing difference in relation to gender, sexuality, ethnicity, culture, class, disability and age.

v) Equal access of service users to professional social work education and training.

16. To support the development of an effective network of local user controlled organisations as recommended in Improving the Life Chances of Disabled People report and working in close and equal relationship with them. This is a key requirement is social work is to be user centred and involve service users meaningfully.

17. To support the development and provision of more user-led services and support, based in user controlled organisations. Evidence highlights that such services are particularly valued by service users, but at present they compete on unequal terms with other sectors of service providers to provide them.

18. To explore the development of appropriate organisational and management structures for social work to maximise the contribution and effectiveness of social work practice. Such structures will need to be accessible in the broadest sense to ensure the diverse and full involvement of service users.

19. To maintain and advance a strategic approach to service user involvement of service users and their user controlled organisations in social work and social care structures and organisations. This will seek to ensure that they are fully accessible and enable effective involvement on equal terms. Such structures include, for example:

i) Social work and social care organisation like SCIE, GSCC, Skills for Care, CSCI, etc.

ii) Editorial boards and refereeing systems for peer review journals, professional journals, books and other publications;

iii) The management and partnerships for qualifying and post-qualification and other social work education and training.

References

Agnew, Elizabeth N. 2004. *From Charity to Social Work: Mary E. Richmond and the Creation of an American Profession.* Urbana, IL: University of Illinois Press.

Barker, Richard 2009. *Making Sense of Every Child Matters - multi professional practice guidance* (1st ed.). Bristol, UK: Policy Press.

Reamer, Frederic G. 2006. *Ethical Standards in Social Work: A Review of the NASW Code of Ethics* (2nd ed.). Washington, DC: NASW Press.

Specht, Harry; Courtney, Mark E. 1994. *Unfaithful angels : how social work has abandoned its mission.* New York: Free Press.

5

Poverty Reduction Policies

Few economists doubt that economic growth is necessary for the long-term reduction of poverty. But how close is the link between the two? If the incomes of the poor rise closely in line with incomes overall, then the key to poverty reduction is rapid economic growth; on the other hand if the relationship is weak, then other policies, such as targeted subsidies, are likely to be important and the concept of "pro-poor growth" might have some relevance.

David Dollar and Aart Kraay address the problem directly, in a paper entitled "Growth is Good for the Poor" that appeared in March 2000. They gathered information on the per capita income of the poor and on overall per capita income. The data come from 80 countries over four decades, and Dollar and Kraay were able to piece together 236 "episodes," - periods during which it was possible to measure changes in the income of the poor and of the country overall.

They first regressed the log of per capita income of the poor and got

$$\ln(\text{poor}) = 1.07 \ln(\text{inc}) - 1.78. \quad R^2=0.87.$$

Two points are worth noting: First, the relatively high value of R^2, which says that 87% of the variation in the log of per capita income of the poor is associated with changes in the log of per capita income overall. Second, the coefficient on the ln(inc) term is 1.07, which means that if average incomes were to rise by 10%, the incomes of the poor would rise by about 10.7%. This coefficient is not significantly different from 1, so perhaps it would be wiser to conclude that the incomes of the poor tend to rise *in line with* those of the country as a whole.

As an alternative, Dollar and Kraay regressed the *change* in ln(poor) on the change in ln(inc). In this case they found.

$$\text{“}\ln(\text{poor}) = 1.17 \ln(\text{inc}) - 0.00. \qquad R^2{=}0.52.$$

The fit is weaker in this equation, with only about half of the variation in the change in the log of incomes of the poorest quintile being attributable to changes in the log of overall income. The elasticity (i.e. 1.17) is still close to unity.

In order to test the robustness of this finding, Dollar and Kraay estimate a number of variations on the original equation - for different time periods, for countries that are growing and countries that are shrinking, for low- and high-growth countries, for poor countries and rich.

There are several important conclusions:

1. The per capita income of the poorest quintile grew in line with overall per capita GDP for the 80 countries in the same over the four decades covered. In short, growth matters.
2. The relationship in equation (1) has not changed over time, and applies both in rich and poor countries. In short, growth still matters.
3. The incomes of the poor do *not* fall disproportionately during an economic crisis.
4. Greater economic openness, the rule of law, fiscal discipline, and low inflation all contribute to faster economic growth, and in this manner help the poor.
5. Democracy, and higher public spending on health and education, do not have a measurable effect, one way or another, on the incomes of the poor.

Other researchers have also found that poverty trends tracked growth trends very closely in 1980s and 1990s. According to Chen and Ravallion on average, growth in the consumption of poorest fifth of the population tracked economic growth one-for-one over this period. In the vast majority of countries that they study, growth led to rising consumption in the poorest fifth of the population, while economic decline led to falling consumption. So pro-growth policies in most cases actually are also pro-poor.

If the incomes of the poor are closely tied to overall economic growth, how much room remains for a poverty reduction policy per se? Put another way, is there any substance in calls for "pro-poor" growth?

In a recent controversial paper, Aart Kraay argues that "in the medium run, most of the variation in changes in poverty is due to growth, suggesting that policies and institutions that promote broad-based growth should be central to pro-poor growth." He goes on to argue, "most of the remainder is due to poverty-reducing patterns of growth in relative incomes," but "cross-country evidence provides little guidance on policies and institutions that promote these other sources of pro-poor growth."

That has not stopped the World Bank and others from trying! The World Bank separates its anti-poverty – as distinct from pro-growth – activities into three groups: promoting opportunity, facilitating empowerment, and enhancing security. We now consider each in some more detail.

5.1. Policies to Enhance Opportunity

The lack of material opportunities such as jobs, credit, and public services, including schools and health services, is a direct cause of poverty. Well-functioning markets are important in generating sustainable growth and expanding opportunity for poor people because poor people rely on formal and informal markets to sell their labour and products, to finance their investments, and to insure against risks. The findings: these policies on average benefit poor people more than others. Case studies of Chile, China, Ghana, Uganda and Vietnam show that agricultural reforms have helped raise producer prices for small farmers by eliminating marketing boards, changing real exchange rates through broader economic reforms, lowering tariffs and eliminating quotas.

The human, physical, natural, financial and social assets that poor people possess – or have access to – affect their prospects for escaping poverty because these assets can enable poor people to take advantage of opportunities. Expanding the assets of poor people can strengthen their position and their control over their lives. A recent study of irrigation in Vietnam has uncovered important complementarities between education and gains from irrigation. Households with higher education levels received higher returns to irrigation.

The World Bank argues that creating more opportunities involves complementary actions to stimulate overall growth, make markets work for poor people, and build their assets, including addressing inequalities in the distribution of endowments such as education. More specifically:

1. Encouraging effective private investment is essential because investment and technological innovation are the main drivers of growth in jobs and labour incomes. Fostering private investment requires reducing risk for private investors—through stable fiscal and monetary policy, stable investment regimes, sound financial systems, and a transparent business environment. Certainly, the rule of law and anti-corruption measures are also important. Special measures are frequently required to ensure that micro enterprises and small businesses can participate effectively in markets that are more vulnerable, yet employ a large number of poor people. Public investment in expanding infrastructure and communications, and upgrading the skills of the labour force have to complement private investment to enhance competitiveness and create new market opportunities.
2. Opening to international markets offers an important opportunity for income growth as long as countries have the infrastructure and institutions to stimulate a strong supply response. Therefore, the opening needs to be well designed with special attention to bottlenecks.
3. Building human, physical, natural and financial assets that poor people own or can use requires actions on at least two fronts. First, sufficient public spending on basic social and economic services such as primary education. Second, reform public delivery or privatise those services in order to ensure good quality service delivery.

4. Addressing asset inequalities across gender, ethnic, racial and social divides. Special action is required to tackle socially-based inequality such as concentrated farm land ownership in rural communities, under-schooling of girls relative to boys, and the limited independence of women due to lack of access to productive means.
5. Getting infrastructure and knowledge to poor areas. Special action is also needed in order to improve the social and economic infrastructure in poor and remote areas, which to a great extent also contribute the poverty problem. Similarly, basic urban services should be provided to city slums so that urban poor people may have chance to participate more actively in over growth.

5.2. Policies to Enhance Empowerment

The premise underlying an emphasis on empowerment is that a lack of representation in the process of policy-making, due to social and institutional barriers, has impeded poor people's access to market opportunities and to public sector services. It follows that empowerment should help. Unfortunately, there is very little empirical evidence, to date, on how well empowerment policies along the lines discussed below contribute to reducing poverty.

Broadly, empowerment refers to being able to make informed decisions and choices effectively. But there is some disagreement about the true content of empowerment. Mahatma Gandhi emphasised self-reliance; Polo Freire stressed the need for concentrations, for helping the poor to learn about and perceive "social, political and economic contradictions" and then to stir to act against "the oppressive elements of society." The World Bank finesses these differences by defining empowerment as "the expansion of assets and capabilities of poor people to participate in, negotiate with, influence, control, and hold accountable institutions that affect their lives." It sees the four major elements of empowerment as (i) access to information, (ii) inclusion/participation, (iii) accountability, and (iv) local organisational capacity.

State institutions must be responsive and *accountable* to poor people. In nearly every country the public sector often pursues activities that are biased against poor people, and poor people have trouble getting prompt, efficient service from the public administration. Accountability is helped when there is good *access to information.*

Example: The Public Expenditure Tracking Survey (PETS) conducted in 1996 in Uganda found that only 22% of the central government funds intended to support schools run at the local level were reaching their intended destination.

Amartya Sen sees poverty as consisting of a "deprivation of capabilities," so that the poor have inadequate resources to participate fully in society; in short, they are socially excluded. It follows that *inclusion*, which encompasses economic and political participation, is inherently part of the solution to poverty. The process of including the poor is likely to require the development of their social capital, the "features of social organisation, such as trust, norms, and networks, that can improve the efficiency of society by facilitating coordinated actions." Social capital takes time to build, but contributes to stronger *local organisational capacity*.

Good social institutions — kinship, community organisations, and informal networks—can play an important role in poverty reduction. For example, many development programs succeed because they mobilise local groups of project beneficiaries in program design and implementation.

Some social norms and practices help generate and perpetuate poverty. Discrimination on the basis of gender, ethnicity, race, religion, or social status can lead to social exclusion and create barriers to upward mobility, constraining people's ability to participate in economic opportunities and to benefit from and contribute to economic growth. For example, one cross-country study indicates that countries that invest in girls' education have higher rates of economic growth.

It is difficult to empower the poor if decision-making is concentrated in a faraway capital city. Hence the conclusion that a major component of empowering the poor is the need to decentralise power, particularly through delegating it to sub-national levels of government, and privatising some activities. Decentralisation is not, however, a panacea; when done badly, power may be captured by local elites, who may be even less concerned about the poor than the central government. In India, for instance, the state of Kerala has used its powers to spread development widely, while in the state of Bihar local decision-making has not been particularly beneficial to the poor.

Empowerment is difficult to measure. The UNDP's *Gender Empowerment Measure (GEM)* includes indicators such as male and female shares of parliamentary seats, managerial positions, and earned income, but also has serious limitations in that it does not include information on the informal sector, or on such items as the right to vote.

To empower poor people, policies need to facilitate active collaboration among poor and other groups in society include strengthening the participation of poor people in political processes and local decision-making; making changes in governance that make public administration, legal institutions, and public service delivery more efficient and accountable to all citizens; and removing the social barriers that result from distinctions of gender, ethnicity, race and social status. Worthy as this sounds, it is not at all obvious how to achieve such changes, but here are some policies that have been suggested:

1. To improve access to *information*, encourage the development of the media. For instance, Besley and Burgess show that there is a robust link between media development and government responsiveness in India; states with higher newspaper circulation also undertake more extensive relief efforts in the wake of natural disasters.

2. To increase *participation and inclusion*, it helps to institutionalise transparent, democratic and participatory mechanisms for making decisions and monitoring implementation. In this context, it may also be useful to provide legal assistance to poor people who usually have limited access to the legal system.

3. *Accountability* is increased by strengthening the mechanisms used to monitor the performance of public administrations and by providing access to budgetary information and participatory mechanisms. There are many possible ways to do this, including:

(i) Publish complete and timely budgetary information. Vietnam does not do this, for instance, so it is impossible to hold the government to account for how it spends its money.

(ii) Institutional and Governance Reviews (IGR), which use surveys and other quantitative measures to analyse the functioning of public institutions.

(iii) Citizen Report Cards, which allow citizens to express their opinions on the performance and quality of government services.

(iv) World Bank Corruption Surveys, which are designed to extract information on corruption from households, the private sector, and public officials. Based on such a survey, for instance, Albania requested an anti-corruption program to undermine patronage in judicial and civil service appointments. Public Expenditure Tracking Surveys (PETS), which have helped ensure that budgeted funds get to their intended recipients in places such as Ghana and Uganda. Private Enterprise Surveys of the Business Environment, and Investor Roadmaps. These indicate the problems and costs faced by entrepreneurs.

(v) Participatory Poverty Assessments (PPA). Using focus groups, in-depth interviews and other measures, these complement survey data to help build a more detailed picture of the nature and roots of poverty; they have been influential in Vietnam, for instance.

4. To increase *local organisational capacity*, it helps to

(a) Promote decentralisation and community development to enhance the control that poor people and their communities have over the services to which they are entitled. Decentralisation needs to be combined with effective participation and monitoring mechanisms.

(b) Promote gender equality by promoting women's representation in decision-making and providing special assistance for women's productive activities.

(c) Tackle social structures and institutions that are obstacles to the upward mobility of poor people by fostering debate over exclusionary practices and supporting the socially excluded participating into political processes.

(d) Support poor people's social capital by assisting networks of poor people to engage with market and non-market institutions so as to strengthen their influence over policy.

5.3. Policies to Enhance Security

Poor people are exposed to a wide array of risks that make them vulnerable to income shocks and losses of well-being. Reducing poor people's *vulnerability* to ill health, economic shocks, natural disasters, and violence enhances well-being on its own and encourages investment in human capital and in higher-risk, higher-return activities as well.

Households and communities respond to their risk exposure through diversification of assets and sources of income and various types of self-insurance and networks of mutual insurance mechanisms. For instance, some family members may travel to the cities to seek work, sending remittances home; if they cannot find work, then return home.

Mechanisms such as these help to reduce the risk or soften the impact, but the effect may be limited. To counter the incentive and information problems that exclude poor people from many market-based insurance mechanisms, the state has a special role in providing or regulating insurance and setting up safety nets. Health, environmental, labour market, and macroeconomic policies can all reduce and mitigate risk.

Large adverse shocks – economic crises and natural disasters – cause poor people to suffer not only in the short run. They undercut the ability of the poor to move out of poverty in the long run as well, by depleting their human and physical assets, which may be irreversible. So it is crucial to prevent economic crises and natural disasters, as well to protect poor people when they occur.

National programs to manage economy-wide shocks and effective mechanisms to reduce the risks faced by poor people, as well as helping them cope with adverse shocks when they occur, are useful. Appropriate measures might include:

1. Formulating programs to helping poor people manage risk. Micro insurance programs, public works programs and food transfer programs may be mixed with other mechanisms to deliver more effective risk management.
2. Developing national programs to prevent and respond to macro shocks—financial or natural.
3. Supporting minority rights and providing the institutional basis for peaceful conflict resolution, to help prevent civil conflict and mobilise more resource into productive activities.
4. Tackling health problems including widespread illnesses such as malaria and tuberculosis, as well as moderately common but serious conditions such as HIV/AIDS.

There is no simple, universal blueprint for implementing this strategy. Each developing country needs to prepare its own mix of policies to reduce poverty, reflecting national priorities and local realities. Given the important complementarities among these three dimensions, an effective poverty reduction strategy will require action on all three fronts, by all stockholders in society—government, civil society, the private sector and poor people themselves.

5.4. Examples of Good Practices

Any good poverty reduction plan has to be based on a comprehensive poverty analysis that identifies the nature and evolution of poverty, the profile of poor people, and all contributing factors of poverty. Building on an accurate understanding of poverty, the strategy for poverty reduction has to priorities the poverty reduction goals and take into account complementarities and compatibilities of various policy tools. Then specific implementation modules including resource allocation and monitoring mechanisms have to be designed.. The participation of poor people at the last two stages is essential since overall they are the main actors in the fight against poverty.

5.4.1. India

India suffers severe deprivations in education and health—especially in the North, where caste, class, and gender inequities are particularly strong. In studies in Bihar and Uttar Pradesh, poor women and men emphasised their extreme vulnerability and the ineffectiveness of state institutions, from schools to police.

In the past, poverty reduction in India lagged behind that of East Asia because of slower growth and significantly less progress in promoting mass education and basic health. More recently, however, growth has accelerated and there is a growing consensus that poverty has fallen substantially.

There are also marked differences within India—with the South, particularly the state of Kerala, having sharply better education and health. The effectiveness of public action in Kerala has been attributed to its strong tradition of political and social mobilisation.

What are the priorities for action in India? Accelerated poverty reduction requires continued solid economic growth, which in turn demands further liberalisation, especially in agriculture, and better provision of infrastructure, sorely lacking in most of India. In areas with deep deprivation in health and education, the development of social infrastructure is critical. Expanding education and health services requires that state governments reverse the deterioration in their fiscal positions, as subsidies to the loss-making power sector crowd out spending in the social sectors. This requires deep improvements in governance, often weakest in India's poorest regions, and in combating teacher absenteeism. Also needed is more equitable service provision, which requires empowering women and members of lower castes.

5.4.2. Tanzania

Since independence, the government has been focused on three development problems: ignorance, disease and poverty. National efforts to tackle these problems were initially channelled through centrally directed, mediumterm and long-term development plans; despite high levels of foreign aid, these efforts were a complete failure, and poverty was higher in 1990 than at the time of independence.

The current poverty reduction strategy takes a decentralised approach, based on broad consultation with all stockholders. The Zonal Workshops, which included a large number of representatives of the poor at the village level, identified priority concerns and requirements for poverty reduction. Through an assessment of the poverty profiles and trends using 6 household surveys of various purposes during the past two decades, the key findings include: a very high incidence of poverty, is more widespread in rural areas than in urban centres; the poor are concentrated in subsistence agriculture; urban poverty is also acute in urban areas other than Dares Salaam, and poor people are mostly in the informal sector; youth, the old and large households are more likely to be poor; the incidence of poverty declined between 1983-1991 and 1991-1993, but rose during 1993-1998; infant mortality rate remains to be high and AIDS is the leading killer of youths in Dares Salaam and several other sampled districts.

Two participatory poverty assessment studies have suggested the following causes of poverty and obstacles to development: insecure land tenure, lack of access to agricultural inputs, credit, technology, transportation, markets, and quality health services, vulnerability to shocks, gender inequality. These factors were reiterated in the Zonal Workshops. The information then was summarised for each dimension of poverty and further discussed with other stockholders.

The poverty reduction strategy aims at (1) reducing income poverty; (2) improving human capabilities, survival and social well-being; and (3) containing the extreme vulnerability among the poor. The key instrument is high and equitable growth. Specifically the strategy aimed to raise, within three years, the annual GDP growth rate from 5.2% to 6%. Agriculture was expected to increase by 5% annually on average, compared to 3.6% during 1990-1998. The growth of the industrial and service sectors was expected to be higher than that of agriculture. At these growth rates, the incidence of poverty is expected to drop to 42% by 2003 and 24% by 2010. In pursuit of the above poverty reduction objectives, reforms aimed at bolstering market efficiency and factor productivity will be implemented. Besides maintaining low inflation and a small fiscal imbalance, special budgetary attention is to be given to rural, export, and private sectors development programs.

Specific goals were also identified for other dimensions of poverty such as education and health, and especially HIV/AIDS related issues. Twenty seven indicators for the monitoring and evaluation of the poverty reduction strategy have been selected and at least two observations will be made during the next three years. These key welfare indicators will be at the heart of further discussion and assessment of the poverty reduction strategy.

References

Axinn, June and Mark J. Stern 2008. *Social Welfare: A History of the American Response to Need* (7th ed.). Boston, MA: Pearson/Allyn and Bacon.

Balgopal, Pallassana R. 2000. *Social Work Practice with Immigrants and Refugees*. New York, NY: Columbia University Press.

Barker, Robert L. 2003. *Social Work Dictionary* (5th ed.). Silver Spring, MD: NASW Press.

Richardson, Virginia E. and Amanda Smith Barusch 2006. *Gerontological Practice for the Twenty-First Ccentury: A Social Work Perspective*. New York, NY: Columbia University Press.

Sowers, Karen M. and Catherine N. Dulmus and others. 2008. *Comprehensive Handbook of Social Work and Social Welfare*. Hoboken, NJ: John Wiley & Sons.

6

Conceptual Issues in Social Work Policies

In the dominant view of economic policy making, the analysis of the links between economic and social policy continues to be dominated by a "leader/follower model", in which consistent macroeconomic policies are supposed to be determined first, and social policies are called to manage their social, gender and environmental effects. There may be exceptions to this sweeping statement. But in most analyses of economic policies, the statement readily applies. Even the widespread use of the concept of "social safety net" tends to reflect this residual view of social policies, particularly in comparison to the older concepts of "social protection" and "social security".

The main argument of this note is that this subordination of social to economic policies is unlikely to lead to good social outcomes, no matter how ambitious social policies are.

6.1. Economic and Social System

Although other typologic could be provided, we can define four major links between the economic and the social system. The first runs from the social to the economic. It relates to human development and, particularly, to the capacity of the social system to facilitate the accumulation of "capabilities", to use Sen's terminology. A second could probably be added: the view that there are positive asynergies between equity and economic growth. However, this view, although exposed masterfully by the World Bank in its 2006 *World Development Report,* continues to be subject to conflicting evidence.

In turn, three of the links run from the economic to the social system. They relate, first, to the capacity of the economic system to provide adequate resources for human development, as well as the equity implications of the way the provision of services is organised. The second is the ability of the economic system to offer opportunities for adequate income generation, primarily through employment opportunities, as well as the factors that affect the primary distribution of income. The third is the management of risks generated by the economic system and the associated economic insecurity.

The mere enumeration of these links indicates that it would be impossible to guarantee adequate social outcomes without "social-friendly" economic development. More generally, the undesirable social effects of economic policies and outcomes cannot be compensated by social policies, no matter how aggressive they are.

6.2. Human Development

The capabilities provided by social policy are much more than "human capital". They directly affect the well-being of individuals as well as social and political development, particularly the quality of social interactions and political participation. For these reasons, even beyond the economic returns, human development should be at the centre of any development strategy.

There is widespread evidence that there can be major advances in human development even at low levels of income.

Low levels of human development can generate poverty traps and, in this sense, human capital is a necessary condition for economic growth. However, the links running from human to economic development are not linear. In the views exposed by Ranis, Stewart and Ramires (2000), there are virtuous and vicious circles in which both dimensions of development reinforce each other. But there are also countries in which high levels of human development are not translated into rapid economic growth as well as the opposite pattern — "economic growth-biased". They provide evidence that, while countries with human development-biased patterns can move into virtuous circles, the same is not true of economic growth-biased countries.

The foregoing considerations have two major policy implications. The first is that the effort to promote human development to break the poverty traps of low-income countries should be at the centre of international cooperation. The second is that it is still necessary to understand much better the ways to maximise the effects of social policy on economic development and, in any case, that a weak economic performance reduces the economic returns of human development.

6.3. Financing and Design of Social Policy

There is a strong association between per capita GDP and the proportion of GDP allocated to social spending. This association is true of spending on human capital and is even more pronounced in relation to social protection. This implies that the capacity of the economic system to allocate resources for human development varies with the level of economic development. However, it is also true that there are significant differences in social spending among countries at comparable income levels. This implies that it is possible for under-per-formers to increase their social effort.

Aside from this long-run relation between social spending and income, the pro-cyclical pattern of social spending of developing countries through the business cycle has become a major issue of concern in recent decades. This has high social and economic costs. It implies that public sector spending enhances rather than mitigates the effects of the business cycle on vulnerable groups. The procyclicality of social spending in developing countries contributes, in turn, to the severity of the business cycle a pattern clearly opposite to that of industrial countries, where the counter-cyclical behaviour of social spending contributes to a Keynesian smoothing of the business cycle. The contraction of social spending may also have long term effects on the efficiency of social service provision, as it may lead to the loss of skilled personnel and the running down of the associated infrastructure. It is therefore essential to place the counter-cyclical management of social spending at the centre of macroeconomic policies.

Most forms of social spending tend to improve income distribution. This is quite important in highly unequal societies. The types of social spending that contribute most to income distribution are those that have universal or close to universal coverage as, by definition, they reach the poor. This implies, in a sense, that the best "targeting" to the poor may be achieved by universal policies. Universality is, furthermore, the only principle that is consistent with the character of rights that most social services have according to the UN Covenant of Economic, Social and Cultural Rights. There may be specific forms of social assistance targeted to the poor but, curiously, they may be more attractive in middle income countries. In low-income countries the high proportion of poor persons indeed implies that targeting should be secondary to the universal objective of social policy, whereas in middle-income countries targeted social assistance should never be a substitute for the advance of the core universal social policies. And, although the redistributive effects of universal social policies are one of the major contributions of social policy to equity, the redistributive effects of taxation cannot be ignored, particularly in highly unequal societies.

The design of social policy should also aim at avoiding segmenting population into different groups for service provision, as such segmentation reinforces inequality. This is indeed why, among industrial countries, the best income distribution is associated with the universal character of the Welfare State. In contrast, targeted social policies run the risk of segmenting the population according to income levels. Targeting, in this sense, works better when it is an instrument to facilitate the access of the poor to universally provided social services. This also implies that mixed systems, in which private and solidarity institutions complement state institutions in the provision of social services should be regulated in such a way as to avoid segmentation of the population according to the quantity and quality of the services provided.

6.4. Opportunities for Income Generation

There is widespread evidence of rising income inequality in a large proportion of industrial and developing countries in recent decades. For example, using the large number of countries analysed by Cornea (2004), it can be estimated that 88 per cent of the population of the world lives in countries where income distribution has worsened in recent decades. Contrary to the fairly widespread trend in intra-country inequality, inter-country inequality has improved due to the rapid rise of incomes in China and India; but if we exclude these countries, inter-country inequality has also contributed to the deterioration of world income distribution.

One major issue that has been underscored in recent debates is the insufficient employment generation in developing countries, even in periods of rapid economic growth. One of its manifestation has been rising labour market dualism, as reflected in the relative growth of informal sectors in most regions of the developing world, as well as the rising long-term trend of open unemployment in some regions.

The poverty-reduction effects of a given pattern of economic growth depend on income distribution. This is reflected in the fact that the elasticity of poverty reduction to growth tends to be lower in more unequal societies. By definition, such elasticity is also lower when income distribution tends to worsen. This means that not all growth is equally "pro-poor". The concept of "pro-poor growth" has come to have many different meanings, including, for some authors, cases in which growth reduces poverty despite worsening income distribution.

The policy implications of this analysis are many. First, the adequate generation of "quality jobs" should be at the centre of macroeconomic policy as well as of sectorial economic policies. Many or even most new jobs will continue to be provided through self employment and small enterprises in most developing countries. This implies that the agenda of spreading the access of the poor to productive assets -inclusive finance, but also access to land and technical and entrepreneurial training — should occupy a central place in the economic agenda. Since in the poor countries, the largest proportion of the poor are in rural areas, this means that the broader agenda of rural development also plays an essential role. More generally, much more attention should be given to the effects of economic policy on income and wealth distribution, particularly through the identification of those types of interventions in the functioning of labour, technology and factor markets that could contribute to better distributive outcomes.

6.5. Economic Insecurity

Employment and income insecurity seem also to have risen in recent decades. Macroeconomic volatility in developing countries associated with pro-cyclical capital flows is one major explanation, to which the links with the more traditional volatility of commodity prices must be added. Persistent structural change, including in the structure of employment, is also an inherent characteristic of development and generates risks for those persons who work in sectors that tend to contract in the process of development. Rapid technological change has undoubtedly contributed to the risks faced by workers in recent decades. Open markets have also increased the risks that economic activity would be displaced.

Increased economic insecurity takes place in an environment characterised by the weakening of traditional, family- and community-based, forms of social protection, and in which there is an increasing "privatisation of risk". The latter trend has many dimensions. Reduced state intervention in agricultural price formation is part of this trend, which has made smallholders more vulnerable to price swings associated with market fluctuations. Reduced protection and state intervention, together with broader exchange rate flexibility, have made exporters and import-competing activities more vulnerable to market fluctuations. The financial risks associated with pensions have been shifted to households in the trend to move from defined benefits to "defined contribution" pension systems a euphemism in the latter case to reflect the fact that benefits are uncertain.

This environment demands, first, building better social protection systems, and giving countries the room to manoeuvre in order to do so. The globalisation debate should clearly give closer attention to this issue, and to identify in particular what sort of flexibility in commitments as well as new forms of cooperation would be necessary for countries to increase the room to introduce active social protection systems. Second, an adaptable labour force is critical in a world characterised by greater macroeconomic volatility, and rapid structural and technological change. On the contrary, greater labour market flexibility without increased social protection may have negative effects in terms of the supply of "quality jobs" and income insecurity. Third, increased room to manoeuvre for counter-cyclical macroeconomic policies in developing countries may have an essential role in reducing economic insecurity.

6.6. Institutional Implications

The major implication of the analysis of this note is that much more has to be done to enhance the positive links between economic and social policies. This implies, in particular, that the "leader/follower" model in the design of economic policies must be abandoned and, on the contrary, that a model must be designed based on mainstreaming social objectives into economic policy making.

In view of the link between economic and social development, it is necessary to design integrated policy frameworks that take into account the links among different social policies and between economic and social policies.

These integrated frameworks ought to start by designing rules to ensure the "visibility" of the social effects of economic policies and by asking macroeconomic authorities to regularly examine the effects of policies on the main social variables. Similarly, finance ministers should be asked to include an analysis of the distributive effects of any budgetary or tax reform initiative they present to their legislative authorities. Likewise, public entities entrusted with technological, industrial or agricultural policy ought to evaluate regularly who the beneficiaries of their programmes are.

The spread of "poverty reduction strategies" as a framework for economic policy in poor countries may be seen as a step in this direction but, unfortunately, the choice of policies in this framework is frequently made independently of their social implications. In fact, orthodox analyses continue to promote a framework in which market liberalisation is predicated with no analysis of its social effects, and macroeconomic frameworks continue to be promoted with no attention to the implications of macroeconomic policy on employment, among other social effects. Much more must be done in all those areas to incorporate the basic principle that we support here: that the choice of economic policies cannot just follow "efficiency" considerations; they must also incorporate their social implications.

6.7. Research on Decent Work Agenda

We know that trade is one of the most direct channels through which globalisation—that is, the external world economy—affects employment. Trade liberalisation allows, indeed forces, economies to restructure in the face of changing domestic and world prices and the changing size of available markets for products and services. Some sectors will grow and some will contract. There is no guarantee that there will be net job creation or that the results will be employment neutral. That will depend on the relative labour intensity and productivity of the gaining and losing sectors, the strength of gains in expanding sectors compared to the intensity of losses in contracting sectors, and so on.

These impacts can be studied through ex ante analysis and ex post analysis.

6.7.1. Exante Analysis

By ex ante we mean the use of economic modelling techniques to explore *in advance* the likely impact of trade policy changes on employment and incomes.

Significant progress has been made in recent years in using computable general equilibrium (CGE) models as laboratories for experiments to determine what the impact of specific trade policy changes would be on national economies, on specific sectors, on trade flows and volumes.

In fact, CGE models are now a staple of discussions about proposed trade policy changes and they have a significant impact on policy makers, negotiators and the public discourse about proposed changes. For example, trade models have been intensely cited and debated in the Doha Round of trade negotiations in the World Trade Organisation.

Generally, the models are created and used by economists who are experts on trade. They tend to have a deep appreciation of the efficiency effects that trade can generate. Typically, they are less likely to be experts on labour markets or poverty. Trade models have been used to probe distributional effects of trade policy changes to only a limited extent. Analysis of employment impacts, returns to labour, income distribution effects across different households and net poverty impacts is either not done at all or is done with less precision than aspects of the models dealing with prices, allocative efficiency and trade flows. The modellers often have less understanding of labour markets and often base the models on unrealistic assumptions about labour that are likely to systematically distort the results. In these models, flexible wages ensure that workers flow smoothly between sectors with no impediments and everyone ends up with a job. This unrealistic assumption means, for example, that unemployment cannot arise as a result of trade policy changes. It also means that, despite the presence of unemployed or underemployed workers in an economy, labour costs will rise, with all of the follow-on implications for competitiveness, income distribution and so forth. Trade models also fail to take into account the adjustment costs that are incurred by workers, their households and owners of sunk capital when structural changes are induced by trade.

These shortcomings make it clear that labour market economists and others concerned with employment, income distribution and poverty issues should engage in the trade modeling process and debate. Failure to do so means that trade policy making will be informed by modelling exercises that do not address employment or social concerns adequately or do not address them at all.

More realistic modeling of labour markets significantly changed the overall results from trade liberalisation measures and also changed the distribution of gains or losses between countries and within countries. However other developing countries that have lower wages but are currently less competitive in overall costs gained less or even lost from global trade liberalisation, because China and other current price leaders maintained their cost advantage as a consequence of their own surplus labour. Poorer countries that were shown to gain from trade liberalisation under models using the full employment assumption experienced smaller gains or even losses under the more realistic employment assumptions.

Obviously these differential impacts are critically important to national governments that want to negotiate trade pacts with an eye to their employment impacts. They are also important to anyone concerned about global development, employment and poverty.

CGE modeling is a very dynamic field at the moment. It can be shaped so that a scientific consensus emerges that trade models should always meet at least minimum thresholds with respect to incorporating empirically sound representation of employment, distributional and social issues. CGE modeling can have a significant impact on trade policy makers, and we should strive to ensure that employment and distributional consequences are important and well-understand elements in the trade-offs of trade negotiations.

6.7.2. Ex post Analysis

Many retrospective studies have been done on the impact of trade liberalisation on employment, wages, income distribution and related matters, compared to the relative scarcity of prospective (ex ante) studies on these topics. Some of the best and most rigorous ex post studies have been done at the sectorial level. However too few studies are undertaken at the economy-wide level, to ascertain the *net* effect of trade policy changes on entire labour markets. How many jobs have been created or destroyed in each sector? What is the overall balance? How has this affected wage levels?

This is a glaring omission. If the jobs in contracting sectors are more labour intensive or have lower productivity than those in expanding sectors, it is quite possible that an economy will experience overall growth while the net impact on jobs will be negative. Whether more jobs are created than destroyed is an empirical question that should always be part of a trade research agenda.

It is not easy to establish the causal relationships between changes in trade and job creation/job destruction, but it can be done with reasonable rigor where there has been a trade policy change that gives rise to expansion or contraction of particular sectors. The change in production volumes can then be traced to employment effects, and perhaps to wage effects. This can help to inform policy making with respect to further trade policy or domestic policy changes in the country under study, and also to inform trade policy makers elsewhere on the choices they face.

6.8. Regulation in a Labour Market

The world of labour is undergoing a profound revolution. The number of low-wage workers connected with the global economy is approaching 3 billion as compared to 1.5 billion in 1995. This fantastic increase in labour supply, which comes mainly from the increasing incorporation of China and India in the world economy, is a phenomenon of historical importance.

Low wage labour is no longer necessarily synonymous with bad work. Education is no longer confined to the rich. It is rising in most of the emerging world and leading to better trained and more productive workers. For both goods and services, quality is rising while prices are coming down.

There are more emotions to come. China has 300 million rural people of working age eager to migrate and work in industrial activities, willing to learn new technologies and to work for salaries which are low in international comparison. India is in the same situation and could shift a large part of its rural labour to urban centres in the next twenty years.

Investments in Education, English and Engineering have played an important role in raising quality and decreasing the price of products, as well as in the massive innovation in goods and processes achieved by many emerging countries. There is no question: labour is becoming more and more global.

At the same time, competition among companies and production networks became extreme. To succeed in this world of innovation and cost reduction, one must be efficient not only in one's own endeavours, but also in the network of alliances in which suppliers play a strategic role.

To work with trustworthy and competent partners makes the difference between success and failure. A mistake in selecting one's partner, in negotiating the right agreement with workers, or in choosing the most appropriate time to innovate can be very expensive. In 2006, General Motors was losing US$ 1 billion per month and Toyota was making US$ 1 billion in profit per month. What really made the difference were creativity and the commitment of the different partners in the two alliances.

For many workers the situation has gotten worse. While it is true that the global labour market has provided opportunities for good quality work in the long term, this outcome has not been the general rule. When companies and jobs migrate to other countries, they leave behind the despair that comes from unemployment, as well as unprotected families. Trade unions are often powerless to deal with this situation.

The fact is that globalisation of the labour market has occurred much faster than globalisation of labour protection. Inequality and informality have increased. Cheap labour often means poor conditions of work. A solution for this imbalance is not easy at all.

Competition is here to stay. Companies can mitigate the suffering, but they themselves must *become* and, more importantly, *remain* competitive if they are to survive. To become competitive is, in itself, increasingly difficult nowadays. To remain competitive is even more challenging — it requires permanent innovation, rapid adaptation, and making good use of new forms of work within existing and new alliances.

To maintain competitiveness, companies widely use new labour arrangements. Subcontracting has become an intrinsic ingredient of modern production. The use of independent work is another. Co-operative networks combine different arrangements and put them together in a variety of ways. Jobs are transferred from country to country, and labour protection is weakened.

Take the case of the European Union. There are large differences in pay between East and West. In 2003-05 average hourly pay in the Czech Republic was about 20 per cent of average pay in Germany, Belgium or The Netherlands; in Estonia it was 16 per cent; in Slovakia 15 per cent, and in Lithuania 12 per cent. Generally speaking, in comparison with Western Europe, working hours in the East are longer. Working on Saturdays and Sundays is common.

The huge differences in salaries and working conditions have led both to massive migration of workers from the lower to the higher income countries, and to a substantial flow of foreign direct investment (FDI) in the opposite direction. FDI amounted to 4 per cent of GDP in the Czech Republic and Hungary, 2.5 per cent in Poland and Slovakia, and 8 per cent in Estonia (UNCTAD, 2005). Many factors affect relocations to Eastern Europe, including: (1) labour costs and labour market regulations; (2) the quality of the labour force; (3) industrial relations and labour conflict; (4) tax rates; (5) explicit subsidies granted by public authorities; and (6) proximity to large consumer markets, mainly the EU15 countries. Similar factors have led to relocations to other parts of the world, especially Asia.

Relocating is of course liable to lead to more precarious conditions for workers in the countries of origin. How can these problems be dealt with? How to assure at least a minimum of protection to workers and their families? In other words, how to move the global labour market in the direction of more, but also more equitable work?

One response to relocation and outsourcing has been a growth of concession bargaining, as one means to reduce risks. In fact, in many countries, employers and workers are renegotiating current labour contracts in order to retain companies and jobs in those countries. The German experience, for example, has been a relatively successful effort to prevent companies from migrating on a large scale to Eastern European countries and other parts of the world. Many firms that might otherwise have moved have decided to stay, based on new negotiations that involved management, trade unions and government authorities. The objective was to reduce unit labour costs and stay competitive. Such arrangements are often unpopular but they do offer one possible solution.

Many workers in developed countries have also been pressed to move from comprehensive and generous social protection systems to partial protection models in order to retain companies and jobs. Private elements have been introduced in public social protection schemes, increasing the responsibility of programme beneficiaries. Two or three tier systems are developing as a result. Such systems of partial protection should not be imposed and cannot be permanent. At the same time, when workers are subject to very diverse labour conditions, and under severe domestic and international competition, attempts to apply a unique system of full labour and social protection leads to informality and labour conflict. This requires understanding of the way the labour market is changing, and the possibilities to change labour institutions.

Let us conclude with a few practical suggestions for the research agenda.

First, it may be useful to explore the combination of a long-term strategy for full protection with short-term tactics for partial protection, of course respecting national realities. Since it is difficult to guarantee, by law or by collective bargaining, a wide range of protection in an extremely competitive environment, legal procedures might be introduced to concede partial protection for those who have none.

Second, for a better understanding of partial protection, it appears that a research effort may be necessary to redefine the concept of minimum protection — not only for employees, but also for the growing group of self-employed, including, of course, informal workers. The most realistic definition of this minimum is one generated from the bottom up. A voice must be given to those who live in zero protection situations.

Third, it is time to recognise that in developing countries, workers zigzag in their careers from formal to informal labour markets and back again. So, protection must be assigned to persons rather than jobs. The question of portability should be the centre of new studies on labour and social protection. Portability must refer to core basic protection in such a way that the broader array of protections that a person enjoys when working in the formal labour market can be maintained when such a person works in the informal sector.

Fourth, as a general strategy, we suggest exploring ways to substantially raise the price of informality, while at the same time reducing the price of formality, within the above-mentioned framework of incremental changes.

Fifth, it is time for researchers to take solutions arranged by the poor and destitute themselves more seriously. Informal markets have their own regulation, based on the creativity of the poor to survive under very adverse conditions. In that context, it is by no means clear that the State will keep its monopoly on regulating labour relations.

Finally, as researchers in the area of labour, we should help to demystify some dreams. Deregulation is the dream of entrepreneurs. Fully applying this is an illusion. Labour markets require regulation. Extending the scope of regulation is the dream of trade unions. It is another illusion in an environment of intense competition.

Re-regulation under extreme competition should be a top priority in our research shopping bag. We proposing an incremental strategy as a way to help countries and workers climb the ladder of social protection. This will require the redefinition of key concepts and the design of dynamic institutions, able to support quick adjustments to assure basic security to workers, companies and the self-employed.

References

Butler, Ian and Gwenda Roberts 2004. *Social Work with Children and Families: Getting into Practice* (2nd ed.). London, England; New York, NY: Jessica Kingsley Publishers.

Davies, Martin. 2002. *The Blackwell Companion of Social Work* (2nd ed.). Oxford, UK; Malden, MA: Blackwell.

Fischer, Joel and Kevin J. Corcoran 2007. *Measures for Clinical Practice and Research: A Sourcebook* (4th ed.). Oxford, UK; New York, NY: Oxford University Press.

Greene, Roberta R. 2008. *Social Work with the Aged and their Families* (3rd ed.). New Brunswick, NJ: Transaction Publishers.

7

Poverty Reduction in Globalised Economy

The close interdependence of economic and social policies has long been recognised. It has indeed been a major feature of the work of the ILO throughout much of its existence and is underlined in the Copenhagen Declaration and Programme of Action. The Copenhagen Declaration stressed the need to "create a framework for action to... integrate economic, cultural and social policies so that they become mutually supportive", while the Programme of Action emphasised the importance of "an integrated approach" to implementation. The clear message that should emerge from the Special Session of the General Assembly is that the *integrated problems of sustainable economic growth and social development cannot be tackled with sectorial solutions*. We have reached the limits of sectorial solutions to integrated global problems.

Yet the manner in which the institutions of the international community operate does not reflect this basic but self-evident truth. In the fundamental area of integrated thinking the multilateral system of international organisations is under-performing. It can clearly do better. The interrelationships between the economic, environmental and social aspects of development, and the asynergies to be built up between them, need to guide the policies and activities of the system as a whole. If not, there will be many missed opportunities. As a result, the activities and operations of the United Nations system will be less than optimally effective, and the world of international organisations lays itself open to criticisms of incoherence, inefficiency and wasteful duplication.

The Special Session should call for a more coherent and integrated approach to policy-making, based on a recognition of the necessary interdependence of economic and social policies to address the core issues of the Social Summit: poverty, employment and social integration. All agencies within the multilateral system should work more closely together in order to make the different dimensions of economic and social progress mutually supportive.. In doing so, they should consider the national conditions and particular needs of different groups of countries. It is necessary to move away from "one-size fits all" solutions by putting the collective experience of the United Nations system at the service of individual countries in their development efforts. In this connection, the challenges that need to be addressed include:

(i) promoting the simultaneous and equal consideration of economic and social objectives in the process of policy formulation. This is essential for overcoming the unwarranted dichotomy between economic and social policies that is regrettably still all too common. The attainment of social objectives is the ultimate justification for economic policies. That being so, the employment and social impact of economic and financial policies need to be taken into account from the outset and not to be left for subsequent treatment. It would thus be important to institute systems for the *ex ante* assessment and continuous monitoring of the social impact of economic policies at both the international and national levels. The latter is often overlooked or mistakenly undervalued, hence reinforcing the bias against social investments and expenditures. This would be particularly relevant to the formulation of macroeconomic policies for dealing with financial crises and the design of economic reform programmes such as trade and financial liberalisation, privatisation and enterprise restructuring, labour market deregulation, and social security reform;

(ii) developing new concepts and measurements that will facilitate the shift to a more integrated approach to policy formulation.

(iii) reforming the institutions and processes for policy formulation to ensure greater participation and transparency. Particularly important are measures to develop strong institutions for social dialogue between business and labour, as well as their involvement with relevant organisations from civil society in policy formulation and implementation. This will need to be based on action to strengthen the capacity of the social partners and civil society to address social and economic policy issues and their inter linkages.

(iv) promoting greater awareness of the continuing importance of the role of the State in dealing with market failures and providing public goods, especially in economies where markets remain underdeveloped and inefficient. This includes the State's role in alleviating poverty and reducing inequality, in maintaining adequate financing for basic social services, and in developing and maintaining the regulatory frameworks and institutions that are necessary for the efficient and equitable functioning of markets. We need a "better" State that is respected and respects itself in the institutional function it performs for the benefit of its citizens;

(v) developing a positive environment for investment and enterprise creation nationally and internationally, considering good practices and major differences among countries. It should be based on the recognition of the interdependence between respect for freedom of enterprise for investors and freedom of association for workers.

(vi) implementing the ECOSOC policy on gender equality defined in the Agreed Conclusions of 1997. This requires the mainstreaming of the gender perspective into all policies and programmes in the United Nations system. Mainstreaming is a strategy for making women's as well as men's concerns an integral dimension in the design, implementation, monitoring and evaluation of policies and programmes in all political, economic and socialite spheres, so that women and men benefit equally and inequality is not perpetuated;

(vii) translating into concrete actions the call from the July 1999 Substantive Session of ECOSOC for "the relevant organisations of the United Nations system to take consistent, coherent, coordinated and joint actions in support of national efforts to eradicate poverty, with particular attention to employment creation and work and the empowerment and advancement of women".

The Special Session of the General Assembly should aim to leave its mark on the international system by creating a framework for an integrated approach to economic and social policy-making in an increasingly integrated world economy.

It should send the same message to national governments, where concerted and coordinated action among several ministries is essential for formulating coherent national financial, economic and social policies to respond to the far-reaching challenges of globalisation. And it should insist on the importance of employers' and workers' organisations and other representative organisations of civil society being informed of the social benefits to be expected from policies of greater openness to the global economy, as well as the possible negative social consequences of such policies, and of their being consulted on the choice of mutually supporting economic and social policies to ensure that the benefits are equitably distributed and adequate assistance and protection provided to those most seriously affected by such changes. The absence of such a dialogue in the past may go a long way to explain why some policies have run up against strong popular opposition and great difficulties of implementation.

7.1. Promoting Decent Work

The initial consultations on the possible content and outcome of the Social Summit in the early 1990s made it clear that two interlinked issues constituted the core of social disquiet in most countries: poverty and social exclusion. At the same time, those consultations made it clear that the first step out of poverty and social exclusion was some form of income-generating activity, described in many ways: jobs, sustainable livelihood, self-employment, micro-entrepreneurship, among others. In this context, the Copenhagen Declaration and Programme of Action recognised that the ILO, "because of its mandate, tripartite structures and expertise, has a special role to play in the field of employment and social development" and requested it "to contribute to the implementation of the Programme of Action." In doing so, the ILO has developed many activities at the operational, research and policy level that it wishes to put at the disposal of the Special Session, as an input for its deliberations and with a view to its eventual support for these initiatives as an integral part of the conclusion of and follow-up to the session. The programme is designed to be a strategic means of reducing poverty and promoting social integration and of giving effect to the more integrated approach to economic and social policies that is being called for. The overall goal of the global economy should be to provide opportunities for all men and women to obtain decent and productive work in conditions of freedom, equity, security and human dignity. This requires the attainment of four objectives: employment creation; promoting human rights at work; improving social protection; promoting a social dialogue.

Given the critical importance of employment creation, the Special Session is invited to call upon all States and international organisations to support, and collaborate with, the ILO in the following key initiatives:

(i) the preparation of and follow-up to a *World Employment Forum* that the ILO will hold in 2001. This will bring together national and international policy-makers, as well as representatives of the ILO's tripartite constituency, to examine critically some of the key problems that have to be confronted in achieving decent work in the global economy for all men and women, and to launch new initiatives to deal with them in the perspective of full employment;

(ii) the preparation and follow-up to a *Global Conference on the Informal Economy* that the ILO is planning to organise in the year 2002.

(iii) the preparation of Country Employment Policy Reviews (CEPRs), carried out in close collaboration with national authorities and employers' and workers' organisations. These reviews are a major instrument for developing the comprehensive approaches that are necessary to overcome the many obstacles in terms of economic structure, market limitations, institutional deficiencies, policy inadequacies and lack of social dialogue that prevent developing countries from reaping fully the potential benefits of globalisation for employment growth;

(iv) the production of future issues of the *World Employment Report*, which explores and highlights key developments and innovations in the employment field and aims to provide the basis for an informed global debate on employment issues.

(v) the implementation of the In Focus Programme on Skills, Knowledge and Employability, which aims at promoting increased and effective investment in training and human resource development for enhanced employability, competitiveness and growth as well as improved access of vulnerable groups to human resource development and labour market opportunities;

(vi) the implementation of the In Focus Programme on Boosting Employment through Small Enterprise Development. Given that the greatest potential for job creation worldwide lies with the small enterprise sector, this programme aims to expand employment in this sector through enterprise creation and growth, improve the quality of jobs in small enterprises, ensure that gender concerns in small enterprise development are mainstream, and promote business networking and representation in small enterprises;

(vii) the implementation of the International Programme for More and Better Jobs for Women, which is directed at expanding employment opportunities for women while enhancing their conditions of employment and eliminating discrimination at work.

(viii)the implementation of the "Jobs for Africa" programme, which is based on a framework for poverty-reducing employment strategies in Africa. The programme has two interlocked objectives: the first is to promote investment-led growth, while the second is to ensure that this growth maximises employment and reduces poverty. With respect to the quality of job creation, the Copenhagen Summit chose seven ILO Conventions and agreed to promote their ratification and implementation as a common objective of the international community.

Subsequently, in June 1998, the ILO approved the Declaration on Fundamental Principles and Rights at Work which set in motion a worldwide process of reporting and analysis within the ILO with respect to the effective realisation of these rights. They refer to freedom of association, collective bargaining, nondiscrimination, forced labour and child labour. Additionally, by unanimous vote of the Governments, Employers and Workers in June 1999, the ILO adopted

Convention No. 182 concerning the prohibition and immediate action for the elimination of the worst forms of child labour.

In this context, the Special Session of the General Assembly is invited to call upon all States:

(i) to ratify and apply the seven basic ILO Conventions identified by the Copenhagen Summit as the social floor of the global economy, as well as the Worst Forms of Child Labour Convention, 1999 which has been adopted since the Copenhagen Summit;

(ii) to cooperate with the ILO in implementing the follow-up to the Declaration on Fundamental Principles and Rights at Work, which aims to ensure universal respect for the rights proclaimed in these Conventions. The support of the private sector in giving direct effect to these rights through corporate practices, as called for in the Global Compact proposed by the Secretary-General of the United Nations, would also be an important contribution.

(iii) to support and participate in the global campaign launched by the ILO for the immediate elimination of the worst forms of child labour. In particular, national and international economic and social development programmes should systematically include urgent measures to this end. All international organisations and bilateral cooperation agreements could include specific objectives with respect to the worst forms of child labour.

In the area of social protection the Special Session is invited to consider support for, and collaboration with, the ILO in the following key initiatives:

(i) the In Focus Programme on Socioeconomic Security, which is directed at developing policies and institutions that provide a growing proportion of the world's population with social and economic security; at identifying ways in which the poor and economically insecure can obtain minimal income security most effectively; and at identifying cost-effective and equitable ways in which social protection can be extended to all groups currently excluded from mainstream statutory social security schemes.

(ii) the In Focus Programme on Safe work, which seeks to create worldwide awareness of the dimensions and consequences of work-related accidents, injuries and diseases and to strengthen practical action to bring about a significant improvement in the situation;

(iii) the ongoing ILO activities to advance gender equality at work and at home significantly by extending and strengthening measures that seek to harmonise work and family responsibilities;

(iv) ILO activities to improve protection of *migrant workers*, large numbers of whom continue to be subjected to exploitation in recruitment and employment, to forced labour, to exclusion from social insurance and to the denial of their human rights.

Finally, the Special Session is invited to consider support for the ILO's efforts to strengthen the systems and institutions for social dialogue. An In Focus Programme on Strengthening Social Dialogue has been launched to promote the benefits of social dialogue, both as an end in itself and as a means of action essential for achieving decent work for all and the reduction of poverty. The programme will seek to demonstrate the effectiveness of social dialogue, and to strengthen the institutions of social dialogue.

The Social Summit was prescient in noting that "globalisation... opens new opportunities for sustained economic growth and development of the world economy, particularly in developing countries", but that "at the same time, the rapid processes of change and adjustment have been accompanied by intensified poverty, unemployment and social disintegration". Accordingly, it identified the key challenge as that of "how to manage these processes and threats so as to enhance their benefits and mitigate their negative effects upon people".

Since then, the processes of globalisation have intensified. Trade liberalisation has advanced further with the implementation of the Uruguay Round and progress under regional trading arrangements. Growth in world trade continued to outstrip growth in world output. As a consequence, the share of world exports in GDP increased from 21.7 per cent in 1995 to 22.9 per cent in 1998. Similarly, liberalisation of foreign direct investment has continued and the total flow of foreign direct investment has increased from US$192 billion in 1990 to $400 billion in 1999. With more countries embarking on financial liberalisation, including the removal of controls over the capital account, and continued progress in information and communication technology, capital flows have surged. For example, net private capital flows to low and middle-income countries increased from US$43 billion in 1995 to $298 billion in 1999. At the same time, rapid technological change has continued, most strikingly with the explosive growth of the Internet and electronic commerce. Continued falls in the cost of international communications and transport, together with reduced governmental barriers to doing business across the world, has led to further growth of global production networks centred around multinational enterprises.

These developments have accentuated the shift from an international economy, characterised by economic relations among nation States with distinct economic boundaries, to a global economy where these boundaries are less significant and where cross-border production and transactions in goods, services, and finance assume more and more importance. This increasing openness of national economies, in conjunction with a growing web of multilateral agreements which constrain national actions, has limited the extent to which national policies alone can effectively solve the growing number of economic and social problems confronting the world. There is a need to move from an "international" approach to a "global" approach in dealing with economic and social problems. "The market economy itself is not merely an international system. Its global connections run beyond the relation between nations: it is very often relations between individuals in different countries, between different parties in a business transaction." There is thus a need "to go beyond the narrow limits of international relations: not just beyond the national boundaries but even beyond international relations into global connections.

Since the Social Summit there has also been the trauma of the global financial crisis of 1997-99. Beginning as a currency crisis in Thailand in July 1997, it spread rapidly to other parts of Asia, to the Russian Federation, and to several Latin American countries. In the crisis-affected countries it inflicted sharp falls in output and much human suffering. But its ramifications were even wider in that it resulted in a significant fall in growth rates across the world. It is imperative that the will to resolve this should not flag, now that recovery from that crisis has begun.

In the period since the Social Summit, the rate of growth of real GDP in the world economy slowed considerably in 1998 and 1999 after having grown by 4.2 per cent in both 1996 and 1997. In 1998 it declined to 1.9 per cent and it is estimated to have been 3 per cent in 1999. The main factors behind this have been the Asian financial crisis, its contagion effects on other regions and the deepening of the Japanese recession during 1998 and most of 1999.

For developing countries as a whole, the growth rate declined from 5.7 per cent in 1996 to 2.1 and 3.0 per cent respectively in 1998 and 1999. Within this overall showdown, there was in fact negative growth in GDP in the worst affected Asian countries in 1997 and a decline of 7.9 per cent in 1998. GDP also declined by 2.7 per cent in the countries of the former Soviet Union in 1998, and by 0.6 per cent in Latin America and the Caribbean in 1999.[2] These developments had a significant negative impact on employment and poverty in many developing countries. Although there has been a decline in unemployment with the stronger than expected recovery that is in place, these rates still remain significantly higher than precrisis levels. In Latin America and the Caribbean urban unemployment increased significantly between 1998 and 1999 in 13 out of the 17 countries for which data are available. In ten countries, the rate was very high, ranging between 10.1 per cent and 19.8 per cent in 1999. There has been a similar rise in unemployment in Eastern Europe and the former Soviet Union.

In the industrialised countries there has been a slight drop in unemployment in 1999 with the stronger than expected growth that has occurred recently. For the OECD countries as a whole the average unemployment rate declined from 6.9 to 6.7 per cent between 1998 and 1999. It should be noted, however, that this is still not a very substantial improvement in relation to the 1995 rate of 7.4 per cent. In the European Union the unemployment rate declined from 10.1 per cent in 1998 to 9.4 per cent in 1999. This remains an unacceptably high average level of unemployment, especially when we take into account the fact that double-digit unemployment still prevails in six out of 15 countries in the European Union. In these countries the unemployment rate dropped significantly from their 1995 levels and was below 6 per cent in 1999. Set against this, however, was the rise in unemployment to a postwar high in Japan.

Against this backdrop, there is widespread anxiety over the effects of globalisation on the lives of ordinary men and women across the world. The advantages of open economies and open societies are an accepted reality for most. What is now becoming increasingly evident is that the benefits are not reaching enough people and that changes in the governance structure of the global economy are required to achieve more satisfactory results. Globalisation has created extraordinary new opportunities for businesses and consumers, which have been a major driving force behind recent growth in the world economy. But the inequality of opportunity has been just as extraordinary, both within and between countries. Imagination and creativity will be needed to meet the overriding challenge: that markets must work for everybody.

In spite of the potential benefits that trade, investment, and financial liberalisation and other aspects of globalisation can confer in terms of a better allocation of resources, greater economic efficiency and higher growth, evidence is accumulating that globalisation is widening inequalities between industrialised and developing countries. This is reflected in the continuing marginalisation of the least developed countries. Another indicator is that 80 countries have per capita GDP that is lower than ten years ago. Furthermore, the income gap between the fifth of the world population living in the richest countries and the fifth living in the poorest has increased from a ratio of 60:1 in 1990 to 74:1 in 1997.

Although causation is by no means clearly established in all cases, globalisation has been accompanied by a host of social problems, many of which are related to the world of work. In many countries increased global competition has led to job losses which have often been concentrated in particular industries and communities, thus magnifying their negative impact in media depictions. In many developing countries without systems of unemployment insurance or adjustment assistance to workers, the social pain of these labour market developments has been particularly acute. The burden has typically fallen most heavily on vulnerable groups within the workforce, especially women workers suffering from continuing labour market discrimination. In addition, hundreds of millions of the working poor and their families on the margins of developing country labour markets, as well as a significant number of workers in the industrialised and transition economies, are largely bystanders rather than participants in the growth of the world economy.

The emerging global economy has also brought increased uncertainty and insecurity, which are no longer the sole preserve of the socially excluded. Today they reach deep into middle-class attitudes and reactions, and many parents fear that their children may not have a better life than their own. Youth unemployment is high in many countries and young men and women worry about the appropriateness of their education and training in helping them to enter and adapt to more competitive and dynamic labour markets. Many workers, particularly women in both North and South, feel caught in a race to the bottom, and believe that intensified global competition is exerting downward pressure on working conditions and labour standards.

Intensified international economic competition has created pressures on enterprises to seek more flexible employment arrangements that are often less secure and provide fewer social benefits than regular jobs. This process has often been intensified by misguided labour market deregulation that has ignored more consensual and productive approaches to responding to heightened international competition. Another problem area has been the rise in income inequality that has been observed in many developing and industrialised countries. The causes of this phenomenon are still poorly understood but one contributory factor is the weakening of the bargaining strength of labour. This has come about because of the increased exit options available to capital in a globalising world economy. The reduced bargaining strength of workers often results in their being denied a fair share of the gains from openness to international competition and economic growth.

The liberalisation of foreign direct investment has added to the competitive pressures faced by local firms, including small and medium-sized enterprises, especially in developing and transition countries. While the longer term benefits of this process are likely to be positive, they initially cause job losses through the restructuring and loss of market share among local producers.

Increased financial liberalisation, especially the freeing of capital accounts, has had a significant impact on social development. There has been a growing frequency and severity of financial and economic crises in the 1990s. As shown by the recent Asian crisis these events have resulted in sudden and severe economic downturns that have inflicted heavy social costs. Apart from exposing the dire consequences of neglecting social protection, the crisis has also highlighted the value of sound labour market institutions, especially systems of collective bargaining, dispute prevention and resolution, and social dialogue, in both preventing and coping with the consequences of economic crises.

7.2. Proposals for Further Initiatives

It follows from the above that the central issue that should be addressed in the follow-up to the World Summit for Social Development *is the adaptation of national economies and national institutions to the emerging global economy, and the management of the process of global change so that it responds to human needs of individuals, their families, and the communities in which they live.*

The objective should be to *make globalisation work for everyone*. The process of the integration of national economies into a global economy has immense potential for eliminating poverty and enhancing human development, and there can be no question of attempting to turn the clock back, even if that were possible. But in order for this potential to be realised, globalisation has to be seen and managed as a social and not only a purely economic process. It has to be judged not only by its impact on the volume of world trade and capital movements, or by the improvements that it brings about in economic efficiency and technological change, but also by its impact on the lives of ordinary men and women throughout the world — by its results in terms of net job creation, poverty reduction, and narrowing inequalities in the reasonably short term rather than in some indeterminate future.

The nature of the problems presented by globalisation and the solutions to be adopted will, of course, vary from one region to another, and there can be no question of attempting to prescribe detailed policies of universal applicability. It is necessary to move away from "one-size fits all" solutions by putting the collective experience of the United Nations system at the service of individual countries in their development. But the essential point is that no country or region is unaffected by the profound changes that are sweeping through the world economy. All nations have a collective responsibility towards each other and towards their own people to respond to this challenge in a manner that guarantees greater fairness, decency and equity for all sections of the world's population than has hitherto been the case.

7.3. Greater Policy Coherence

This will require a more coherent and integrated approach to policy-making, based on a recognition of the necessary interdependence of economic and social policies to address the core issues of the Social Summit: poverty, employment and social integration. It is, of course, self-evident that social progress is facilitated by a high and stable level of sustainable economic growth. Decent jobs cannot be created and poverty reduced in an economic desert. But this does not mean that economic policies can or should be pursued in blind disregard for their social consequences. In other words, the sustainability of growth depends quite as much on the distribution of its benefits as it does on continued improvements in economic efficiency. And the economic liberalisation that is required to stimulate growth cannot be viable without simultaneous action to contain its negative social effects. Another important connection between the economic and the social lies in the fact that enlightened social policies such as investments in human development have a high payoff not only in social but also in economic terms. Moreover, the sustainability of economic progress, the efficient functioning of markets and improvements in productivity depend on democratic and transparent governance and the existence of institutions which permit the main productive forces of society to receive a fair share of the wealth they have contributed to creating and to be informed of, and involved in, decisions that directly affect them.

The close interdependence of economic and social policies has long been recognised. It has indeed been a major feature of the work of the ILO throughout much of its existence and is underlined in the Copenhagen Declaration and Programme of Action. The Copenhagen Declaration stressed the need to "create a framework for action to... integrate economic, cultural and social policies so that they become mutually supportive", while the Programme of Action emphasised the importance of "an integrated approach" to implementation. The clear message that should emerge from the Special Session of the General Assembly is that *the integrated problems of sustainable economic growth and social development cannot be tackled with sectorial solutions*. We have reached the limits of sectorial solutions to integrated global problems.

Yet the manner in which the institutions of the international community operate does not reflect this basic but self-evident truth. In the fundamental area of integrated thinking the multilateral system of international organisations is underperforming. It can clearly do better. The interrelationships between the economic and social aspects of development, and the asynergies to be built up between them, need to guide the policies and activities of the system as a whole.

The different organisations and agencies of the international system bring different perspectives to bear on the issues of growth and development. Full advantage needs to be taken of the richness of experience and expertise that each can contribute to the common effort. They need to work more closely together, in order to make the different dimensions of economic and social progress mutually supportive. They then need to promote policy asynergies which deal in an integrated and unitary fashion with the interrelated aspects of economic and social policy in order to address more effectively the social problems that are intensifying in the wake of globalisation.

References

Alice O'Connor; (2000) "Poverty Research and Policy for the Post-Welfare Era" *Annual Review of Sociology*.

Betson, David M., and Jennifer L. Warlick . (1998) "Alternative Historical Trends in Poverty." *American Economic Review* 88:348-51.

Firebaugh, Glenn. (2000) "Empirics of World Income Inequality." *American Journal of Sociology*. 104:1597-1630. in JSTOR

Paugam, Serge. (1998). "Poverty and Social Exclusion: A Sociological View." Pp. 41–62 in *The Future of European Welfare*, edited by Martin Rhodes and Yves Meny.

8

Women Empowerment and Poverty Reduction

There is an important connection between the social construction of gender roles and the social construction of dominant paradigms, or social theories, particularly in sociobiology and the economics disciplines. These influential fields provide intellectual rationale for the way societies attribute 'masculinity' and 'femininity' to various activities and even concepts. Economic models and social theories have embedded subjective premises; they reflect certain interests and biases of those thinkers that create them.

Influential social theories in the 1960s and 70s, particularly those in sociobiology, have reinforced the beliefs regarding gender roles. Such theories emphasised the biological paternal and maternal functions of female and male species, including humans, in determining their "natural" traits. Accordingly, a woman's nature is to be compliant, not competitive; nurturing, not instrumental. Her primary role is to provide a haven for her family and if she works for pay, she will do best in jobs compatible with her household responsibilities and her "feminine personality." Man's "natural" role, on the other hand, is to be the principal provider and protector. "Rationality, logical, and territorial" are attributes of the 'stereotypical' male.

Dominant economic thinking tends to foster these gender roles as well. Mainstream economic thought focuses on individual rationality, market competition, and market activities including trade, finance, and monetary exchanges. Topics such as unpaid work, non-market production, and social norms as well reproductive work and responsibilities in the family are considered 'feminine' and are largely marginalised in mainstream thinking.

The influential works of new household economists such as Edward Phelps, Gary Becker and Jacob Mincer in the sixties and seventies provided economic rationale behind the prevailing division of labour at home and the specialisation of men and women in market work and household work respectively. Using the economic framework of utility maximisation and adopting the basic premises of neoclassical economics, their household models avoided questions regarding patriarchy, conflicting interests, and socially constructed roles of women and men.

In recent decades, such views have been challenged both theoretically and empirically in both biological and social sciences, including economics. Recent developments in the field of sociobiology showed increasing evidence contrary to the traditional view of male dominance and rationality and of female passivity and compliance. Feminist economists developed new theories and conceptulasations, broadening the definition of economics to "provisioning of human life." By examining the economy in its totality, including market and non-market economic activities, and by highlighting the interrelation between unpaid and paid labour, feminist economics has made an important contribution in rethinking economics. The implications of feminist economics are far-reaching, including a deeper understanding of women and men's conditions in the world of work. The implication is that the provision of equality of opportunity will require changes in both domains. The new framework recognises that macroeconomic policies, development strategies, employment policies, family policies, social policies, and working time regimes along with social, political and demographic forces, affect the extent and form of women and men's participation in both the labour market and reproductive work.

8.1. Role of Soco-political Institutions

The roles performed by men and women reflect existing gender relations, which are shaped by the interplay of cultural practices and social norms, economic incentives, political institutions and legal provisions. We provide some examples drawn from different regions of the world to illustrate how these factors help maintain patriarchal norms that privilege and empower men in social and economic relationships.Norms regarding family and kinship ties have been a central force in shaping women's lives in many parts of the world. In parts of the Middle East and North Africa, culture and the strength of patriarchy contribute to women's relatively low rate of labour force participation and high fertility rates. In Africa, social identity, the division of labour, and property transfers are often anchored in various forms of kin relationships.

Religion plays a role in determining women's status as well, both directly through its interpretation and preaching, and indirectly through its influence in law and governance. Political institutions and the law, particularly those governing land rights, also have shaped women's and men's economic roles, as examples from Latin America show.

Political institutions and state intervention have been crucial to the recognition and upholding of women's rights, including the right to work, in Scandinavian, socialist and post-socialist countries. These, however, have not necessarily led to the complete abandonment of patriarchal norms in the labour market. The tension between women's maternal and household responsibilities and the recognition of women's right to work has brought about debates on Sweden's family policy. The parental leave model may also affect gender equality in the labour market. The expectation of long leaves, for instance, produces more unequal conditions for women if employers see more risks than advantages in hiring women as employees. The persistence of patriarchal norms is witnessed in socialist countries as well. In Hungary, the strategies adopted by the socialist government in the 1970s and 80s for advancing women's claims for equality in the labour market took the male patterns of full-time, lifelong employment as the norm against which all citizens, men and women, were required to perform.

8.2. Challenges to Traditional Gender Roles

While traditional roles of men and women have been maintained by the interplay of varied forces, they can also be challenged or modified by changes in the socioeconomic environment. Again using country examples, we examine the manner by which men and women resolve the tensions between tradition and social norms, on the one hand; and the new opportunities as well as burdens brought about by technological change, demographic factors and economic restructuring, on the other.

Women have already adopted new roles across the globe. Specifically, an increasing number of women have taken on the role of income earners and even "breadwinners" in both the developed and developing world. The increasing rates of women's economic activity observed in many countries in the OECD, Latin America, Middle East and Sub-Saharan Africa regions have sometimes been shadowed by declining rates for men. Evidently, not only are more women entering and remaining in the labour force throughout their childbearing years, but they are also finding more ways to combine family responsibilities with market work. But the roles of women and men have evolved in an uneven manner. While some women have benefited from new opportunities in terms of access to income or higher earnings, others face precarious work conditions, increased burdens and more stress.

One reason for these trends is related to demographic changes particularly in the last fifty years. Decreases in mortality rates and fertility rates, and increases in life expectancy resulted in fewer family responsibilities for women. In addition, increasing numbers of women began to postpone marriage and childbirth in many countries.

These have contributed to the increased share of single and married women in the labour force.

Political changes have also brought about social and political interaction, mobilisation, and participation. Women gained the right to vote and demonstrated ever-expanding social and political activism. Together with population shifts and urbanisation, enabling political institutions brought about landmark legal changes and brought women's issues to the centre stage in policy making and social practices. Likewise, the rise of women's movements and gender advocacy groups in many parts of the world generated international discourses, dialogues and pressure to address the different forms of women's exploitation and subordination, and gave emphasis to promoting gender equality in economics and society as a whole.

Technological change in the global economy has had a profound effect on gender roles vis-a-vis its effect on economic incentives and relative prices. In some countries like Japan, the United States and the former Soviet Union, labour-saving technologies both in agriculture and industry raised productivity and output in the sixties and seventies. This contrasted with the labour-intensive technologies adopted in the seventies by newly industrialising countries, which increased the demand for women's labour.

In recent decades, macroeconomic policies, particularly trade and financial liberalisation policies have had extensive effects on the structure and types of employment. Like changes brought by technology, the changes brought about by market liberalisation have not yielded gender-neutral results. Results differ for men and women in terms of earnings, employment, and level of unpaid work; neither is its effect uniform across countries and among women and men.

It should be noted that the global growth in trade has not been equally distributed across countries. Much of the enormous growth in trade over the last fifty years has occurred in developed countries and a few developing countries concentrated in East Asia and Latin America. By contrast, Sub-Saharan African countries not only have had difficulties in shifting to manufactured exports, but have also seen the purchasing power of their main exports decline. Foreign capital flows have been highly concentrated, flowing to the OECD nations, and to a smaller extent, a handful of developing countries – primarily to the East Asian and the more highly industrialised Latin American economies.

8.3. Potential Backlash

A growing body of research by feminist economists has demonstrated that economic policies and development strategies are seldom gender-neutral. Since the 1980s, the idea that liberalisation of financial markets increases investment and hence employment and growth, has been promoted by neighbourly economic theories and has taken hold in most policy and academic circles. But trade, foreign investment and overall economic growth have not guaranteed an increase in decent work or equitable participation between women and men. Macroeconomic policies can help promote new opportunities and incentives for gender equality, but they can also reinforce gender inequalities and enable them to exist in new forms. However, the effects on women and men's access to decent work are complex and not always positive.

In many parts of the developing world including Bangladesh, the Dominican Republic, (South) Korea, Malaysia, Taiwan, and Thailand, employment expansion has significantly increased women's labour force participation. Moreover, tax concessions given to foreign investors and their impact on public finances, the establishment of export processing zones (EPSs), the tacit endorsement of global subcontracting work chains, and the relaxation of labour laws have important gender implications, since the majority of the industries and enterprises in the EPSs and in subcontracting work chains generally employ women. The latter trend refers to firms developing links to informalised production through outsourcing and subcontracting. Studies conducted by the ILO, Women in Informal Employment Globalising and Organising (WIEGO), Home workers World Wide (HWW) and Home Net show that firms, including multinational corporations, increasingly use subcontracting of women home workers at very low wages to replace core, full-time workers. The growing informalisation of employment is part of the dramatic transformation of employment patterns towards more precarious forms. With little bargaining power, subcontracted women workers and home workers in the informal sector face low piece wage rates and work without occupational safety and health standards, benefits and job security.

Moreover, working conditions such as job security, health and occupational safety and pay do not automatically improve for women as employment increases; indeed, these conditions may deteriorate under the pressure of international competition. Recent studies also show that much of the export-led growth experienced by the 'miracle growth' economies e.g. Taiwan and South Korea has relied on prevailing gender wage inequalities and gender norms in these countries. Berik, Rodgers, and Sveglich's 2004 study on Taiwan and Korea suggests that even if trade liberalisation enhances women's employment opportunities, their 'competitive advantage' as workers remains rooted in lower pay and poorer working conditions.

Studies examining the relationship of foreign direct investment and women's employment also argue that while foreign direct investment may have helped bring about the feminisation of the labour force, this feminisation trend can be reversed. In some cases, including parts of Latin America and Africa, even short-term employment effects are not positive. A shift to cash export crops has often undercut women's subsistence production and replaced these with contingent and seasonal employment, leaving them with less real income than before. In turn, women increasingly migrate to impoverished urban zones and expand women's presence in the informal sector, working in precarious jobs. Local producers, especially self-employed women and men in the informal economy, have lost their market share to cheaper imports.

A complicating factor is the interplay of social norms and economic forces. Although female integration into the global market provided opportunities for some women to challenge and/or defy socially ascribed roles, other women remain limited by persistent social forces and patriarchal norms. Women in Uganda for example, were relegated to the role of unpaid family workers in export crop production. They continue to work for men, and have gained little in terms of legal rights or their share of resources. This also happened in cocoa production in Nigeria, and in irrigated rice in Zambia.

An increase in women's time in the labour market (or paid work) does not fully inform us about the resulting changes in women's access to decent work or about their welfare. Further, while having an independent scurce of income tends to be valued by women not only for what it buys, but also for the greater dignity it brings; it may also have serious costs on their health and well-being that counter these beneficial effects.

Currently, and in recent decades, the global economy has become prone to financial and severe economic crises. As governments liberalise financial markets, financial institutions and investors have increasingly taken on excessive risks, created complex financial instruments, and undertaken short-term capital flows with lightning speed. Financial liberalisation policies for the most part, have contributes to economic slumps, collapse of many financial institutions and dramatic increases in unemployment and underemployment, as was witnessed during the East Asian crisis,

Russian crisis, and currently, the US-led, global financial and economic crisis. Market instability and economic downturns tend to disadvantage both men and women, with the latter serving as "safety net of last resort."

The preceding discussion illustrates that gender roles are not static; they evolve and are affected by the interplay of economic, social, political and demographic forces. This evolutionary process is complex, however, and one needs to situate the analysis within a broader framework of the 'tensions' that have been created by rapid technological and scientific changes on the one hand, and the sluggishness of addressing gender inequalities on the other.

8.4. Emerging Patterns of Work

We use labour force participation rates to measure access to employment. Women's labour force participation is among the best measured of the variables we use to evaluate access to decent work. Still, the data should be used with caution. Some data is based on censuses, whereas other data is based on much smaller labour force surveys. Measures based on labour force surveys can vary significantly from year to year.

For the world as a whole, female labour force participation rates held steady from 1996–2006, at about 53%. These rates compare to male participation of about 80%, so women still significantly flag behind men in their access to, or at least take up of, paid employment. Three regions showed clear gains in women's participation in paid work. In Latin America and the Caribbean, the female labour force participation rate rose from 1996–2006, from 46% to 52%, while in the Middle East it rose from 25% to 33%. In developed countries, rates rose slightly, from 51% to 53%. In most other regions, female labour force participation rates fell, although most of these declines were small and may not be statistically significant. Male labour force participation rates worldwide fell slightly over this period, from 81% in 1996 to 79% in 2006, so that the gap between female and male rates narrowed slightly.

While women's participation in paid employment has increased worldwide, women are still segregated into certain types of employment. Due to a complex mix of factors, including household duties, educational background, discrimination, social norms and personal choice, women are more likely than men to be in part-time or temporary work, to be in the informal sector or to be doing home work, or unpaid labour in family enterprises, and to be concentrated in certain types of jobs, usually those at the lower end of the pay and status scale.

Worldwide, in all regions and in developing as well as industrialised economies, women's jobs are more likely to be part-time or temporary. In European countries examined by Janet Gornick, 10–60% of women worked part-time in the early 1990s, compared to 3–11% of men.

In many countries, women are likely to work in the informal sector, and the share of workers in this sector appears to be increasing. In Sub-Saharan Africa, about half of women are estimated to work in the informal sector, where 75% of employment is found. In Asia and Latin America, the situation is similar. In most countries for which we have data, the vast majority of home-based workers are women.

Within both the formal and informal sectors, women continue to be segregated into certain jobs. Looking at data from formal sector employment in 41 countries around the world from years in the late 1980s and early 1990s, Richard Anker found a high level of occupational segregation worldwide. He found that 60% of male and female workers in OECD countries would need to change jobs in order to have equal occupational representation. About the same level of occupational segregation existed for the non-Asian developing countries and European transition economies he examined, while the level of segregation in Asia was slightly lower and the level in the Middle East was slightly higher.

8.4.1. Fairness of Income

One common measure of wage fairness by gender is the ratio of female to male wages – the gender wage gap. To properly measure fairness, estimates of the gender wage gap should correct for selectivity (caused by the fact that a smaller share of women than men engage in paid work, and women who expect to earn higher wages are more likely to engage in such work), and control for differences in education, experience, hours of work, and other factors relevant to wage determination.

From 1980 to the end of the 1990s, the gender wage gap closed significantly in Latin América, where women now earn more than 80% of what men do. Estimates suggest that the wage gap also narrowed in the 1990s to about the same level in most OECD countries. And many post-socialist countries. In some countries in each region the gap increased, however. Information for African countries is very limited. A study using data from the mid-late 1980s in Cote devoir found a small wage gap, while data from Ethiopia and Uganda in the early 1990s showed women earning 60–75% of male wages.

A number of studies have found that wage gaps are greater in the informal than the formal sector. The gap is significantly larger in the informal sector in countries as diverse as Egypt, India and South Africa.[42] If unchanged, the higher informal sector wage gap may undermine the narrowing of the gap in the formal sector, as employment shifts increasingly to the informal sector. Finally, the closing of the gender wage gap has occurred during a period of wage stagnation worldwide, so that while women have gained with respect to men, absolute gains in earnings are limited.

8.4.2. Security at Work

Worldwide, work has become more insecure as global competition has contributed to a shifting of jobs from the formal, legally-regulated and large-firm sector to smaller and informal firms and home work. While it is difficult to generalise about the nature of informal work and self-employment, it certainly offers less security than formal employment. Informal and home workers, and in many cases even part-time workers, lie outside the protections of labour laws and lack rights to social benefits. Even in cases where there are labour codes in place for home work (in the Philippines and India, for example), these are very weakly enforced. The 1996 ILO Convention on Home Work has not been widely ratified, although it provides a framework for future action.

Workers in the formal sector also face significant insecurity in much of the world. Deregulation of labour markets has become a norm, driven by the increasing acceptance of the idea that firms should shed workers quickly in periods of downturn. In most regions of the world.

women are shed more quickly than male workers, exhibiting higher unemployment rates than males for the period 1991–2000.

8.4.3. Social Protection

Social protection considered in measures of decent work often include the share of national budgets spent on public health and education, and access to pensions and healthcare insurance. Changes in these protections may have a greater impact on women, as women do a greater share of caring for the sick and small children. Changes in infrastructure support may also particularly affect women as they are traditionally responsible for collecting water and fuel.

Using the share of national budgets devoted to public health and educational services provides only a rough measure of state delivery of these services. The percent of Gross Domestic Product (GDP) devoted to these services might rise due to price increases. At the same time, the percent of GDP devoted to the services might fall if GDP rises rapidly, while services remain at the same level. But, with these caveats in mind, data suggests significant reductions in state support for these services from the mid-1980s to 2004. The vast majority of these countries were low or middle income countries, and in many cases the decline was more than 50%. In many countries, the share of GDP spent on education also fell.

Data on public expenditure on unemployment benefits, pensions and health care is harder to find, but spending in these areas has followed the same downward trends in many countries. Spending may also be unequal across gender lines, as these social benefits are often in the form of insurance and thus offered only to formal sector and full-time employees.

In some developing countries, efforts have been made to develop alternative forms of social protection, in response to the shift in jobs from the formal to the informal sector and reductions in the state role in providing education and health care services. A pilot seminar entitled "Social Protection, Informality, and Gender" hosted by the global research-policy network "Women in Informal Employment: Globalising and Organising (WIEGO)", the Centre for Women's Studies (CEM), and the ILO-Latin America regional office, held in Santiago, Chile in 2001 facilitated discussions and dialogue among policymakers, researchers, advocacy groups and worker organisations. Such dialogues and the pressure from Service National de la Mujer (SERNAM) have helped bring about a number of changes in working terms and conditions for women temporaries in Chile. These include the provision of childcare facilities for horticultural and other agricultural workers and the establishment of four national commissions on Health and Safety at Work, Childcare, Pesticides and Training, to deal at the policy level with conditions of temporary work. SEWA's Integrated Social Security Scheme in India is another example. SEWA is a trade union comprised of poor, self-employed women workers. It provides its 959,698 members vital supportive services such as savings and credit, legal aid, health care, child care and insurance services. Some states have also expanded protections to those outside formal sector employment. But it is the NGO efforts that may become the basis for a new model of social protection in developing countries, especially for women, who are more likely to work outside the formal sector.

Two other forms of social protection which particularly affect women are maternity protection and subsidised childcare. These protection allow women to maintain their labour force attachment during childbearing and rearing, ensuring that the costs of child bearing are shared across male and female workers. While only 37 countries had signed the ILO Convention 103 on maternity protection as of 2004, an ILO review of maternity protection legislation in 167 countries found that all had some legislation in place. In industrialised and former socialist countries, only the US offered less than 14 weeks of leave, while many countries offered 18 weeks. Most industrialised and former socialist countries offer at least two-thirds pay for at least 14 weeks.

In most OECD countries, these benefits have expanded significantly in recent years, increasing the length of possible leaves, the financial protections which accompany them, and the possibilities for sharing the leave between male and female parents, which helps to equalise the impact of childrearing on men's and women's careers. In developing countries, however, it is unclear what share of workers can actually access maternity protections. And as the formal, large-firm sector has shrunk, the share has clearly declined.

A further issue is the take-up of benefits. Kawaguchi shows that in 2001 very few women in Japan used the mandated leave of up to one year with partial wages. Women cited social norms as well as low benefits and lack of information about leave rights as reasons for failing to take advantage of benefits.

The availability of subsidised child care is limited in many parts of the world. Almost half of all countries have no formal programs for children under 3, and for those that do have programs, coverage is limited. In OECD countries, the share of children under 3 served by publicly financed care varies significantly, from 2% in the UK to 74% in Denmark. For children between 3 years and school age, more care is provided, although the share of children reached still varies, from 53% in the US to 99% in Belgium and France. Former socialist countries achieved high rates of participation in preschooling, ranging from around 70% or more in the European areas to about 20–50% in Central Asia and the Caucuses. In other developing countries, for the most part, there are few public programs. While private daycare centres are expanding, such market-based care facilities are often beyond the means of poor households or nonexistent in rural communities.

Even when day care programs are available, they often do not meet the needs of workers with children in terms of the hours and the duration of programs. Most programs run between 15 and 40 hours per week, although many countries offer fewer hours. Child care remains a problem even for school age children, as the hours of primary and secondary schools are typically shorter than the usual work day. Parents with two or more children can face a host of problems trying to patch together different childcare solutions for the different age related needs of their children. In many places, women choose part-time, home and informal work because of the possibilities this offers for combining child care with paid work.

Finally, women can benefit from the availability of legal protections against discrimination. The vast majority of countries have ratified the ILO conventions on elimination of discrimination in respect of employment and occupation. However, there are serious problems with their enforcement. An ILO Director General Report on discrimination notes the ways through which some countries have used labour inspections to raise awareness about the issues and mediate problems. Other countries, including a number of developing countries, have used numerical targets in hiring for under represented groups.

8.4.4. Freedom of Association

One measure for the degree of freedom of association in a given country is the share of workers represented by labour unions. Labour unions have been under pressure due to globalisation. Efforts to make labour markets more "flexible" have led to reductions in workers' rights to organise in many countries, and firms' ability to shift jobs overseas has reduced the bargaining power of labour. Sectorial shifts in employment from manufacturing to services have also reduced the share of workers with access to unions. Of the 58 countries for which the ILO publishes data, union density fell in 42 from the mid-1980s to the mid-1990s. In numerous cases, the decline exceeded 20%.[57] In developing countries, a shift of economic activity to subcontracting and informal firms has accelerated this shift from union coverage.

In many countries, unions have responded to declining membership by organising previously under-organised sectors, including the service and the informal sector, where women predominate. As a result, female union membership has increased significantly in industrialised countries and some developing countries.

However, increases in women's membership do not always mean increased power for women workers. Union leadership is traditionally male and focused on the interests of male, full-time workers. Women, and union leaders focused on increasing women's membership, have often used separate women's structures within unions to give women more voice and then bring these to the attention of central leadership. Many unions in both industrialised and developing countries have also turned to quotas on national committees to increase women's participation in leadership.

In some countries – much of the evidence comes from Asia – unions and, to a greater extent NGOs, have begun organising women in the informal and home work sectors. Such organisations include Home Net, SEWA, PATAMABA WIEGO, and PSWS (Malaysia). Enforcement of legal gains is sometimes weak, but legal rights provide a basis for further action and demands.

8.5. Labour Market and Reproductive Work

The link between decent labour market work and the reproductive, unpaid work that individuals also perform is multifaceted. First, the time spent by a person in growing food for subsistence, gathering fuel and water, doing childcare, sick and elder care, and performing domestic chores is co-determined by the time spent in paid, market work. Thus, reproductive work time directly affects individuals' labour market options. The areas of overlap in the diagram refer to the multiplicity of work arrangements in the labour market sectors. These include home-based work that allows workers to combine paid market work with reproductive work, as well as subcontracting and outsourcing activities that link formal and informal work in a production chain.

Second, unpaid work also affects the rate at which time in paid work is rewarded, by limiting women's time available for work and their ability to specialise. Third, unpaid work activities such as domestic chores, fuel and water gathering, subsistence production and care work in the household are crucial to the production of the labour force, generation of knowledge and overall social reproduction. As Nancy Folbre puts it: "Children grow up to become workers as well as taxpayers, and the older generation is not the only group that benefits from their existence. The benefits are realised by all consumers of commodities, whether they have raised children or not."

Finally, the interrelatedness of paid and unpaid work is reinforced by the complementary and substitution between goods and services purchased with earned income and the non-marketed goods and services produced with unpaid labour. Market-produced goods and services are inputs in household production of meals, clean clothes, and backyard gardening. Households which can afford them also make use of purchased goods and services as substitutes for home production, thereby reducing unpaid work. Although increasing numbers of women in most of the world have become income earners in the last few decades, the majority of them continue to perform their traditional roles as household managers and care providers.

A number of developing as well as developed countries has undertaken time use surveys. Although estimates of unpaid work can vary considerably and many countries have yet to conduct time use surveys on a systematic basis, available empirical studies on time use and gender division of labour in both developed and developing areas show that women, both employed and non-employed, do substantially more unpaid work than men. In contrast, men typically spend more hours in paid economic activities than women. However, the contributions hardly even out; when hours in paid and unpaid work are totalled, women tend to have longer work weeks than men and less time for leisure or sleep.

8.5.1. Effect of Unpaid Work

The fact that women do most of the unpaid reproductive work strongly affects their ability to be available for paid work. When women do participate in the labour market, family responsibilities affect the amount and type of work that women can undertake.

While labour available for performing paid work seems to be directly related to the time use in reproductive and domestic activities among women on average, this is not necessarily the case for men. Regardless of their position in the life course, a study using 1992 Australian time use data shows that men's weekly hours of unpaid work tend to be a fixed quantity. Hence a reduction in men's paid work hours generally results in greater leisure time, so that men literally can choose between work and leisure. For women, however, it is more likely to be a choice between paid and unpaid work.

Gender roles in social reproduction can also affect a worker's choices of employment and work location. Home-based work has enabled some women to resolve the contradictions between socially defined roles and their need for income, while also meeting the demand for cheap, flexible labour by firms facing increased competition in both domestic and global markets. Not surprisingly, women are disproportionately represented among home-based workers across countries, as it allows them to combine paid work in time and space with their domestic responsibilities. Home-based work also results in "spillovers" through which some market risk and volatility are shifted onto the informal sector and particularly to unpaid family workers. In many small enterprises and agricultural production, unpaid family labour, mainly that of women and children, may be shifted in and out of production in order to absorb some uncertainties of production.

8.5.2. Labour Time Allocation

The level of household production and the gender division of household labour are not static, however. They change in response to changing wages and conditions in paid work, to policy reforms and to a host of demographic, economic and social forces. Changes in educational attainment, technology, and relative returns to different skills cause households and individuals to shift time between activities and change how labour is used. Demographic and social changes such as urbanisation, migration, fertility and divorce rates can influence the allocation of labour time as well.

Time use studies show that while large differences persist in men's and women's allocation of time between market and non-market work, these began to converge between the 1960s and 90s. However, this convergence pattern does not take into account the extent to which multiple tasks are performed simultaneous by women, which can lead to intensification of work. While men have compensated for some of the time that women are now working outside the home, women are likely to accommodate increased labour market participation by reducing leisure time and by doing simultaneous activities.

Another impact of the recent changes in economic, demographic and social factors, is the blurring of boundaries between paid and unpaid work and the movement of labour between formal and informal markets, and between market and non-market sectors. Encouraged by market liberalisation policies, this has increased the link between the formal and informal sectors, and in some cases, between paid and unpaid work. These firms have tapped into the "seemingly abundant female supply of labour" by creating new forms of putting out systems, involving multilayered networks of parent firms, subsidiaries, subcontractors and home-based workers. The resulting firm restructuring and work arrangements have diminished the bargaining power of labour. As firms lay off workers, informal activities and household activities partially offset the drastic drop in access to market purchased goods and services. In the face of insecurity, the burden of survival falls on unpaid workers in the household and community, particularly women.

The increase in paid employment for women and the shift from formal to informal work has come at a time when social welfare schemes in industrialised countries and post-socialist countries have eroded. In developing countries, social security, healthcare and pension systems have remained limited. This lack of security on a social level has increased the demand for care work. For households affected by HIV/AIDS, the situation is quite grave as the demand for caring services increases at a time when additional income is needed for medical expenses and to compensate for the possible loss of the income of the infected family member.

8.5.3. Market Work and the Need for Care

A crucial aspect of reproductive work is care service provided to dependent and sick household members. In both developing and industrialised countries, family members have been a major source of caring labour. With women increasingly employed, dual-earner couples or working single parents who have traditionally been able to count on the unpaid care work of predominantly female relatives and kin find themselves more constrained in employment choices. Urbanisation, migration, and the growth of single-mother households have further undermined extended family support networks.

The conflict between the roles as income earners and care providers is, therefore, likely to intensify. Attempts to balance the demands of market work and the unpaid work in household maintenance and social reproduction have lead to long hours of work and can undermine both men's and women's capacities not only in their jobs, but also in meeting care responsibilities.

Growing concern about potential crises of the family based care system and social reproduction as a whole has reached both developed as well as developing countries. Yet, policymakers tend to continue neglecting the non-market sector and its important linkages to the market sector, particularly labour markets. Workers and their families are left alone to find their own solutions to deal with family and care responsibilities as there is few or no government support or public sector provisioning.

Hiring domestic workers, typically women, is a common solution for middle-income families in developing and developed countries. Throughout Latin America, for example, domestic workers are approximately 17% of employed women. They are about 9% of all employed women in South Africa, about 9.5 % in the Philippines, and are found in 1 out of every 2 Kenyan homes.

This private solution to the demand for care work comes with its own problems and may undermine the ability of women to have decent work. Domestic workers are predominantly women, often from poor communities, rural areas, ethnic and racial minorities, or immigrants. Enforcement of labour laws is often very weak, in part because of the "hidden" nature of the work. As a result, most domestic workers are employed informally, at very low wages, with few legal rights or social protections and little access to voice and representation. In fact, the large numbers of domestic workers, and the growing evidence of abusive working conditions that many face around the world, have compelled the Governing Body of the ILO to place a standard-setting activity for domestic workers on the agenda of the ILO in June 2010.[75]

For the working poor, hiring domestic help is simply unforgettable, and workers in these households are compelled to engage children in paid work and unpaid domestic work to enable the family to meet its survival needs. In many countries, it is typically girls who are removed from school to care for younger children and accomplish domestic tasks, thus contributing to household survival at the expense of long-term education and employment opportunities.

The lack of social policy measures and supports for unpaid family responsibilities hits poor and vulnerable families the hardest, as they have the weakest economic capacity to purchase goods that can free up their time for paid work. They are often forced to choose between employment and care, or to combine them – choices which require painful sacrifices in terms of quality of employment and/or quality of care. These choices also have longer term welfare and economic consequences. With no childcare at hand, poor families cope by leaving children home alone or by taking children to work with them. In Nairobi, 54% of poorer mothers were found to bring their babies to work, whereas 85% of better-off mothers had house-girls.

The overall work burden and extent of role conflicts are heightened during periods of economic recession and crises, decline in real wages and cutbacks in government expenditures. Economic policies that cause workers to be both 'time-poor' and 'money-poor' contribute to the rise in stress and eventual deterioration of their well-being. The level and scope of non-marketed goods and services, and by extension, the volume of unpaid work invariably increases during this period. Poor women, in ensuring the daily survival of their households, perform more unpaid work during periods of market volatility. A working life characterised by the 'double day' and 'high work intensity' is an often ignored impact of economic policies.

Some countries have made important strides in reducing the tensions between paid market labour, and unpaid non-market labour in the home. The Nordic countries in particular have priorities the balancing of work and family, through policies such as extended paid parental leave, the creation of incentives for more equal sharing of this leave, set limits on the expected work week, and expanded public and subsidised child care. The labour market entry of women became a gender-enabling process, in part due to the democratic institutional space that allowed women's needs and interests to find their way into the policy process. Cash benefit for childcare schemes encourage gender-differentiated family models. Even in countries with the best policies, domestic responsibilities continue to disadvantage women in their access to decent work on a par with men. In most of the world, women continue to face much greater pressures, combining income-generating work with domestic responsibilities, in a context of decreasing state support.

Certain circumstances and characteristics of men and women particularly affect their labour market outcomes. Among these are education, household structure, race, class, and government policy. However, it is important to recognise that although these influence access to decent work, access to decent work can also influence these variables.

Household structure may adjust to economic need, as an individual's access to decent work changes. An adequate treatment of the relationship between labour market outcomes and the related factors would require careful econometric analysis. Here, we provide only an overview of some of the key relationships documented to date.

Education plays an important role in access to decent work. More educated individuals are less likely to be unemployed, are more likely to work in the formal sector, and typically earn higher wages than less educated individuals. Men still get more education than women in many countries, although since 1980 the gap has narrowed everywhere except the Middle East/North Africa region, where it has widened as men have increased their educational levels faster than women. Men and women also continue to pursue different types of schooling, with women more often preparing for traditionally "female" jobs.

Another important factor in explaining differences in access to decent work, particularly for women, is household structure. Women do a significantly larger share of household work than men, and this impacts the time, energy, and mobility that they are able to dedicate to paid work. Households with more children or other dependent require more time in care-giving and other household work, which may reduce women's ability to access or keep decent work. Like education, household structure is, thus, partly endogenous, resulting from household efforts and success in accessing and keeping decent work.

Unequal distribution of assets also affects access to decent work in a number of ways. Land ownership may allow owners to work for themselves, instead of taking work in the informal or home work sector, or migrating to cities in search of other work. Other forms of assets may also provide direct opportunities for self-employment and they may be used for collateral when taking loans to start a small business. Assets may also affect access to work when they are used to finance the education of children, additional training for adults, or assistance with household work, in the form of hired labour or purchase of timesaving technology. Finally, when women increase their access to assets relative to men in their household, they may increase their household bargaining power.

Differences in government policy are clearly important in explaining variations in access to decent work across countries. Policies can play a significant role in reducing gender inequalities in access to decent work, as well as inequalities related to differing educational, racial, and class backgrounds and household structures within a country. Perhaps the most fundamental policy is the assurance of equal educational opportunities. Facilitating policies more directly oriented toward labour markets include fiscal policies, which do not disadvantage two-worker households. Paid maternity leave of up to one year increases women's labour force attachment and reduces the negative impact of career interruptions, while leaves of longer than one year have negative effects on future earnings and labour force attachment, and unpaid leaves have no positive effect. Requirements for fathers to take at least part of the (parental) leave can also help equalise the impacts of child-rearing on men's and women's employment.

Protecting workers' rights to organise collectively and have voice in workplace affairs also increases access to decent work, particularly for women and minorities who are likely to be at the lower end of the wage distribution. While the collectively bargained wages do not always reduce the gender wage gap inside the union compared to outside, by reducing overall income inequality, unions contribute to a lower overall gender wage gap.

Finally, recent efforts to quantify household work, incorporate it into national accounts, and measure its distribution among family members will contribute to better recognition and valuation of this work. This, in turn, is likely to contribute to changing perceptions about this work and also to its more equal sharing.

8.5.4. Policy Recommendations

Structural and economic realities have shaped today's world of work and the lived experiences of women and men. The examples given throughout juxtapose the varied, emerging patterns of work and the new challenges brought about by forces of rapid change. These new conditions in the world of work offer new opportunities to women and men but, at the same time, seem to have limited the ability of many to find decent work in the labour market and in the home. Women with few assets and in weak bargaining positions are particularly prone to being 'time-poor', 'money-poor', or both.

Economic, social and labour policies in many countries remain gender-blind to date. In fact, they directly and indirectly have contributed to rising stress and growing tensions that underlie persistent gender inequalities and disempowerment of women. Worldwide, work has become more insecure as global competition, firm restructuring and economic downturns contributed to a shifting of jobs from the formal, large-firm sector to smaller and informal firms, and home-based work. Informal and home workers, and in many cases, temporary and part-time workers, lie outside the protections of labour laws and lack rights to social benefits. In cases where there are labour codes in place, they remain limited and weakly enforced, particularly in most of the developing countries.

The issue of decent work cannot be comprehensively addressed without examining the unpaid work that individuals also perform. As increasing numbers of women have taken on the role of income earners, the majority of them continue to perform their socially ascribed roles as household managers and care providers. In both developing and industrialised countries, family members remain a major source of caring labour. Although men in several countries have increasingly taken on more household chores, much of the unpaid work at home and in the community still falls on women. Even when women do participate in the labour market, family responsibilities affect the amount and type of paid work that women can undertake. The prevalence of women in informal and home-based work is linked to their other responsibilities, foremost to their duties of raising children. Women in households with few or no assets have the fewest options to deal with the conflicts between economic and care responsibilities.

Policy concerns and discourses regarding job creation, the balance between paid and unpaid work, equal opportunity, childrearing and care-giving and labour standards have brought the issues of social reproduction and human maintenance provisioning to the forefront of many discussions. These issues are central to providing women with equal opportunities to achieve decent work.

8.6. Role of Governments and NGOs

Achieving decent work for all requires a coherent yet strategic approach that includes a wide-ranging policy agenda, from gender-aware macroeconomic, social and labour policies to poverty reduction strategies and strengthened rights for workers to organise. While policies that promote trade and attract foreign investment can expand employment opportunities to some, they may simultaneously undermine the well-being of other workers including micro-entrepreneurs, subsistence farmers and care-providers, and thus raise policy concerns. This calls for governments to have plan of action to create a socioeconomic environment that upholds rights at work, decent employment, social protection, social dialogue, and policies that enable men and women to balance their paid and reproductive work responsibilities and to share the latter equally.

In order for governments to successfully promote decent work and workers' rights, a number of actions and strategies are suggested below:

1. Undertake, support and disseminate gender-aware analyses of the effect of macroeconomic policies including trade, fiscal, investment and financial policies as well as social/family policies, on access to decent work and on the level and distribution of reproductive work.
2. Undertake, support and disseminate gender-aware analyses of financial flows, investment policies and the impact of financial/economic crises on availability and quality of employment and unpaid work.
3. Develop and adopt legal frameworks that effectively address gender biases and discrimination in the ownership of and access to productive resources, especially land, credit, education, market knowledge and technology.
4. Undertake and support the collection of sex-desegregated data on employment, work conditions, earnings and time use.
5. Promote the use of such data and indicators, along with qualitative information, in the formation of policies on issues such as access to social protection, social services, union representation and collective bargaining, and the impact of changing work conditions on reproductive work.
6. Use such analyses for the development and formulation of gender-aware macroeconomic policies.
7. Establish gender-sensitive rules to guide employment practices of domestic and foreign firms, including global corporations, by building on existing multilateral instruments such as the ILO conventions on fundamental workers' rights and other conventions with regard to home-based work and part-time work.

8. Develop and implement gender-aware employment assistance measures and programs in order to protect, retrain and assist laid-off workers and displaced entrepreneurs, particularly small and micro-entrepreneurs, in both formal and informal sectors, including through employment creation.
9. Carry out country-specific and gender-aware assessments of labour laws and standards, with special attention given to those applied in export processing zones as well as those related to subcontracted, home-based work.
10 Increase the resources allocated for inspection of work sites and enforcement of local labour laws, especially those that relate to fundamental worker's rights as specified by the Declaration on the Fundamental Rights at Work.
11. Increase gender-awareness in labour ministries by increasing financial resource and technical capacities in this area.
12. Develop export strategies that rely on the upgrading of workers' skills and capacities as opposed to those that jeopardise their capabilities, health and safety.
13. Promote the development and implementation of social policies and social protection systems that enable men and women to balance both their paid and reproductive work responsibilities.
14. Strengthen broad-based participatory policy formulation and decision making processes. Involve researchers and civil society, especially labour groups and women's groups.

References

Alsop, R. and Heinsohn, N. 2005 *Measuring Empowerment in Practice: Structuring Analysis and Framing Indicators*, World Bank Policy Research Working Paper 3510

Fiedrich, M. and Jellema, A. 2003. *Literacy, Gender and Social Agency: Adventures in Empowerment*. A Research Report for ActionAid UK

Norwegian Agency for Development Cooperation. 1999. *Handbook in Gender and Empowerment Assessment,* NORAD

Pradhan, B. 2003. *Measuring Empowerment: A Methodological Approach, Society for International Development* (www.sidint.org) 1011-6370 46:2; 51-57; 033500 Palgrave Macmillan.

9

Governing Poverty Reduction Strategies

The debate about policy and poverty reduction touches on three interrelated issues: the measurement of poverty, the arithmetic decomposition of poverty reduction into growth and distribution effects, and the causal relationships between growth, distribution and policy variables affecting them. The appropriateness and accuracy of measures of poverty have come under repeated scrutiny. There are wide variations in the measures, and small changes in underlying measurement techniques can have significant effects on measured poverty. These measurement problems make it difficult enough to identify trends, and certainly make it very difficult to test complex causal relationships with satisfactory degrees of confidence. On the other hand, the arithmetic relationship among mean incomes, income distribution and poverty is relatively simple, and can be used to decompose poverty reduction into income growth and distribution components. But these decompositions do not directly tell us much about the *causal* relationships among growth, distribution and the variables that jointly affect them, which have been the subject of considerable debate.

9.1. Measurement Issues

Poverty is typically measured by the headcount measure, the proportion of the population below a commonly agreed poverty line. In recent years, the $1 a day line used by the World Bank has achieved wide usage. The first set of poverty measures using this line was published in the *World Development Report 1990* for 22 countries for

1985, using 1985 PPP to convert the dollar a day line into local currencies. In 1993, PPP data were substantially revised and improved, and using these numbers, a new poverty line was chosen from the median of the ten lowest national poverty lines which gave a figure of $1.08 at 1993 PPP. This figure was the basis of subsequent World Bank estimates of national and global poverty till the international poverty line was further updated to $1.25 in 2005 PPP prices. The new 'dollar-a-day' line emerged as the mean of the national poverty lines of the fifteen poorest countries converted into 2005 PPP dollars. Rather the particular level of the line was derived as the mean or median of an arbitrarily chosen set of national poverty lines converted into PPP dollars. As a result, it is not clear that the Bank's headcount poverty measures over time identify the proportion of population below a fixed absolute consumption level.

A further problem with these standard World Bank poverty measures is that they are very sensitive to estimates, both of the conversion rate of the PPP dollar poverty line into local currency using the PPP conversion rate for the benchmark year, and then the conversion of this local currency poverty line for the benchmark year into a poverty line for the current year using consumer price indices. Changes in the estimates of the PPP conversion rate or the consumer price index can significantly alter estimates of poverty. Updating price data explains some of the significant changes in the estimates of global poverty that the World Bank has been forced to announce. For instance, the revision of PPP estimates in 2005 and the revision of the poverty line from $1.08 at 1993 PPP dollars to $1.25 at 2005 PPP dollars resulted in the estimate of the proportion of global population living in poverty increasing from 17.2 per cent to 25.7 per cent, an obviously massive change in the numbers.

Finally, computing the conventional headcount poverty measure requires the use of national income distribution statistics typically derived from expenditure or income surveys, and these vary significantly in quality across countries and over time within countries. These data issues need to be kept in mind when we comment on changes in poverty in developing countries based on these numbers. Even so, the headcount ratio is the simplest and crudest of the measures of poverty. It ignores the distribution of poverty under the line. Other measures of poverty that take the distribution of poverty below the poverty line into account are even more difficult to estimate. These significant data issues mean that we are not in a position to trace the effects of policy with any precision. Ten data are at best able to indicate very broad trends, and even that with significant qualifications.

9.2. Income Distribution and Poverty Reduction

Poverty reduction is arithmetically related to growth and changes in income distribution. The density function describing the share of the population that receives each per capita income provides all the information required to estimate any measure of poverty. That density function, in turn, can be described by its mean and the shape of the distribution around that mean.

Changes in the level of poverty can be related to changes in per capita incomes and changes in the distribution of this income. If the distribution of income stays constant, income must have changed for all income groups at the same rate. The logarithmic horizontal axis ensures that a rightward shift of the density function will entail the same percentage change in the incomes of all groups. Moving the density function to the right therefore shows a pure growth effect with no change in the distribution of relative incomes. If distribution worsens, poverty reduction will be slower because incomes of poorer groups will be rising at a rate lower than the average. In contrast, if distribution improves, poverty reduction will be faster because the incomes of poorer groups will be rising faster than the average, so that not only is the density function moving to the right, it is also moving downwards at the bottom end. When both mean incomes and the distribution of relative incomes change, the overall change in poverty can be decomposed into a growth component and a distribution component.

The decomposition of poverty into growth and redistribution provides a number of arithmetic insights that are not in dispute. First, poverty reduction will be faster if the growth of per capita income is higher, and/or if income distribution is improving. Secondly, since income distribution cannot keep improving and has, in any case, an arithmetic upper bound when all incomes become equal, the long-term driver of poverty reduction must be growth. But thirdly, income distribution in most developing countries is so far away from equality that significant poverty reduction is arithmetically possible for a while if distribution improves. Fourthly, for any given growth rate of per capita income, poverty reduction will be faster if incomes are more equally distributed to begin with. These arithmetic facts are not in dispute, but they do not help to resolve the intense disputes about *causality* and the appropriate content of poverty reducing policies.

9.3. Growth, Redistribution and Governance

A wide range of contradictory causal relationships have been suggested between growth and redistribution. The inconclusive empirical testing of these possible hypotheses suggests that the relevant relationships may vary significantly across countries, regions and periods. The causal relationships relevant for particular countries are nevertheless important, because it may be that higher growth may require policies that slow down or reverse improvements in distribution, or it may be that higher growth requires improvements in income distribution. For instance, if improvements in distribution have a negative effect on growth, an excessive focus on redistribution may have negative growth effects that could more than offset the positive redistribution effects for poverty reduction.

The causality between growth and redistribution can also run in both directions. Growth may, in turn, have causal effects on distribution that may be positive or negative, and again, there are obvious implications for poverty reduction. Finally, both growth and distribution are likely to be responsive to policy and these policies can be judged in terms of their impact on growth and redistribution. The optimal policy mix would depend on the effective relationships between growth and distribution. In turn, both growth and income distribution can determine the effectiveness of specific policies, because the political feasibility of implementing particular policies may depend on the environment of growth and distribution. As we are particularly concerned with governance reform.

An important link operates through the savings-investment effect. The classical position on the direction and sign of the savings-investment effect was articulated by Kaldor, drawing on the classical political economy insight that growth in capitalist economies is driven by the investment of profits. As profits are the incomes of capitalists, the higher investments that drive growth may be associated with a more unequal distribution of income.This argument can be interpreted to imply that greater equality would have a negative effect on growth. What is often not clearly articulated is that even if higher profits were associated with greater in-equality, this would only imply higher growth rates if other factors were conducive to sustaining high levels of investment. There is no point having high levels of profits if expectations of future profitability are weak and investments in potential growth sectors do not take place. So we should not be surprised if we do not find an overall relationship between inequality and growth in cross-sectional analysis looking at all countries together.

The savings-investment effect can also directly suggest the opposite relationship between equality and growth. Amartya Sen capabilities approach to development can be interpreted as saying that greater equality would be good for, or at least compatible with, poverty-reducing growth. Redistribution to the poor would allow higher investments in areas like health and education that enhance the capabilities of the poor to participate in growth. Variants of this argument point out that a failure in capital markets can prevent the poor from accessing capital if their initial endowments of assets are too low. These arguments are also theoretically plausible, but equally, there is likely to be little point in building capabilities for the poor, in the way Sen's argument suggests, if employment opportunities for the somewhat educated poor do not also emerge. Thus, it is not surprising that some developing countries and regions with above average education underperforms in terms of growth because of poor employment generation. These economies often become exporters of skilled labour rather than high growth economies. The cases of Kerala within India and of the Philippines in South East Asia are particularly relevant.

A second linkage between distribution and growth operates through the mechanism of political redistribution. Examples are Alesina and Rodrik as well as Person and Tabellini who suggest that inequality would have a negative effect on growth by creating pressures for taxation and redistribution. Attempts by political organisations to achieve this redistribution, in turn, have a dampening effect on growth.

The political economy behind many of these models is implausibly simplistic. It is not possible to say much that is useful even about the sign of the relationship between initial distribution and political responses to it without a fuller picture of the political structure of a country, its level of development, the structure of its economy and so on. For instance, a society that is very unequal may have fewer distributive conflicts if the poor are really poor and disorganised compared to one that was more equal but had powerful intermediate classes who could lead the mobilisation against the rich.

Finally, growth can directly affect distribution as suggested by Kuznets. Kuznets suggested that as the capitalist or modern sector in developing countries grew, income inequality would initially worsen and then eventually improve, implying an inverse-U shaped relationship between per capita income and inequality. His argument depended on the possibility that mean income in agriculture was lower and distribution is relatively more equal than in the emerging industrial sector. As labour moved from agriculture to industry, income distribution would initially worsen despite overall mean incomes growing. However, even in poor countries, poverty would be unlikely to increase as a result of growth because for the economy as a whole, the positive growth effect would be likely to at least balance, if not outweigh, the negative redistribution effect.

Not surprisingly, given the number of plausible theoretical relationships between growth and distribution with opposite signs and directions of causality, the empirical evidence is indeterminate. Each of these plausible mechanisms depends on implicit institutional, political and economic conditions being appropriate. In cross section studies where country-specific conditions are almost impossible to fully account for, the overall relationships observed are likely to be either indeterminate or spurious. Alesina and Rodrik as well as Persson and Tabellini provide some empirical support for the hypotheses that higher initial inequality results in lower growth. On the other hand, Forbes using a better data set on income inequality and using panel data to limit the impact of regional effects, finds a positive relationship between inequality and growth at the level of countries.

The panel data analysis suggests that the negative relationship between inequality and growth in some cross section regressions may have been capturing regional effects because many low growth regions happened to have relatively poor income distribution. A positive relationship between inequality and growth along the lines of Forbes is also reported by Lie and Zou. In their test of Kuznets using panel data, Deininger and Squire find very weak relationship between growth and inequality. Since a relationship does exist in cross-sectional data, they suggest that the Kuznets relationship could also be picking up regional effects. None of these studies attempt to test these relationships using more sophisticated theories which identify the specific conditions under which relationships of a particular sign and direction of causality may hold.

9.4. Good Governance

Keeping these fundamental questions about the relationship between growth, distribution and poverty in mind, we can look at the important policy area of governance reform to see how these reforms may affect poverty. We can examine this by looking at the possible effects of governance reforms on growth and distribution. Much of the emphasis of good governance reforms has focused on the likely effect of these reforms on growth. The anomalous nature of good governance on growth has been examined elsewhere.

Governance reforms refer to strengthening state capabilities to enforce institutional rules that are important for economic and social development. Ten dominant 'good governance' paradigm identifies a series of capabilities that, it argues, are *necessary* governance capabilities for a market-friendly state. These include, in particular, the capabilities to protect stable property rights, enforce the rule of law, effectively implement anti-corruption policies and achieve government accountability. Many of these capabilities are clearly desirable as they help to achieve conditions that are desirable. But in the good governance framework, these capabilities are not just *desirable for achieving some of the goals of development.* Rather, good governance capabilities are identified as *preconditions for development* because they ensure that markets will be efficient and less subject to market failures.

The new consensus draws on a particular reading of the New Institutional Economics to derive these conclusions. A core proposition is that efficient markets are achievable in developing countries, and efficient markets will drive development. Unstable property rights and welfare-reducing interventions, in turn, persist because of corruption and rent seeking because some individuals and groups benefit from these instabilities and interventions. And finally, damaging rent seeking and corruption continue because of weak accountability and a lack of effective democracy, which allow a minority to benefit at the expense of the majority.

The good governance agenda therefore aims to reduce the market transaction costs which are theoretically the source of important market failures. Ten expectation is that strengthening the requisite capabilities will reduce market transaction costs, which in turn will drive development. Ties is why in Khan and elsewhere, we described the 'good governance' agenda as one of *market-enhancing governance*. To the standard liberalisation strategies which have been the core component of the international development consensus, the good governance agenda adds a number of simultaneous reform priorities.

States have to achieve capabilities for protecting property rights and contracts using the rule of law. These require capabilities for fighting corruption and rent seeking, which, in turn, have to be bolstered by reforms promoting democratisation, decentralisation and accountability. The final component often added to the package by development agencies is the promotion of pro-poor service delivery as a way of mobilising the poor who are the majority or close to the majority in poor countries. If this group can be mobilised to hold the state to account by ensuring that the state delivers to them, then the accountability essential in this framework can be kick-started. The importance of pro-poor service delivery in this governance approach is therefore not simply the direct effect on poverty but primarily to establish the virtuous cycle of governance which, in theory, will sustain market-led growth.

9.4.1. Good Governance and Growth

We have argued elsewhere that the expectation that implementing good governance reforms in developing countries will drive growth is unlikely to be met. This is not because the theory is implausible, but because there are structural and fiscal constraints that prevent the achievement of significant improvements in the good governance capabilities. As a result, the achievement of lower market failures through this route is likely to be very limited. Indeed, when we compare high-growth and low-growth developing countries, we do not find significant differences in their scores on good governance. High-growth developing countries do not, in general, have better governance compared to other developing countries in terms of their good governance capabilities. But case study evidence suggests that developing countries that have sustained high growth over long periods did have significant governance capabilities to identify and address significant market failures.

These observations suggest that developing countries that focus exclusively on good governance reforms are not likely to achieve significant improvements in their growth rates as a result. Indeed, they are unlikely even to achieve significant improvements in good governance across the board given the structural and fiscal constraints that we have referred to. The achievement of good governance goals – like the stabilisation of property rights, the achievement of good rule of law or the significant reduction of corruption – require fiscal capabilities not available in the typical developing country. In this context, market failures are likely to remain significant and serious, and are unlikely to be significantly reduced by good governance reforms. Developing countries therefore also need to focus on alternative governance capabilities that enable them to directly address market failures.

9.4.2. Good Governance and Distribution

While the impact of good governance on growth is unclear at best it is possible that good governance reforms may have an impact on poverty reduction by improving income distribution in poor countries. If so, the implementation of good governance capabilities may have a positive impact on poverty in poor countries. This is primarily likely to happen through the pro-poor service delivery aspect of good governance reforms, but also through the protection of property rights and the rule of law, through anti-corruption policies and democratisation, all of which could, in theory, allow the poor to protect their rights better, demand better services from the state, and ensure that a greater part of the public goods that they are entitled to are in fact delivered.

The linkage between the implementation of good governance reforms in poor countries and its effects on poverty through distribution depends on the types of implicit assumptions that we make about a series of background conditions. Making some of these assumptions explicit may help us to assess the plausibility of the claims made for poverty reduction through good governance reforms in specific country contexts.

The growth effects of the good governance reform agenda are theoretically plausible, but unlikely to be strong. We have discussed elsewhere that structural weaknesses of poor countries are likely to prevent them from significantly implementing good governance reforms. At the same time, growth in the modern sector is likely to be constrained by significant market failures unlikely to be addressed by the limited improvements in market efficiency achieved through good governance reforms. If the growth of employment opportunities does not materialise, then this aspect of pro-poor spending will effectively have been a limited period of enhanced consumption for the poor. Sustainable improvements in the incomes of the poor and therefore the effects on poverty through growth will only materialise if these investments in human capital are supplemented with a growth in job opportunities.

There is however a second and more direct effect on distribution and poverty through the effect of good governance reforms and support for pro-poor spending on the mobilisation of the poor to hold governments to account. The provision of pro-poor public goods through the state together with good governance reforms that encourage accountability, attack corruption and strengthen the rule of law could induce the mobilisation of the poor to demand effective delivery of what has been promised to them by law. If the response of the poor is to form sustainable and viable organisations to ensure effective service delivery, these could continue to operate to hold the state to account over time. If this happens, the redistributed effect could be permanent, not just limited to the period for which aid is available.

For the political redistribution effect to be positive in this case, without a negative impact on investment or investor confidence, we require some further implicit assumptions. We have to assume that the distribution of power in society is such that once the poor mobilise to sustain the allocation of a greater share of public goods to the poor, or to demand redistributive programmes through the tax system, the rich will not be able to resist, and therefore will not try to resist. This assumption is necessary to ensure that adverse effects on investment do not follow. With these assumptions, the improvement in accountability – triggered by a combination of good governance reforms and the catalyst of aid-financed pro-poor spending – could result in a sustainable improvement in distribution.

These political assumptions may be unrealistic in most developing countries. Pro-poor spending is typically targeted at the bottom ten to fifty per cent of the population who are, by definition, the very poor, and mainly targeted to the population below the poverty line. This part of the population may be very numerous, but, typically, they are not collectively very powerful in developing countries.

As a result, most of the redistributive conflicts in poor countries are between different fractions of the rich and the 'intermediate classes'.The relatively small amounts of aid-funded pro-poor spending in poor countries are unlikely to change this fundamental distribution of power or result in an alternative set of powerful poor-led organisations emerging that can change the way governments are held to account.

The most optimistic of the realistic outcomes is that dominant political factions do not react adversely to protect their interests in the face of aid-financed pro-poor spending. The more pessimistic outcomes are that the politically dominant organisations of the not-so-poor will work out ways to capture much of the pro-poor spending. When this happens, this 'rent seeking' by intermediate class interests to capture more aid resources can quickly have adverse effects. Not only is delivery to the poor likely to be affected, but more seriously, the attention of the political elites is likely to be diverted towards sustaining the aid economy rather than being focused on the enhancement of productive capacity.

A combination of adverse conditions can result in the focus on pro-poor spending having much more limited or even adverse effects on distribution and growth. Here, pro-poor spending and good governance reforms fail to achieve growth acceleration, and on the political redistribution side, the main result is the diversion of mainstream patron-client factions into particular types of rent seeking.

The effect of good governance reforms and pro-poor spending in many countries has been to induce an elaborate set of rent seeking activities, beginning with the consultants and stockholders who produce the Prizes As the pro-poor spending preferences of donors are well known, governments and stockholder in developing countries have rapidly evolved skills in defining national priorities in line with activities likely to be funded. Ministries, departments and service providers of different types of pro-poor services have also frequently become aligned to absorbing and spending the inflow of resources. The most pessimistic outcome is when the leading elites of the country begin to become dependent on pro-poor aid flows as sources of rents. The difficult and risky task of organising the productive transformation of society can then take a back seat.

The good governance reform package is easy to support as a set of desirable objectives for developing countries to aspire to. There is considerable doubt as to whether this package is implemental to the extent that it can make a dent on the serious market failures that developing countries are subject to. There is therefore an argument that the good governance agenda may divert attention from the task of developing growth-enhancing governance capabilities in poor countries. On the other hand, there is the possibility that good governance reforms, particularly when bolstered by support for pro-poor spending as a way of improving government accountability, can have a direct effect on redistribution.

The available data provides no evidence that good governance is associated with improvements in distribution. The weakness of the data has to be kept in mind, but there are also theoretical reasons to question the presence of strong relationships between good governance reforms and sustainable redistributive changes in favour of the poor. Given the weak political power of the poor and the implausibility of significant shifts in that power balance coming about as a result of pro-poor spending, it is more likely that good governance reforms will themselves be subject to new forms of rent seeking by elites. If so, any improvements in distribution are likely to be largely the result of aid-funded spending that is not likely to be sustainable over time. The reduction in poverty that is arithmetically achieved is therefore also likely to suffer if aid is eventually removed.

The theoretical analysis of the relationship between growth and distribution suggests that sustainable improvements in distribution have to be consistent with a growth strategy, and the analysis of the arithmetic of poverty reduction reminds us that while improvements in distribution are important, the long-run reduction of poverty can only be assured by sustainable growth. Aligning redistributive agendas with the needs of growth strategies so that an acceptable mix of growth and distribution is achieved is obviously the only viable strategy.

A growth-enhancing governance strategy would focus on assisting developing countries to identify critical constraints to growth and develop the institutional capacities to address them. There may be many strategies, each prioritising different sectors and market failures, each with different distributive implications. Keeping poverty reduction in mind means we should rule out growth strategies where the poor have to pay a significant price, even if only in the short term. The desirable mix of growth and distribution is obviously a political judgment and different political parties could well reach different judgments. The second part of the argument is very important. Whichever strategy a political leadership assesses as optimal is likely to have distributive implications that some powerful groups may resist. A successful growth strategy will therefore also have to give some attention to its feasibility. But all policies are likely to require some realignment of political power through the construction of appropriate new coalitions or the political weakening of specific distributive coalitions who would have opposed successful implementation of that specific growth strategy.

References

Agere, Sam (2000). *Promoting good governance*. Commonwealth Secretariat.

Khan, Mushtaq Husain (2004). *State formation in Palestine: viability and governance during a social transformation: Volume 2 of Political economy of the Middle East and North Africa*. Routledge

Poluha, Eva; Rosendahl, Mona (2002). *Contesting 'good' governance: crosscultural perspectives on representation, accountability and public space*. Routeledge.

The IMF's Approach to Promoting Good Governance and Combating Corruption — A Guide. International Monetary Fund. 20 June 2005.

10

Institutional Approach to Development

Five years after the Millennium Summit - and with ten years remaining towards the goals set for 2015 - it is essential to take stock and to adjust course where needed. This includes ensuring that the following fundamental conditions for economic growth to achieve the MDGs are in place in both OECD and partner countries:

1. A peaceful and secure environment.
2. A reliable macroeconomic framework.
3. Sustainable approaches to meeting growing energy needs.

10.1. Fostering a Secure Environment

"Security and political stability are fundamental to long-term growth, development and poverty reduction in developing countries. Poverty reduction and the promotion of human rights are mutually reinforcing approaches and of immediate relevance for a peaceful and secure environment. Efforts to reduce poverty and promote human rights are more effective in countries with sound institutions and policies. These countries represent 13 per cent of the developing world but account for an estimated one-third of people living on under a dollar a day. They have a major impact on regional and global security and present an enormous challenge for the MDGs.

Conflict has devastating human and economic costs and a profound impact on the political, social and economic development of a country - and often its surrounding region. All too often the outbreak of violent conflict reverses the benefits of development. Much remains to be done to ensure that awareness of conflict-related issues gets integrated into policy areas such as development co-operation, foreign affairs, defence and trade.

The OECD's recent report, *Security System Reform and Good Practice,* concludes that accountable and efficient security systems operating under civilian control in a democratic context can create an enabling environment for development. OECD countries can effectively contribute to security-system reform through joined-up government approaches that respond to the needs of partner countries and their populations. Support for regional and sub-regional efforts will complement support at the country level.

The DAC recommends that development and other agencies remain engaged, even in countries where institutions and policies are weakest and partnership is difficult. The OECD is building consensus on the special requirements for engaging effectively with fragile states in terms of aid allocations; alternate practices for harmonisation and alignment; service delivery; and coherence of aid with diplomacy, trade and other policies.

The UN Security Council has called for assistance from countries adhering to the *OECD Guidelines for Multinational Enterprises* for a specific fragile state, the Democratic Republic of Congo (DRC), because of the illegal exploitation of its resources. The OECD has responded with its broad package of integrity instruments - not only the *Guidelines*, but also its *Convention on Combating Bribery of Foreign Public Officials, Corporate Governance Principles*, and *Guidelines for Managing Conflict of Interest in the Public Sector*. While complementing broader efforts to enhance multinational enterprises' contributions to these difficult investment environments, this work also recognises that the primary responsibility for policy reform lies with the host country itself and that multinational enterprises cannot substitute for governments that are unable or unwilling to assume their responsibilities.

10.1.1. Macroeconomic Framework for Shared Growth

High and sustainable rates of growth are essential for poverty reduction. Studies at the OECD and elsewhere stress the importance of a stability-oriented macroeconomic framework for ensuring sustainable long-run growth in per capita incomes. Economic stability allows consumers, firms and governments to plan more effectively for the long term, improving the quality and quantity of investment in physical and human capital – two key long-run determinants of economic growth in all economies.

Clear and sound macroeconomic policies of OECD countries provide considerable benefits for developing economies. Sound medium-term public finances help to reduce pressures on global interest rates, providing more favourable financing conditions and low and stable rates of inflation, thus reducing uncertainty about the returns from long-term investments and loans. Clear medium-term policy objectives also help to enhance policy transparency and lower market uncertainty about future policy actions. Reduced uncertainty should be favourable for global financial market conditions, lowering risk premiums in interest and exchange rates and output and inflation volatility in all economies. OECD analyses and peer reviews are geared to ensuring macroeconomic stability in member countries.

The experience of OECD countries also offers useful lessons for the design of macroeconomic policy frameworks in developing countries. Well-designed policy rules can support medium-term goals while leaving sufficient flexibility for macroeconomic policies to react to unexpected short-term economic fluctuations. Equally, a focus on medium-term price stability permits monetary policymakers to respond to deflationary as well as inflationary shocks.

The benefits from adopting clear and transparent macroeconomic frameworks will likely rise as national economies become ever more integrated with each other. Stable frameworks also provide a favourable setting in which microeconomic and regulatory reforms can be introduced to help improve productive potential and in which barriers to international trade and investment can be lowered. A macroeconomic framework designed to maintain long-term stability should help policy makers in all economies to minimise the adverse impact of such external events on long-term growth prospects.

Growth episodes in some developing countries have been weak and unsustainable, and the patterns of growth often have not significantly reduced poverty. Efforts to increase growth have focused on the social sectors, given the critical importance of factors such as health and education in long-term growth prospects. Stable economic growth and its other determinants have been somewhat neglected, a perspective now being addressed in the DAC and Povnet agenda to promote sustainable growth and poverty reduction.

Developing country experiences with pro-poor growth vary considerably. In some developing countries growth and distributional objectives have not been well integrated. In other countries, growth and poverty reduction have gone hand in hand. Studies reveal that programmes and policies need to target poverty reduction, to involve the poor in the process by making markets work for them, and to be integrated with a locally owned poverty reduction strategy. Gender equality is fundamental to achieving shared growth and attaining the MDGs.

A dynamic private sector, agriculture and infrastructure are key strands of the pro-poor growth agenda. Jobs and self employment constitute the main pathway out of poverty. Most poor people live in rural areas, and agriculture is a major contributor to developing countries' GDP. More and better infrastructure is essential for broad-based growth, increasing international economic linkages and mobilising investment.

10.1.2. Promoting Sustainable Approaches

Economic growth and energy consumption are fundamentally linked. Access to energy is an essential requirement for economic development and a key contributor to social development. Energy services enable basic human needs to be *in* met and contribute to social development by improving education, sanitation and public health. In many poor countries, under-investment in public utilities, inefficient management, underpricing and a generally unattractive climate for private investment can cause energy shortages and hold back economic growth and development. The International Energy Agency (IEA) estimates that the investment requirements for electricity generation, transmission and distribution in developing countries will amount to over USD 185 billion per year from now until 2030. Domestic capital, FDI and development aid will all be necessary, especially in the poorest countries. Public-private partnerships that may include host-country governments, donors, multilateral development banks, NGOs and private companies represent an important option for mobilising the needed investment.

The IEA's *World Energy Outlook 2004* analyses the energy implications of meeting MDG1: Eradicating extreme poverty and hunger. One yardstick for this is halving the proportion of people living on less than USD1 a day by 2015. Modelling work by the IEA demonstrates a strong link between income and access to modern energy services.

Meeting the target also implies extending the use of modern cooking and heating fuels to over 700 million more people from 2002 to 2015. The use of traditional biomass and waste for energy, usually a characteristic as well as a cause of persistent poverty, is both inefficient and the source of the indoor smoke pollution responsible for the deaths of more than 1.6 million women and children in developing countries every year.

The Clean Development Mechanism defined under the Kyoto Protocol to the UN Framework Convention on Climate Change, promotes investments in developing countries that help to reduce global greenhouse gas emissions. Many of these investments will flow toward energy projects that are more sustainable. The OECD and IEA have been active in recent years in helping to define the criteria under which abatement credits for CDM activities will be provided to developed countries. They have provided technical assistance in developing standardised baselines for use in approving CDM projects, thereby contributing to speeding up low-cost energy-improving investments that will ultimately help to alleviate poverty in many developing countries.

The IEA has introduced an Energy Development Index (EDI), a composite measure of energy use in developing countries. The EDI seeks to capture the quality as well as the quantity of energy services provided and is calculated to mirror the UNDP's Human Development Index (HDI).

The EDI and the HDI are strongly correlated, but the correlation is non-linear; the indices appear to educable at higher levels of wealth and human development. EDI projections to 2030 indicate that although EDI scores should continue to rise in all developing regions, only a few countries in the Middle East and Latin America will have reached by 2030 the stage of energy development already attained by OECD countries three decades ago.

10.2. Improving Policy Implementation

The OECD and its members are striving to improve aid policies and to leverage their effectiveness through asynergies with other policy areas. A major international effort is under way to focus the whole aid process more sharply on results and to reduce unnecessary donor-generated demands on countries with overstretched capacities. Efforts to untie more aid continue. OECD countries are devoting greater attention to interactions between policies and their impact on development. Of highest priority is strengthening the aid-trade-investment-migration nexus in support of shared growth and poverty reduction. These issues are taken up under four headings:

1. Aid effectiveness: harmonisation, untying and complementarity with partner strategies and programmes;
2. Improved coherence and asynergies between OECD member country policies that impact on development;
3. Enabling partners to benefit from open markets;
4. Policies that help attract business investment.

10.2.1. Making Aid more Effective

The international development community committed in Rome to align development assistance with partner-country strategies, to harmonise donor policies and procedures and to implement principles of good practice in development co-operation.

On *harmonisation:* Donors have made a start in using simplified procedures and practices, joint analytical work, a focus on delivery of development results, delegated co-operation, common procurement and financial management procedures, and common arrangements for programme-based approaches.

On alignment: By October 2004 some 43 countries had prepared poverty reduction strategies, and many other low- and middle-income countries had nationally owned development strategies. Information from DAC and other sources suggests a promising trend toward increased donor alignment behind country strategies and more joint support of these strategies. Interest has surged in sector wide approaches (SWAps) to align all aid modes around sectorial priorities, and a growing number of SWAps include use of countries' existing frameworks for allocating and accounting for funds.

Several factors hamper further progress. Some partner country policy and investment priorities are still poorly defined. The links between medium-term plans and annual budget decisions are often missing. It is difficult to agree upon indicators that can trigger disbursement of donor funding. More use of strengthened country systems along with arrangements that allow one donor to manage aid on behalf of another and joint financing would increase harmonisation and alignment. Two other areas require attention: the special needs of fragile states, where harmonisation and alignment have proved even more critical than elsewhere.

Building on growing momentum for change, on 2 March 2005 Ministers of OECD and partner countries and Heads of multilateral and bilateral development institutions adopted the *Paris Declaration on Aid Effectiveness.* It commits donors and partner countries to "take far-reaching and monitorable actions to reform the ways [they] deliver and manage aid as look ahead to the UN five-year review…" Donors resolve to base their overall support on partner countries' national development strategies, institutions and procedures. Donors commit themselves to providing reliable indicative commitments of aid over a multi-year framework and to disbursing aid in a timely and predictable fashion according to agreed schedules.

The tying status of aid has long been considered a key test of donors' commitment to coherent policies and effective aid delivery. In the context of improving aid effectiveness, partners challenge a system in which a significant part of ODA goes back to donor countries and recommend that aid should become untied. Tying raises the cost of many goods, services and projects by 15 to 30 per cent on average. This implies that tied aid reduced the value of total bilateral aid by USD5 billion to USD 7 billion in 2002, a conservative estimate that ignores the indirect costs. It is incompatible with country owned procurement systems and their integrity, a basic component of the *Paris Declaration* process.

A DAC Recommendation to untie ODA to the Least Developed Countries entered into force on 1 January 2002. In 2003 total bilateral ODA in the categories covered by the recommendation more than doubled and amounted to USD 9.4 billion. Of that amount members reported 91% as untied. Many donors have further increased the share of untied aid in their bilateral programmes. A few have untied all or large parts of their programmes. Based on incomplete coverage, about half of total bilateral aid is reported as untied. The Recommendation's contribution to aid effectiveness remains limited, however, by its present coverage. The Recommendation invites members to study the possibilities of extending untied aid to the areas beyond its coverage. The need for and the value of increasing the Recommendation's impact on broader aid effectiveness objectives are receiving growing acknowledgement: developing countries ask for more untied aid as part of the implementation of the aid-effectiveness agenda.

10.2.2. Improving Coherence and Synergies

Policy coherence for development means ensuring that the objectives and results of an OECD member government's development policies are not undermined by other policies of the same government that impact on developing countries. Policy coherence increasingly features as a key item on the international agenda. The experience of OECD countries suggests that governments and institutions can seek greater policy coherence at the national, regional and international levels, including the consistency of policies adopted by donor and recipient countries to achieve shared development objectives.

To complement the traditional focus on internal consistency of development policy, OECD countries began in the early 1990s to stress the other dimensions of policy coherence for development, particularly intra-country coherence. The DAC strategy *Shaping the 21st Century*, adopted in 1996, brought this to the fore by emphasising the importance of ensuring that the entire range of relevant policies is consistent with and does not undermine development objectives.

Many OECD governments have promoted joined-up government approaches to avoid the wasted resources, missed objectives and lost credibility associated with inconsistent policies in different fields. OECD experience suggests that the success of such approaches depends on the acceptance by development people that coherence requires a "two-way street".

An OECD project, begun in 2002, has been examining ways of mainstreaming climate change policy objectives into the development assistance efforts of OECD donors, as well as into the national planning activities of developing countries. National level case studies in six developing countries have been completed. The main emphasis is on delivering cost-effective adaptation to climate change in developing countries, using sectorial and aid policies as vectors for doing so. Policy guidance to aid agencies is currently in preparation; the work is also examining ways of mainstreaming climate policy objectives into specific development instruments, such as the Poverty Reduction Strategy Papers (PRSPs).

Challenges to achieve policy coherence for development call for a combination of institutional and sectorial policy actions. Given the numerous forms of assistance to partner countries, the diverse government ministries responsible for various aspects of development assistance and for other policy areas that impact on developing countries, the sheer number of actors at the supra-national level and the multiplicity of decision-making forums, the need for co-ordination and coherence in policy making is easily recognised but still difficult to implement.

Based on good practice, the OECD has developed an analytical framework for institutional approaches to policy coherence for development that helps assess the progress of DAC members, as well as recommendations for improvement. Some OECD member countries have already embraced strategic actions for institutional change by adopting this analytical framework for assessing political will and institutional capacity. OECD's systematic application of this framework with subsequent monitoring is recommended as part of the peer reviews.

Sectorial approaches to policy coherence complement the institutional efforts. OECD frameworks are being developed for better understanding the impacts on partner countries of macroeconomic, agricultural and fisheries policies. Discussion of the conclusions and follow-up continues in relevant OECD committees. In agriculture, an analytical framework has been designed to help OECD countries assess the effects of their policies on partner countries in relation to the MDGs. In the fisheries sector, a meeting planned between development and fisheries experts in 2006 will take up issues such as access agreements, trade, income effects and development co-operation policies.

The MDGs explicitly include providing access to affordable essential drugs and making available the benefits of new technologies, especially information and communication technologies (ICT). Rapid advances in science and technology open new opportunities for fighting poverty. Greater asynergies between development policies and science and technology for sustainable development, access to medicines, and eradication of "neglected diseases" should receive greater attention in efforts to reduce poverty.

The OECD will seek to address in a more concerted fashion how member countries might encourage innovation that meets the health needs of developing countries. This will include incentives for the development of new drugs, availability, affordability and access to medicines as well as the need to address more explicitly the threat posed by emerging and neglected diseases. Several developing countries have seen decades of slow, painstaking improvement in standards of living wiped out in just a few years by the ravages of disease.

A regional case study of East Asia's development recently examined a range of OECD country policy vectors – trade, investment, migration, aid and others – and their impacts on Asian economies. The central findings of this study show that policy coherence in OECD countries can bear fruit only when partner economies have the capacity to respond: coherent policies are necessary, but not sufficient.

Interactions among OECD countries' policies in Asia, as well as Africa, Latin America and Eastern Europe, are being further examined through eighteen country case studies. When do such policies complement each other and when do they work at cross-purposes. How do OECD member countries' policies interact with those of developing and transition economies to overcome or reinforce development bottlenecks? The comparative analysis of the case studies will provide a rich source of policy-oriented insights in support of economic reform in OECD countries and developing countries alike.

As part of the OECD's evolving partnership with Africa, the *Mutual Review of Development Effectiveness* takes up a range of themes of mutual accountability between African and OECD countries, including policy coherence. The issues taken up in the *Mutual Review*, together with the African country cases and other studies, will inform the OECD's next regional case study, which will focus on the impacts of OECD member country policies on Sub-Saharan Africa.

This regional case study work aims to solidify the case and quicken the momentum for development coherence, as well as to provide better understanding of policy impacts, through empirically based analysis of concrete regional and country experience. Such as between trade, aid, migration and investment policies. More positively, it could suggest best practices and more channels through which policy asynergies can be created to strengthen developmental impacts in support of the MDGs.

10.2.3. Adopting Policies to Attract Business Investment

Investment has proven to be a powerful catalyst for innovation, sustainable growth and poverty reduction. Despite positive trends in the past decade, business investment and enterprise development in most non-OECD regions need to grow more strongly to meet development needs.

A *Policy Framework for Investment* is being developed by a Task Force of OECD and partner governments in co-operation with civil society and other international organisations. Drawing on a wide spectrum of policies such as trade, competition, tax and corporate governance, it will function as a checklist for governments engaged in domestic reform, regional co-operation or international policy dialogue aimed at creating an environment that is attractive to domestic and foreign investors and that enhances the benefits of investment to society. The *Framework* could serve as a reference point for investment promotion agencies and donors as they assist recipient countries in improving the investment climate, as well as for businesses, trade unions and NGOs in their dialogue with governments.

Bilateral and multilateral donors spend a sizeable share of their official development assistance on activities that mobilise more and better private investment, both domestic and foreign. These include initiatives at the macroeconomic level at the institutional level and at the enterprise level. They use a wide range of instruments including grants and concessional loans, equity stakes, guarantees, debt relief and technical co-operation. As the Monterrey Consensus recognised, meeting the internationally agreed development goals requires the mobilisation of all available resources, domestic and international, including aid. ODA can be used to leverage additional investment. To understand what works, what doesn't work and why, the OECD has identified a need for more detailed information on the impact and efficiency of the different ways ODA is used to stimulate private investment and the asynergies between FDI and ODA. The OECD is lending its investment expertise to this task.

The Monterrey Consensus states that multinational enterprises have an important role to play in helping to achieve the internationally agreed development goals. The OECD *Guidelines for Multinational Enterprises* are a government-backed, voluntary code of conduct for international business; they aim to strengthen the basis of mutual co-operation between multinational enterprises and the societies in which they operate so as to enhance economic, social and environmental well-being. The *Guidelines* provide voluntary principles and standards for appropriate conduct by multinational enterprises in such areas as labour relations, human rights, disclosure of information, anti-corruption, environment and consumer protection. They apply to the global operations of multinational enterprises based in adhering countries.

The governments adhering to the *Guidelines* represent countries that are home to most multinational enterprises and the source of most global trade and international investment. Adhering countries comprise all 30 OECD members and to date nine non-OECD partner countries.

While observance of the *Guidelines* is voluntary for companies, the adhering governments have committed to promote them actively. The most visible signs of this commitment are the National Contact Points which are government offices charged with promoting observance of the *Guidelines* by multinational enterprises operating in or from the national territory.

NCPs have significant flexibility in determining how they go about promoting the *Guidelines* and dealing with specific instances. They engage in annual peer reviews of their activities and publish an annual report. According to the 2004 Annual Report on the *Guidelines*, some 80 specific instances have been brought to National Contact Points' attention since the 2000 Review of the *Guidelines* dealing with a range of concrete problems of business ethics.

The *Guidelines* are part of the broader package of OECDintegrity instruments that summarises an extensive body of analysis and experience in how to design and implement good public policy and, in some cases, about the business sector's role in the overall governance framework. By taking steps to cut off this side of bribery in international markets, OECD countries take responsibility for their role in curbing world corruption and poverty reduction.

10.3. Mobilising Resources to Achieve the MDGs

Resource mobilisation is fundamental to achieving the MDGs. For many of the poorest countries, aid will continue to be the principle source of finance for some time. Significant aid increases have been promised by OECD countries: these amounts need to be reliable and provided for predictable time periods. But OECD members can do more. They can help partner countries reap trade benefits by freeing their markets and strengthening trading capacity. OECD experience can also be put to work to help developing countries mobilise new financial resources and better exploit existing ones, as well as to reduce the costs of corrupt practices and conflicts of interest in the public and private sectors. What are the OECD and its membership doing to:

1. Increase aid volume and aid predictability;
2. Help partners mobilise domestic sources of finance through taxes, user charges and economic instruments;
3. Share special finance strategies for achieving water-related goals;
4. Help use remittances efficiently and productively;

5. Analyse innovative sources of financing;
6. Promote partnerships and results-based management of resources;
7. Work against conflicts of interest and bribery?

10.3.1. Increasing Aid Volume and Predictability

In 2004, aid reached its highest level ever USD 78.6 billion – in both nominal and real terms. Aid levels fell during 1992-97, and the trough continued through 2001. Since then, total aid from DAC members has risen in each of the past seven years, by over a quarter in real terms.

Yet ODA growth has not matched donors' economic growth over the past decade, so its recent recovery becomes less impressive when measured as a share of DAC members' combined GNI. The ODA/GNI ratio rose to 0.25 per cent in

2003 and 2004, up from 0.23 per cent in 2002 and 0.22 per cent in 2001, but still well short of the average of 0.33 per cent achieved in 1970-92.

One can expect further substantial growth in real ODA in line with the Monterrey commitments. Denmark, Luxembourg, the Netherlands, Norway and Sweden remain the only countries meeting the United Nations ODA target of 0.7 per cent of GNI. So far seven others have committed to reach it before 2014: Belgium, Finland, France, Germany, Ireland, Spain, and the United Kingdom. Canada and Switzerland have also made commitments to reach higher ODA targets, and the United States has already increased its aid by more than the 50 per cent it pledged at Monterrey. If these existing commitments are met, ODA will reach some USD 115 billion by 2010 — still short of estimates of the amounts required to help many more countries attain the MDGs by 2015 than those currently expected to do so.

Aid flows from non-DAC/OECD donors are growing, a development that is welcome and encouraging. A dialogue with these donors is being built around aid flows, statistics and effectiveness. At a joint meeting in February 2005, it was acknowledged that significant scope exists for stronger co-ordination and mutual learning between DAC donors and the growing non-OECD donor community.

Effective ODA flows must be predictable. Aid programming is vital for recipients' fiscal planning and has always played a key role in the World Bank Consultative Groups and UNDP Round Table discussions. Unpredictability deeply compromises the ability of governments to plan future public expenditure. The problem arises mainly in programme-type assistance, particularly if the time frame extends to three or five years. The absence of such commitments or at least indications undermines the credibility of recipients' medium-term budget planning, which is intended to provide the centrepiece for donor-supported Poverty Reduction Strategies.

Among African recipients, volatility is lower in more stable countries and higher in those more fragile. A substantial number of recipients experience year-to-year ODA variations averaging only 10 per cent to 20 per cent, but the figure can rise to 50 per cent or more for recipients suffering conflict or unrest. The problem is most acute in aid-dependent countries with low international reserves, where donors are unsure about government commitment and capacity to reform. Some success stories of countries that have managed to increase aid predictability provide lessons that could have application elsewhere.

10.3.2. Mobilising Domestic Resources

Taxes: The Monterrey Consensus recognises the need for and responsibility of developing countries to finance their own development. In addition to the mobilisation of domestic savings, proper tax design and administration also have a major role to play, not least in ensuring a growth-friendly environment.

Yet many developing countries have difficulty in raising revenue to finance physical and social infrastructure to support market-based economies. To some extent, these difficulties arise from the structures of their economies, often with large informal sectors and many people below any acceptable poverty line.

Yet most developing countries still have scope to increase revenues by improving tax design and administration. Bringing enterprises into the formal economy has important fiscal implications. They can ensure effective taxation of corporate income, regardless of home country. This may call for measures to check tax evasion and cross-border tax avoidance. The experience of OECD countries can provide useful input to the improvement of tax collection.

The OECD Model Tax Treaty is a major contribution to improving the operation of tax systems worldwide. It provides a framework within which countries can agree bilaterally about how to minimise and resolve cross-border tax issues and ensure taxation in the appropriate country, while giving migrant workers and multinational companies certainty about their tax liabilities and ensuring no double taxation.

Two provisions of the Model Treaty have particular relevance for ensuring effective taxation of FDI and reducing tax avoidance and evasion opportunities: the allocation of profits to subsidiaries of multinational companies through the arm's length principle and the exchange of information between tax authorities. The *Transfer Pricing Guidelines* aim to ensure that rights to tax the profits of multinationals are allocated equitably between countries. Correct application of these principles reduces the tax that companies can avoid by making their profits appear in low-tax jurisdictions.

User charges: No country claims to have found the ideal tax system, and all countries look continually for ways to improve theirs. This, combined with the general unpopularity of taxes, has prompted a search for non-tax revenue sources. One source gaining ground in many countries but rarely a major source of revenue is user charges: payments made by users of government services. They have a number of advantages. They are relatively easy to collect, can be used to motivate the providers of government services and are seen as less onerous than taxes. They also often fall disproportionately on individuals rather than companies and on residents rather than nonresidents. Experience with user charges within OECD countries is growing quickly, making this an area where developing countries can draw on OECD expertise.

Using economic instruments for environmental policy: The OECD has also worked extensively on improving environmental effectiveness and economic efficiency through economic instruments for environmental policy. Such instruments include reform of environmentally harmful subsidies, environmental taxes and charges, domestic tradable permits and voluntary approaches, as well as public environmental expenditures. OECD has also analysed the environmental effectiveness and economic efficiency of other policy instruments, in particular, voluntary approaches.

Giving greater prominence to such instruments in the mix of policies used to address environmental and sustainable development objectives can help cost-effectively to meet MDG 7, and "... reverse the loss of environmental resources". It may help to alleviate poverty directly by addressing environmental problems that impact the poor and indirectly by generating or freeing resources for investment in infrastructure, such as water supply and sanitation, which is critical for the poor. Such instruments can also free budgetary resources for other kinds of pro-poor investments, like health and education.

10.3.3. Developing Finance Strategies

The international community has agreed to halve the proportion of people without access to safe water and sanitation by 2015.[1] This presents a major challenge demanding strengthened efforts from all stockholders and, according to the Camdessus Panel, a doubled financial commitment. Currently, 1.1 billion people do not have access to safe water, and 2.6 billion have no access to basic sanitation. Achieving them would provide important support for attaining several other goals including those on poverty, education and gender equality.

Substantially increased financial flows to the water sector are necessary but not sufficient for reaching the water targets. Fundamental reforms in the governance of the water sector must ensure that existing and increased resources get used efficiently and effectively. OECD and the Danish government have developed a decision-support tool to support developing and transition countries in this task. The FEASIBLE model focuses on the realism and affordability of water-related financing. It also provides a basis for addressing the social issues often associated with raising water tariffs to consumers connected to water networks and the policy and institutional reforms needed to use financial resources efficiently.

DAC data on aid to the water sector show a recent decline but the most recent data are for 2002 and thus may not reflect the more recent upturn in overall aid trends. Some other key findings include:

1. Half of donor commitments were allocated to just ten countries;
2. A significant proportion of resources went to countries with already high access to water services, although it was not clear whether they were used to improve access; and
3. On average commitments for water projects took eight years to complete disbursement.

These issues will need to be addressed if donors are to make a more decisive contribution to achieving the internationally agreed water targets.

10.3.4. Using Remittances Productively

Remittances have grown due, in part, to renewed interest in migration for employment, the international mobility of skilled *a* and highly qualified workers, and the increase in the number of foreign students. Emigrant workers' remittances of savings from wages and other work income are a considerable source of hard currency for countries of emigration.

The OECD has long experience in migration issues. It has studied the role that remittances have played in the development of sending countries such as Italy, Ireland, Greece, Spain and more recently Portugal, Turkey and Mexico. It can share this experience and draw the lessons of best practice for optimal use of emigrants' money transfers through savings and investment. In co-operation with other organisations such as the World Bank and the IMF, the OECD could contribute in other ways. It is also important to explore ways to increase the use of new technologies to reduce transfer costs, help modernise the formal transfer system, and offer better banking services to migrants.

The OECD is working on the role that remittances play in the economic and social improvement of receiving countries, especially their impact on poverty reduction and improving levels of education and healthcare. Greater coherence is needed between migration policies and development policies. New forms of co-operation between sending and receiving countries are necessary to optimise transfers of funds by emigrants and consolidate development and job creation in countries of origin.

10.3.5. Developing Innovative Sources

Recent pledges by donor countries in Monterrey and elsewhere have improved prospects for higher aid flows but still leave the annual target to achieve the MDGs under financed. The simplest solution is to raise aid further, but government budgets are tightening, and new sources of development finance need to be explored for governments to have certainty of keeping their pledge to the world's poor. OECD research has helped to rationalise the debate on alternative forms of development finance.

The most popular new forms for financing the MDGs are now inventoried and classified. The classification criteria derive from public-finance principles, *i.e.* according to funding sources and criteria for choice. This exercise has structured and informed the debate and clarified the policy choices, analysing the advantages and risks associated with various approaches.

10.3.6. Partnerships and Results-based Management

The present consensus model of development co-operation unites donors and partner countries around the shared goals of poverty reduction and the fulfilment of the MDGs by 2015.

Implementation is complicated by donor diversity and fragmentation, making stronger partner leadership of development co-operation a challenge for many countries.

Poverty Reduction Strategy Papers are being reviewed by the World Bank, International Monetary Fund and the UN Economic Commission for Africa's PRSP Learning Group, following an evaluation by independent evaluators, to improve their usefulness as a basis for donor alignment.

As a result, a "second generation" PRS model is emerging that integrates the goals and the growth agenda, including the central role of the private sector. This model is based around domestic policy and consultation processes to achieve shared results, rather than being driven by the process of multilateral institutions and other donors. As a contribution to evolution of the consensus model of development co-operation, the OECD is researching successful models of stockholder involvement, predictable financing, and results-based management.

10.3.7. Preventing Bribery

Significant resources are lost through dubious and illegal practices by economic agents. By adopting and implementingthe Convention on Combating Bribery of Foreign Public Officials, OECD countries have taken responsibility for their role in reducing corruption and poverty in developing countries, but effective results also depend on the capacity of partner countries to combat bribery of their own officials.

As conflict of interest in both the public and private sectors has become a major problem worldwide, partner countries are also using more extensively the OECD *Guidelines for Managing Conflict of Interest in the Public Service.* They provide a unique international benchmark for developing and implementing a comprehensive conflict-of-interest policy. The *Guidelines* introduce a deliberately simple definition of conflict of interest and a principle-based approach to support public organisations' review and modernisation of their policies and practices. In addition, a set of practical tools, such as checklists, self tests, model provisions and training materials have been developed and tested to help managers in the daily application of the conflict-of-interest policy.

10.4. Harnessing Policy Networks

Improving OECD country policies and scaling up resources to meet the MDGs require sufficient capacity in partner countries for them to bear fruit. The OECD has intensified its capacity building programmes in several key areas, notably in statistics, investment, taxation, trade, entrepreneurship, environment, budget management, and science and technology, as well as in helping make aid more effective. All capacity building efforts require long-term commitment.

10.4.1. Statistical Capacity Building

Timely, reliable statistics that support and monitor development policy and progress towards the MDGs are of increasing international interest. This has led to a formal call for low-income countries to design and implement National Strategies for the Development of Statistics (NSDS) by 2006. Achieving the

MDGs, and indeed reaching all development objectives, requires good statistics, which in turn require a healthy national statistical system that produces and analyses reliable data. Because statistics furnish an essential input to policy formulation, the NSDS is intended to align with wider poverty-focused national development programmes and strategies.

The Partnership in Statistics for Development in the 21st Century parries – a Consortium hosted by the OECD and guided by representatives from developing countries, bilateral donors, and multilateral institutions – drives this work. It promotes NSDS development so that countries can have, *inter alia*, nationally owned and produced data for all MDG indicators by the next major MDG review in 2010. Paris has already produced a guide for designing an NSDS and an advocacy document, which makes the case for adopting a strategic approach to developing national statistical capacity.

10.4.2. Investment in Capacity Building

In support of the Millennium Declaration and the Monterrey Consensus the OECD launched the *Initiative on Investment for Development* in 2003 in Johannesburg. It includes three closely interrelated projects: the development of a *Policy Framework for Investment*; drawing lessons on the use of ODA in support of efforts to mobilise investment for development; and sharing the OECD's experience with investment policy peer reviews as capacity-building mechanisms.

The OECD has a long history of peer learning and consensual approaches towards the development of best practice. It has become a forum for countries to share their experiences, develop common understanding and elaborate policy guidance and capacity aimed at enhancing the contribution of domestic and foreign investment to development. Multiple initiatives support this function. *Global Fora on International Investment* have been held in Mexico, China, South Africa and India. OECD investment policy reviews of China and Russia have recently been completed. And regional programmes to date include the OECD-SEE Investment Initiative and the new OECD-MENA Initiative on Governance and Investment for Development.

An important complement to these efforts concerns OECD work on legal issues associated with international investment, as for example recent work on most-favoured-nation treatment in international law.

10.4.3. Capacity Building in Taxation

Through its multilateral, regional and country-specific tax programmes, the OECD provides developing countries with assistance over a range of tax issues important to the twin goals of attracting investment and collecting fair tax revenues from domestic and foreign investment. Tax advice and technical support have been provided most recently to countries in South East Europe. Follow-up capacity building continues in the form of workshops on micro-simulation tax modelling, tax incentive policies, and tax expenditure reporting for proper budget management. Work currently under way will provide similar assistance under the MENA-OECD investment programme.

A host country's tax regime may negatively or positively impact investment flows. Poorly designed tax systems discourage capital investment. Experience shows that a high host-country tax burden is not just a question of tax rates. Too often, imprecise or non-transparent tax rules and their application add to compliance costs, perceived risk and uncertainty over investment profitability. Systems leaving excessive administrative discretion in the hands of tax officials have also repeatedly invited corruption, thus undermining the good governance objectives so crucial to attractive investment environments. Moreover, all countries should target tax incentives with care, because tax revenues must provide the main source of finance for public programmes critical to business, investment and social development.

While treaties, transfer pricing and exchange of information provide a framework for effective taxation of cross-border activities, they can benefit a country only if it develops a treaty network and has the technical expertise to make full use of it. The tax events provide for sharing experience on tax administration issues, such as the administration of value-added tax and the auditing of taxpayers to help in efficient and effective revenue collection. They include discussions of tax policy experience and methods of tax policy analysis, so that developing countries can learn from both the successes and failures of tax policy in other countries in designing tax systems that suit their own circumstances.

Exchanges with OECD countries can play a vital capacity-building role in tax administrations and ministries of finance, and help mobilise domestic resources. The International Tax Dialogue is a recent joint initiative of the IMF, the World Bank and the OECD in response to the call in Monterrey for greater international tax co-operation. To be successful, this process must involve real dialogue and not promote a single OECD position.

10.4.4. Trade Capacity Building

At Doha in 2001, trade ministers made clear that trade negotiations alone cannot address all the trading challenges facing the poor countries. To reap the maximum benefits from future trade liberalisation these economies need to address the supply-side constraints they face. This typically involves domestic policy reforms to reduce trade costs at the border, help domestic firms meet the price, quality and technical requirements of global supply chains, and build legal and physical infrastructures conducive to international business development.

OECD countries have intensified their trade-related technical assistance and capacity building programmes, which the Doha Ministerial Meeting in 2001 called "core elements of the development dimension of the multilateral trading system". The OECD *Guidelines on Strengthening Trade Capacity for Development* is a reference document for donors and their partners. In November 2002 it created jointly with the WTO the Trade Capacity Building Database, a user-friendly tool to help the development and trade communities share information, improve co-ordination and monitor the implementation of the Doha commitments.

In 2003 bilateral donors and multilateral agencies significantly increased their aid commitments for trade-related technical assistance and capacity building. Commitments to activities aimed at supporting beneficiary countries in trade policy and regulations increased in real terms by 31 per cent to almost USD 1 billion in 2003, while aid committed to trade development rose by 18 per cent to almost USD 1.8 billion.

Bilateral donors and multilateral agencies increased their funding to multilateral trust funds and programmes-such as the Doha Development Agenda Trust Fund, the Integrated Framework and the Joint Integrated Technical Assistance Programme (JITAP)-by 24 per cent between 2002 and 2003. Donors also focused more of their assistance on Least Developed Countries (LDCs). In 2003, LDCs represented 40 per cent of total commitments for support to trade policy and regulations and 27 per cent of commitments for support to trade development.

These public-sector initiatives need enhancement with new partnerships featuring recipient and donor governments, business and civil society. They offer a way to resolve complex issues of policy ownership and implementation so that the benefits of trade-linked investment actually materialise and improve the lot of the poor. Public-private partnerships are integral to capacity building, and OECD countries can contribute much to their successful creation and operation.

10.4.5. Increasing Capacity for Entrepreneurship

Fostering entrepreneurship – including women's entrepreneurship – and developing small and medium-sized enterprises are key drivers of economic growth, job creation, regional and local development and social cohesion. SMEs play a crucial role in transition and developing countries. Globalisation, the acceleration of technological change and innovation create opportunities and challenges for SMEs in both developed and developing countries.

Capacity building to promote entrepreneurship is vital for local development strategies to combat poverty. It can work through at least three channels. First, entrepreneurship works as an important catalyst for employment and income creation in distressed urban areas. Second, the non-profit sector, which tends often to contain many relatively small and highly entrepreneurial groups, plays a fundamental role in making OECD member countries more inclusive through "social entrepreneurship". Third, an asset building approach, through small savings and loans from microfinance institutions, is rapidly developing as an effective tool for job creation and social inclusion.

With its long standing expertise and peer review methodology, the OECD has become a renowned forum for policy dialogue and co-operation on SMEs, entrepreneurship and local development. Building on this, and for the past five years, the *OECD Bologna Process* for SME and Entrepreneurship Policies, provides guidance *SME* to both member and non member governments to help entrepreneurs and SMEs worldwide meet the challenges and reap the benefits of globalisation. Based on multidisciplinary analytical work and policy recommendations, *the OECD Bologna Process* is further deepening and improving the high-level dialogue and co-operation among the different stockholders at the global level. In this context, the dialogue with developing economies, at national and local levels, is well advanced.

10.4.6. Enhancing Capacity for Environmental Management

Environmental institutions in partner countries face severe challenges to devise and implement policy reforms and to undertake and facilitate priorities investments. To strengthen capacity for achieving environmental sustainability (MDG 7), the OECD works with partner countries in a number of ways. Co-operative programmes have been established with several UN regional organisations to share OECD experience with environmental information and indicators and in undertaking environmental performance reviews (EPRs). In 2005, the OECD and UNECLAC reviewed Chile's environmental performance, and plans are under way for an EPR of China. Several nonmembers are full participants in the mutual acceptance of data programme, which facilitates chemical risk management.

The OECD has developed a range of tools, including guidelines, good practices, handbooks and software applications, to enhance the environmental management capacity of non-member countries, mostly in the fields of environmental expenditure management, water supply and sanitation, environmental permitting and environmental compliance assurance. Demonstration projects in pilot countries have been used to test the tools and adapt them accordingly. Policy dialogues between OECD and partner countries through the *Global*

Forum on Sustainable Development also enhance capacity for environmental management.

10.4.7. Strengthening Budgeting

Aid effectiveness depends on strengthened partner capacities and systems. Donor alignment with country priorities depends on sound development strategies for poverty reduction that are guided by clear priorities, are linked to budgets and expenditure plans, and are results oriented. The effectiveness and efficiency of assistance depends crucially on the capacity of the budgeting and public expenditure management systems in the recipient countries to effectively allocate, manage and account for all the funds spent and to show development results.

The OECD provides assistance to developing countries in this area through its series of regional and country-specific programmes on budgeting. Senior budget officials from OECD countries provide unique insights for fellow practitioners, offering immediate credibility and operational value for partner countries. The OECD has also developed guidelines for various aspects of the budget process including the *Best Practice Guidelines for Budget Transparency,* which have become a recognised reference in this field. As part of its work on aid effectiveness, the DAC has issued guidelines on *Strengthening Procurement Capacities in Developing Countries*.

10.4.8. Science and Technology for Sustainable Sevelopment

A major conclusion of the World Summit on Sustainable Development in Johannesburg was that science and technology (S&T) should play a greater role in contributing to sustainable development. The Task Force on Science, Technology and Innovation of the UN Millennium Project likewise stresses furthering the role of science, technology and innovation in meeting the MDGs. To harness S&T, developing countries need to develop capacities to conduct research in response to local needs and to transfer and adapt necessary scientific and engineering knowledge. Building such capacities encompasses science and engineering education at all levels, creating or strengthening research institutions, building research infrastructures and recruiting and retaining qualified scientists and engineers.

Effective, efficient technology transfer implies fostering a dynamic private sector that can choose, adapt, develop and market advanced technologies suited to local needs and has the necessary incentives to do so. Markets and appropriate institutions need development. OECD and partner countries could draw lessons about how to build scientific and technological capacities from the countries that have done so and from their experiences with well-designed international co-operation programmes.

References

Alsop, R. and Heinsohn, N. (2005) *Measuring Empowerment in Practice: Structuring Analysis and Framing Indicators*, World Bank Policy Research Working Paper 3510

Betson, David M., and Jennifer L. Warlick . (1998) "Alternative Historical Trends in Poverty." *American Economic Review* 88:348-51.

Fiedrich, M. and Jellema, A. (2003) *Literacy, Gender and Social Agency: Adventures in Empowerment*. A Research Report for ActionAid UK

Paugam, Serge. (1998). "Poverty and Social Exclusion: A Sociological View." Pp. 41–62 in *The Future of European Welfare*, edited by Martin Rhodes and Yves Meny.

Pradhan, B. (2003) *Measuring Empowerment: A Methodological Approach, Society for International Development* (www.sidint.org) 1011-6370 46:2; 51-57; 033500 Palgrave Macmillan.

Norwegian Agency for Development Cooperation, (1999) *Handbook in Gender and Empowerment Assessment,* NORAD

Bibliography

Agere, Sam 2000. *Promoting good governance*. Commonwealth Secretariat.

Agnew, Elizabeth N. 2004. *From Charity to Social Work: Mary E. Richmond and the Creation of an American Profession*. Urbana, IL: University of Illinois Press.

Alice O'Connor; 2000. "Poverty Research and Policy for the Post-Welfare Era" *Annual Review of Sociology*.

Alsop, R. and Heinsohn, N. 2005. *Measuring Empowerment in Practice: Structuring Analysis and Framing Indicators*, World Bank Policy Research Working Paper 3510

Axinn, June and Mark J. Stern 2008. *Social Welfare: A History of the American Response to Need* (7th ed.). Boston, MA: Pearson/Allyn and Bacon.

Balgopal, Pallassana R. 2000. *Social Work Practice with Immigrants and Refugees*. New York, NY: Columbia University Press.

Barker, Richard 2009. *Making Sense of Every Child Matters - multi professional practice guidance* (1st ed.). Bristol, UK: Policy Press.

Barker, Robert L. 2003. *Social Work Dictionary* (5th ed.). Silver Spring, MD: NASW Press.

Betson, David M., and Jennifer L. Warlick . (1998) "Alternative Historical Trends in Poverty." *American Economic Review* 88:348-51.

Butler, Ian and Gwenda Roberts 2004. *Social Work with Children and Families: Getting into Practice* (2nd ed.). London, England; New York, NY: Jessica Kingsley Publishers.

Davies, Martin. 2002. *The Blackwell Companion of Social Work* (2nd ed.). Oxford, UK; Malden, MA: Blackwell.

Fiedrich, M. and Jellema, A. 2003. *Literacy, Gender and Social Agency: Adventures in Empowerment*. A Research Report for ActionAid UK

Firebaugh, Glenn. (2000) "Empirics of World Income Inequality." *American Journal of Sociology*. 104:1597-1630. in JSTOR

Fischer, Joel and Kevin J. Corcoran 2007. *Measures for Clinical Practice and Research: A Sourcebook* (4th ed.). Oxford, UK; New York, NY: Oxford University Press.

Greene, Roberta R. 2008. *Social Work with the Aged and their Families* (3rd ed.). New Brunswick, NJ: Transaction Publishers.

Grinnell, Richard M. and Yvonne A Unrau (2008). *Social Work Research and Evaluation: Foundations of Evidence-Based Practice* (8th ed.). Oxford, UK; New York, NY: Oxford University Press.

Khan, Mushtaq Husain (2004). *State formation in Palestine: viability and governance during a social transformation: Volume 2 of Political economy of the Middle East and North Africa*. Routledge

Mizrahi, Terry and Larry E. Davis (2008). *Encyclopedia of Social Work* (20th ed.). Washington, DC; Oxford, UK; New York, NY: NASW Press and Oxford University Press.

Norwegian Agency for Development Cooperation. 1999. *Handbook in Gender and Empowerment Assessment*, NORAD.

Paugam, Serge. 1998. "Poverty and Social Exclusion: A Sociological View." Pp. 41–62 in *The Future of European Welfare*, edited by Martin Rhodes and Yves Meny.

Poluha, Eva; Rosendahl, Mona 2002. *Contesting 'good' governance: crosscultural perspectives on representation, accountability and public space*. Routeledge.

Popple, Philip R. and Leslie Leighninger 2008. *The Policy-Based Profession: An Introduction to Social Welfare Policy Analysis for Social Workers* (4th ed.). Boston, MA: Pearson/Allyn and Bacon.

Pradhan, B. 2003. *Measuring Empowerment: A Methodological Approach, Society for International Development* (www.sidint.org) 1011-6370 46:2; 51-57; 033500 Palgrave Macmillan.

Reamer, Frederic G. 2006. *Ethical Standards in Social Work: A Review of the NASW Code of Ethics* (2nd ed.). Washington, DC: NASW Press.

Richardson, Virginia E. and Amanda Smith Barusch 2006. *Gerontological Practice for the Twenty-First Ccentury: A Social Work Perspective*. New York, NY: Columbia University Press.

Sowers, Karen M. and Catherine N. Dulmus and others. 2008. *Comprehensive Handbook of Social Work and Social Welfare*. Hoboken, NJ: John Wiley & Sons.

Specht, Harry; Courtney, Mark E. 1994. *Unfaithful angels : how social work has abandoned its mission*. New York: Free Press.

Statham, Daphne (2004). *Managing Front Line Practice in Social Work*. New York, NY: Jessica Kingsley Publishers.

The IMF's Approach to Promoting Good Governance and Combating Corruption — A Guide. International Monetary Fund. 20 June 2005.

Thyer, Bruce A. and John S. Wodarski. 2007. *Social Work in Mental Health: An Evidence-Based Approach*. Hoboken, NJ: John Wiley.

Turner, Francis J. 2005. *Canadian Encyclopedia of Social Work*. Waterloo, ON: Wilfrid Laurier University Press.

Wittenberg, Renee. 2003. *Opportunities in Social Work Careers* (Revised ed.). Chicago, IL: VGM Career Books.

Index